WITHDRAWN
FROM
UNIVERSITY OF PLYMOUTH
LIBRARY SERVICES

D0421381

OXFORD ECHR SERIES

General Editor: Professor John Merrills
University of Sheffield

FREEDOM OF RELIGION
UNDER THE EUROPEAN CONVENTION
ON HUMAN RIGHTS

Freedom of Religion
Under the European Convention
on Human Rights

CAROLYN EVANS

OXFORD
UNIVERSITY PRESS

OXFORD

UNIVERSITY PRESS

Great Clarendon Street, Oxford OX2 6DP

Oxford University Press is a department of the University of Oxford.
It furthers the University's objective of excellence in research, scholarship,
and education by publishing worldwide in

Oxford New York

Athens Auckland Bangkok Bogotá Buenos Aires Cape Town
Chennai Dar es Salaam Delhi Florence Hong Kong Istanbul Karachi
Kolkata Kuala Lumpur Madrid Melbourne Mexico City Mumbai Nairobi
Paris São Paulo Shanghai Singapore Taipei Tokyo Toronto Warsaw

with associated companies in Berlin Ibadan

Oxford is a registered trade mark of Oxford University Press
in the UK and in certain other countries

Published in the United States
by Oxford University Press Inc., New York

© Carolyn Evans 2001

The moral rights of the author have been asserted
Database right Oxford University Press (maker)

First published 2001

All rights reserved. No part of this publication may be reproduced,
stored in a retrieval system, or transmitted, in any form or by any means,
without the prior permission in writing of Oxford University Press,
or as expressly permitted by law, or under terms agreed with the appropriate
reprographics rights organization. Enquiries concerning reproduction
outside the scope of the above should be sent to the Rights Department,
Oxford University Press, at the address above

You must not circulate this book in any other binding or cover
and you must impose this same condition on any acquirer

British Library Cataloguing in Publication Data
Data available

Library of Congress Cataloging in Publication Data
Evans, Carolyn, lecturer in law.
Freedom of religion under the European Convention on human rights / Carolyn Evans.
p. cm.—(Oxford European Convention on human rights series; 1) •
Includes bibliographical references and index.
1. Freedom of religion—Europe. 2. Convention for the Protection of Human Rights and
Fundamental Freedoms (1950). I. Title. II. Series.
KJC5156. E927 2001
341.48'1—dc21 00-065243
ISBN 0-19-924364-6 ✓

3 5 7 9 10 8 6 4 2

Printed in Great Britain
on acid-free paper by
Bookcraft Ltd., Midsomer Norton, Somerset

UNIVERSITY OF PLYMOUTH	
Item No.	9005221119
Date	– 5 AUG 2002 B
Class No.	341.481 EVA
Cont. No.	✓
PLYMOUTH LIBRARY	

To my husband, Stephen Donaghue,

with love and gratitude

General Editor's Preface

The European Convention on Human Rights, which was concluded in 1950, came into force in 1953 and will therefore soon celebrate its first half-century. As well as setting out a list of rights guaranteed, the Convention contains institutional arrangements for their supervision which have now been functioning for more than forty years and have produced a large detailed body of case law. Both the supervisory machinery and the rights guaranteed have, of course, been significantly added to and modified over the years; the latter by a number of protocols extending the list of rights protected, and the former by various institutional changes, the most recent being the creation of the new Court of Human Rights by Protocol No. 11 in 1998

Interest in the Convention has naturally generated a considerable body of literature, including many works providing an overview of the Strasbourg system and its jurisprudence. Less common are studies like Dr Evans's book concerned with the interpretation and application of individual provisions. However, as she shows in this comprehensive analysis of the concept of freedom of religion, such an approach is now feasible, not only with regard to provisions such as Articles 5 and 6 which furnish, so to speak, the staple diet of human rights lawyers, but also with regard to Article 9 and Article 2 of Protocol No. 1, where, as with other provisions, the cases may be less numerous, but in terms of principle and policy the issues presented are no less important.

To examine freedom of religion under the Convention Dr Evans carefully reviews the relevant jurisprudence against the background of international human rights law generally and an incisive appreciation of theory. While the bulk of the case law discussed is the product of the Commission and the old Court, post-1998 developments are not neglected. The author argues that 'freedom of religion or belief appears to have been given significant protection under the Convention. Yet the case law interpreting Article 9 has not demonstrated an appropriate understanding of the importance of freedom of religion or belief in the lives of individuals and has shown an undue deference to the concerns of the States'. It is clear thererfore that in her view the verdict on the record to date at Strasbourg is 'could do better'.

It is particularly apt that the present volume should appear at a time when, as as result of the Human Rights Act 1998, courts in the United Kingdom are for the first time being called upon to take account of the European Convention. In a multicultural society religious freedom is plainly fundamental and lawyers, judges and others with responsibilities in this area will find Dr Evans's book extremely useful. This thoughtful, systematic and critical study provides an excellent start to the *Oxford ECHR* series.

Faculty of Law   J. G. Merrills
Sheffield University
10 November 2000

Acknowledgements

This book is based on the doctoral thesis that I completed at Oxford University in December of 1999 and there are a number of people whose contribution to the thesis deserves acknowledgement. In particular, I wish to thank my two supervisors, Professor Mark Janis, now of the University of Connecticut, who supervised the thesis from 1995 to 1997 and Professor Guy S. Goodwin-Gill of Wolfson College, Oxford who took over from 1997 to 1999. In their different ways they both gave me encouragement and support, as well as a great deal of practical advice and assistance. My examiners, Professor Vaughan Lowe and Professor Kevin Boyle, deserve mention for the thorough reading and the helpful comments that they made upon my thesis.

I also wish to acknowledge the funding that I received from the Rhodes Scholarship, without which this book would not have been written. In particular, I wish to thank Sir Anthony Kenny for the efficient and flexible manner in which he responded to my requests to suspend the scholarship to allow me to take up a two-year lectureship at Exeter College. My thanks also go to the Rector, Fellows, and students of Exeter College, especially my colleague Professor Sandra Fredman, for their support and encouragement during my time there. Professor Alan Ryan at New College and Dr Alison Riding of Balliol College were also most helpful in discussing the theory/jurisprudence of religious freedom with me.

A number of people associated with the European Commission on Human Rights were kind enough to allow me to interview or correspond with them regarding religious freedom. Professor Christos Rosakis and Mr Hans Christian Krüger gave me useful insights into the decision-making of the Commission. Mr Stephen Naismith was helpful in assisting me to gain access to unpublished materials. My particular thanks go to Dr Stephanos Stavros of the Secretariat who was most generous with his time and introduced me to a number of his colleagues. While these colleagues have asked not to be named, I am grateful to them also for their insights.

Finally, I wish to thank my family. To my parents for their unfailing love and support. To my husband, Stephen Donaghue, who spent huge periods of time discussing and debating religious freedom, setting up computer facilities, proof-reading, and editing chapters, not to mention washing, shopping, and nappy changing in order to give me time to work. Without this practical assistance the book could never have been completed, but it is his love, encouragement, and belief in me that have meant the most. And to my daughter Caitlin, for learning to sleep for long enough to keep me sane and for learning to smile early enough to make me happy.

The material in this book is up to date as of May 2000.

Contents

Table of Authorities

EUROPEAN COMMISSION OF HUMAN RIGHTS CASES

UNITED NATIONS CASES

DOMESTIC CONSTITUTIONS AND STATUTES

List of Abbreviations and Defined Terms

Commission	European Commission of Human Rights
Convention	European Convention on Human Rights and Fundamental Freedoms, 4 Nov. 1950, 213 U.N.T.S. 221
Court	European Court of Human Rights
Declaration on Religious Intolerance and Discrimination	Declaration on the Elimination of All Forms of Intolerance and Discrimination Based on Religion or Belief, G.A. Res. 36/55, U.N. GAOR, Supp. (No. 51) 171, U.N. Doc. A/36/684 (1981)
General Comment on Article 18	United Nations Human Rights Committee, General Comment No. 22(48) on Article 18, Freeedom of Thought, Conscience and Religion, U.N. Doc. CCPR/C/21/Rev.1/Add.4, para 2 (1993); see reprint in 15 Hum. Rts L.J. 233 (1994)
I.C.C.P.R.	International Covenant on Civil and Political Rights G.A. Res. 2200 A, 21 U.N. GAOR, Supp. (No. 16) 52, U.N. Doc. A/6316 (1966)
Krishnaswami study	Arcot Krishnaswami, Special Rapporteur of the Sub-Commission on Prevention of Discrimination and Protection of Minorities, Study of Discrimination in the Matter of Religious Rights and Practices, E/CN.4/Sub.2/200/Rev.1 (1960)
U.N.	United Nations
V.C.L.T.	Vienna Convention on the Law of Treaties, 23 May 1969, U.N. Doc. A/Conf.39/27, 8 ILM 679

1

Introduction

The right to freedom of thought, conscience and religion is probably the most precious of all human rights, and the imperative need today is to make it a reality for every single individual regardless of the religion or belief that he professes, regardless of his status, and regardless of his condition in life. The desire to enjoy this right has already proved itself to be one of the most potent and contagious political forces that the world has ever known. But its full realization can come about only when the repressive action by which it has been restricted in many parts of the world is brought to light, studied, understood and curtailed through cooperative policies; and when the methods and means appropriate for the enlargement of this vital freedom are put into effect on the international as well as the national plane.

Arcot Krishnaswami[1]

Religion and belief have been the cause of controversy in Europe for centuries. Minority groups have been persecuted for their religion or belief since before the time of the Roman Empire,[2] torture and killing were once a common way of dealing with heretics or non-believers,[3] and this century saw an attempt at genocide against the Jewish people of continental Europe. The war in the former Yugoslavia[4] is a reminder that, even today, people can be capable of the most appalling acts against others on a religious/ethnic basis.[5] Yet, over time, the peoples of Europe came to see the need for some

---

[1] Arcot Krishnaswami, Special Rapporteur of the Sub-Commission on Prevention of Discrimination and Protection of Minorities, Study of Discrimination in the Matter of Religious Rights and Practices, E/CN.4/Sub.2/200/Rev.1 (1960) [hereinafter the 'Krishnaswami study'].

[2] For an overview of early notions of religion and religious freedom in Europe see MALCOLM D. EVANS, RELIGIOUS LIBERTY AND INTERNATIONAL LAW IN EUROPE chapter 1 (1997).

[3] Myres S. McDougal, Harold D. Lasswell, and Lung-chu Chen, *The Right to Religious Freedom and World Public Order: The Emerging Norm of Non-Discrimination*, 74 MICH. L. REV. 865, 866–72 (1976).

[4] *Case Concerning the Application of the Convention on the Crime of Genocide* (Bosnia and Herzegovina v. Yugoslavia), 1996 ICJ 603 (Preliminary Objections) gives an outline of the crimes alleged to have been committed against Bosnians, in part on the basis of religion.

[5] Theo van Boven, *Advances and Obstacles in Building Understanding and Respect between People of Diverse Religions and Beliefs*, 13 HUM. RTS Q. 437, 442 (1991) claims that in the 1980s some 25 regional or civil wars were based 'to a significant degree' on disputes 'evolving at least in part from religions or beliefs'. See also Kevin Boyle, *Religious Intolerance and the Incitement of Hatred, in* STRIKING A BALANCE: HATE SPEECH, FREEDOM OF EXPRESSION AND NON-DISCRIMINATION 61–2 (Sandra Coliver ed., 1992).

degree of religious tolerance and began to develop protection for freedom of religion or belief.

This book deals with one form of protection for freedom of religion and belief in Europe, the European Convention on Human Rights and Fundamental Freedoms ('the Convention').[6] This treaty sets out both a series of rights to which all persons within the jurisdiction of Contracting States are entitled, and also mechanisms for the protection of these rights. It is considered by many to be the most effective treaty for the protection of human rights.[7] The bodies which have authority to deal with matters under the Convention have developed an extensive case law on the complex and controversial issue of freedom of religion or belief, yet until recently there has been little in the way of detailed discussion of this jurisprudence.[8]

This book provides a detailed examination of the articles of the Convention that deal with freedom of religion and a critical analysis of the case law that has developed around those articles. It argues that the bodies responsible for protecting freedom of religion and belief under the Convention have approached their task in an incoherent and inconsistent manner. The principles which they have developed to assist in interpreting articles relevant to freedom of religion or belief have generally been favourable to States and have given little consideration to the importance of freedom of religion and belief, both to those whose freedom is being denied, and to the development of pluralistic and tolerant democracies where the risk of serious persecution based on religion or belief is less likely to occur.

---

[6] European Convention on Human Rights and Fundamental Freedoms, 4 Nov. 1950, 213 U.N.T.S. 221 [hereinafter 'the Convention'].

[7] e.g. Thomas Buergenthal, International Human Rights 84 (1988); D. J. Harris, M. O'Boyle, and C. Warbrick, The Law of the European Convention on Human Rights 28–32 (1995); Francis G. Jacobs and Robin C. A. White, The European Convention on Human Rights chapter 28 (2nd edn. 1996). For more cautious assessments see Andrew Drzemczewski, European Human Rights in Domestic Law: A Comparative Study 3–6 (1983); Brice Dickson, *The Common Law and the European Convention, in* Human Rights and the European Convention (Brice Dickson ed., 1997).

[8] The most detailed analysis of these issues can be found in Evans, above, note 2, at chapters 11, 12, and 13. See also Stephanos Stavros, *Freedom of Religion Claims for Exemption from Generally Applicable, Neutral Laws: Lessons from Across the Pond?*, 6 Eur. Hum. Rts Rev. 607 (1997); Peter W. Edge, *The European Court of Human Rights and Religious Rights*, 47 Int'l & Comp. L.Q. 680 (1988); T. Jeremy Gunn, *Adjudicating Rights of Conscience under the European Convention on Human Rights, in* Religious Human Rights in Global Perspective: Legal Perspectives 305 (Johan D. van der Vyver and John Witte Jr. eds., 1996); Carolyn Evans, *Religious Freedom in European Human Rights Law: The Search for a Guiding Conception, in* Religion and International Law 385 (Mark Janis and Carolyn Evans eds., 1999); Malcolm Shaw, *Freedom of Thought, Conscience and Religion, in* The European System for the Protection of Human Rights 445 (R. StJ. Mcdonald, F. Matscher, and H. Petzold eds., 1993).

1.1 SCOPE OF THE BOOK

1.1.1 Overview

The book is divided into three parts. The first part sets the context in which the interpretation of religious freedom in the Convention takes place. The second looks at the meaning of the Article 9(1) provisions for the protection of freedom of religion and belief, and the third part explores the limitations that a State may place on that freedom.

This chapter outlines the key religious freedom provisions of the Convention and the role of the Court and Commission in determining whether there has been a breach of these provisions. It goes on to examine the issues of admissibility that arise in the context of claims under Article 9. Chapter 2 briefly outlines some theories of religious freedom and argues that the Court needs to develop a philosophy of freedom of religion or belief that gives emphasis to the autonomy of the individual and the development of a pluralistic and democratic society. Chapter 3 deals with the drafting history of the relevant articles of the Convention and discusses the way in which they assist in the interpretation of the right to religious freedom. These three chapters set the context—textual, theoretical, and historical—in which questions about the way in which Article 9 has been interpreted can be raised.

The second part of the book deals with Article 9(1), which outlines the freedom to have and to manifest a religion or belief. Chapter 4 deals with the definition of the term 'religion or belief' in Article 9 jurisprudence. The Commission has tended to be broad and inclusive in defining this term but has given no clear indication of how 'religion or belief' is to be defined. While this is a complex task, it is argued that it would be appropriate for the Court to develop a tighter and more sophisticated definition. Chapter 5 explores the nature of the right to have and to change a religion or belief. This right is sometimes said to protect the *forum internum* (or matters of internal conscience) but, despite the importance that the Court says should be attributed to this area, the case law does not develop any test for distinguishing the freedom to have a belief from the freedom to manifest a belief. Nor does the Court take a particularly sophisticated view of the circumstances in which the State may intrude on the *forum internum*, particularly in the areas of the State Church and the education of children in State schools. Chapter 6 deals with the issue of the right to manifest a religion or belief, focusing particularly on the test set out by the Commission in the leading case of *Arrowsmith v. the United Kingdom*.[9] The chapter looks at this case and the way it has been applied and suggests that the test both

---

[9] *Arrowsmith v. the United Kingdom*, App. No. 7050/75, 19 Eur. Comm'n H.R. Dec. & Rep. 5 (1978).

involves the Court in inappropriate intrusions into the beliefs of applicants and also pays undue deference to the role of organized religions or similar groups.

The third part of the book deals with permissible limitations on the right to freedom to manifest a religion or belief under Article 9(2). Unlike the freedom to have or to change a religion, the right to manifest that religion or belief in 'teaching, practice, worship and observance' is subject to restriction by States if this is necessary in a democratic society for the protection of other enumerated social goals. Chapter 7 looks at the general scope of the limitations on religious freedom and the criteria by which the Court and Commission have determined whether State restrictions on religious freedom are permissible under the Convention. Chapter 8 looks at the problems caused by a general and neutral law, which does not appear to breach religious freedom, but nevertheless requires some people to act inconsistently with their religion or belief. The Court and Commission have dealt inconsistently with these cases, sometimes suggesting that they are not capable of raising Article 9(1) issues and sometimes dealing with them under Article 9(2). It is argued that the second approach better protects both freedom of religion in general and the position of religious minorities in particular.

The final chapter draws together the criticisms outlined in the earlier chapters and concludes that the manner in which Article 9 has been interpreted is inconsistent with the mandate of the Court and the Commission to protect freedom of religion or belief in Europe. Some suggestions are made as to possible alternative approaches that could be taken to interpreting the Convention in a manner that is more respectful of religious freedom and less inclined to take the State's part in areas of contention.

1.1.2 Materials

The two main primary sources of material that are drawn upon in the book are the *travaux préparatoires* of the Convention and the cases on freedom of religion or belief that have been heard by the Commission and Court. There is, of course, extensive case law on freedom of religion and belief in many States but this book does not attempt to give a comprehensive survey of the position of any State or international organization. Where it has proved useful, however, comparisons are drawn between the case law of the Convention and that of other courts or human rights bodies, particularly those bodies set up under the auspices of the United Nations and the Supreme Court of the United States of America. While much of the material from the United States is not directly transferable to the European context (especially given the strict separation between Church and State in the

United States[10]), the Supreme Court has developed over time a sophisticated and useful jurisprudence on the free exercise of religion and comparisons with this approach are illuminating. The position of many Contracting States can be seen through the case law of the Court and Commission, which often refer to the law of the respondent State in their decisions.

I.2 AN OVERVIEW OF THE KEY PROVISIONS ON FREEDOM OF RELIGION AND BELIEF IN THE CONVENTION

Any interpretation of a treaty must begin with an interpretation in good faith of the words of the treaty itself.[11] In the Convention there are three key articles that deal with freedom of religion or belief and a number of other articles that have been or could be used for the protection of religious freedom, even though their primary purpose is not related to religion. The most important article in the Convention dealing with freedom of religion is Article 9, which states that

1. Everyone has the right to freedom of thought, conscience and religion; this right includes freedom to change his religion or belief, and freedom, either alone or in community with others and in public or private, to manifest his religion or belief, in worship, teaching, practice and observance.

2. Freedom to manifest one's religion or beliefs shall be subject only to such limitations as are prescribed by law and are necessary in a democratic society in the interests of public safety, for the protection of public order, health or morals, or for the protection of the rights and freedoms of others.

Another important article in the Convention regarding the protection of freedom of religion is Article 14. Article 14 sets out the general protection of rights contained in the Convention without discrimination on the basis of religion or other grounds. It reads

The enjoyment of the rights and freedoms set out in this Convention shall be secured without discrimination on any grounds such as sex, race, colour, language, religion, political or other opinion, national or social origin, association with a minority, property, birth or other status.

---

[10] CONSTITUTION OF THE UNITED STATES OF AMERICA, 1787. The relevant clauses of the First Amendment read, 'Congress shall make no law respecting an establishment of religion, or prohibiting the free exercise thereof . . .'. There is no equivalent explicit prohibition of establishment in the Convention or any other international human rights treaty.

[11] Vienna Convention on the Law of Treaties, 23 May 1969, U.N. Doc. A/Conf.39/27, 8 ILM 679 [hereinafter the 'V.C.L.T.']. Art. 31(2) states that treaties should be interpreted 'in good faith in accordance with the ordinary meaning to be given to the terms of the treaty in their context'. While the V.C.L.T. is not retrospective in its application, Arts. 31–3 were accepted by the Court as customary international law and thus applicable to the Convention in *Golder v. the United Kingdom*, 18 Eur. Ct. H.R. (ser. A) at 14 (1975).

The final significant protection of freedom of religion in the Convention is Article 2 of the First Protocol.[12] This Article states that

No person shall be denied the right to an education. In the exercise of any functions which it assumes in relation to education and teaching, the State shall respect the rights of parents to ensure such education and teaching in conformity with their own religious and philosophical convictions.

This Article was one of the most controversial in the Convention and had to be included in a separate Protocol because agreement on its wording could not be reached in time for the signing of the main instrument.[13]

The Convention also contains other articles that could be used to protect aspects of freedom of religion or belief, although they do not refer directly to them. These include Article 8 ('respect for ... private and family life'), Article 10 ('freedom of expression'), and Article 11 ('freedom of peaceful assembly'). Clearly there is potential for overlap between the various articles.[14] A group that wishes to organize a religious procession, for example, may attempt to claim a right to both freedom of religion and freedom of assembly.[15] Someone claiming the right to religious speech will rely on both their general freedom of expression and their specific right to manifest their religion or belief.[16] Some types of religious persecution, such as the use of torture against people to attempt to force them to change religion or belief, or the imprisonment of people for this reason, would also give rise to claims under other articles of the Convention.[17]

In some of the earlier cases, the Court and Commission separately considered each of the Articles under which a claim was made. In *Arrowsmith v. the United Kingdom*,[18] for example, a pacifist who was convicted for distributing leaflets that urged soldiers to refuse to accept a tour of duty in Northern Ireland, had her claim dealt with under both Article 9 and Article 10. The potential importance of such separate examination can be seen in the decision of Mr Opsahl who was prepared to hold that, while the United Kingdom's actions did not breach Article 9, they did breach Article 10.[19] Increasingly, however, the Court or Commission determine that a particular Article is the *lex specialis* of the claim and articles raising

[12] First Protocol to the European Convention on Human Rights, 20 Mar. 1952, 213 U.N.T.S. 262.

[13] See the discussion at Chapter 3.2.4.

[14] Shaw, above, note 8, at 461–2.

[15] e.g. *Plattform 'Artze fur das Leben' v. Austria*, App. No. 10126/82, 44 Eur. Comm'n H.R. Dec. & Rep. 65 (1985); *Rai, Allmond and 'Negotiate Now' v. the United Kingdom*, App. No. 25522/94, 81-A Eur. Comm'n H.R. Dec. & Rep. 146 (1995).

[16] e.g. *Kokkinakis v. Greece*, 260-A Eur. Ct. H.R. (ser. A) (1993); *Arrowsmith v. the United Kingdom*, App. No. 7050/75, 19 Eur. Comm'n H.R. Dec. & Rep. 5 (1978).

[17] Such as Art. 3, the prohibition on torture, inhumane and degrading punishment.

[18] *Arrowsmith v. the United Kingdom*, App. No. 7050/75, 19 Eur. Comm'n H.R. Dec. & Rep. 5 (1978).

[19] *Id.* at 26.

other issues are therefore ignored.[20] In *Riera Blume v. Spain*,[21] for example, the Court held that the actions of Spain in permitting parents to forcibly imprison their children (who were members of a 'cult') in order to 'deprogramme' them, was a breach of Article 5(1) of the Convention (the Article that deals with false imprisonment) and thus decided that there was no need to consider whether there had also been a breach of Article 9. While the effect of this judgment was a considerable advance in the protection of freedom of religion, the indirect path by which the Court chose to extend the protection of the Convention to members of cults allowed it to ignore some complicated but important issues that would have been raised by consideration of the applicants' arguments based on freedom of religion. Many applicants make claims arising under a large number of Convention articles and it is generally a sensible practice for the Court to focus its attention on the most important of these claims. Too great a use of the *lex specialis* doctrine, however, may inappropriately limit the range of issues considered by the Court.

Despite the fact that freedom of religion may be indirectly protected under other articles in the Convention, the focus of this book is Article 9. Article 14 discrimination issues are addressed to the extent that they are relevant to Article 9 but no further. Article 2 of Protocol 1 is a complex Article that is relevant to a wide range of issues, most of which are at best tangentially linked to freedom of religion or belief. Some of these education cases, however, do make important points about freedom of religion or belief in education and are often raised together with an Article 9 claim. Only these types of education cases are considered here.[22] Cases arising under other articles will be addressed only in so far as they shed light on issues that are directly relevant to freedom of religion.

The other main development in the Council of Europe that is relevant to the protection of religious freedom is the Framework Convention for the Protection of National Minorities.[23] Again, this Convention will not be considered in detail, although it will be referred to when it makes a useful contribution to understanding the provisions of the Convention. As it deals only with the religious freedom of national minorities, has only been ratified by 23 Member States and one non-member (Armenia), and its main enforcement mechanism is five-yearly self-reporting, it does not add particularly to an understanding of religious freedom or to the judicial protection

---

[20] e.g. *Rai, Allmond and 'Negotiate Now' v. the United Kingdom*, App. No. 25522/94, 81-A Eur. Comm'n H.R. Dec. & Rep. 146 (1995) (Art. 11 was the *lex specialis*); *Handyside v. the United Kingdom*, 24 Eur. Ct. H.R. (ser. A) (1976) (Art. 10 was the *lex specialis*); *Johnston v. Ireland*, 112 Eur. Ct. H.R. (ser. A) (1986) (Art. 12 was the *lex specialis*).

[21] *Riera Blume and others v. Spain*, App. No. 37680/97, Eur. Ct. H.R., 9 Mar. 1999, unreported.

[22] For a fuller discussion of the education cases see Chapter 5.5.

[23] Framework Convention for the Protection of National Minorities, 1 Feb. 1995 ETS 157.

of religious freedom by the Council of Europe. It certainly should not be seen as a substitute for an appropriate interpretation of Article 9 of the Convention.[24]

1.3 THE ROLE OF THE COURT AND THE COMMISSION

Much has been written about the role of the European Court and Commission of Human Rights under the Convention and it is not the purpose of this book to replicate the work done elsewhere in this area.[25] This section gives a brief overview of the system that was used to adjudicate claims until 11 November 1998 and the new system that has now replaced it.

One of the purposes of the Convention, as set out in the Preamble, was to 'take the first step for the collective enforcement of certain Rights stated in the Universal Declaration'.[26] The Convention created the European Commission of Human Rights[27] and the European Court of Human Rights[28] to 'ensure the observance of the engagements undertaken'[29] by the Contracting Parties. Until 1 November 1998, when the structure for taking complaints under the Convention was changed under Protocol 11,[30] these two bodies had the primary role in determining whether there had been a breach of any of the rights set out in the Convention or its various protocols. Therefore most of the Article 9 case law was determined under the old system.

1.3.1 Procedure of the Commission

Before 1 November 1998, the Commission could receive petitions from 'any person, non-governmental organization or group of individuals claiming to be the victim of a violation by one of the High Contracting Parties of the rights set forth in [the Convention]'.[31] The Commission had the power to determine that a petition was inadmissible if the applicant had not exhausted all domestic remedies[32] and could not deal with a

---

[24] Stavros, above, note 8, at 626, suggests that some perceived inadequacies in the application of Art. 9 could be best overcome by the drafting of a new framework convention on religious minorities.

[25] HARRIS, O'BOYLE, AND WARBRICK, above, note 7, at chapters 22–5; P. VAN DIJK AND G. J. H. VAN HOOF, THEORY AND PRACTICE OF THE EUROPEAN CONVENTION ON HUMAN RIGHTS 26–65 (3rd edn. 1997); JACOBS AND WHITE, above, note 7, at 6–14; MARK JANIS, RICHARD KAY, AND ANTHONY BRADLEY, EUROPEAN HUMAN RIGHTS LAW: TEXT AND MATERIALS chapters 3–4 (1995).

[26] Convention, final paragraph of the Preamble.

[27] Art. 19(1) [hereinafter 'the Commission'].

[28] Art. 19(2) [hereinafter 'the Court'].

[29] Art. 19.

[30] Protocol 11 to the European Convention on Human Rights and Fundamental Freedoms, 11 May 1994, 155 E.T.S. The Protocol entered into force on 1 Nov. 1998.

[31] Art. 25.   [32] Art. 26.

petition which was anonymous or which was substantially the same matter as one which had already been examined by the Commission or another international investigation.[33] These powers do not raise any particular issues in the context of religious freedom. [34]

Under Article 27(2), however, the Commission had the power to deem inadmissible a petition that it considered 'incompatible with the provisions of the present Convention, manifestly ill-founded, or an abuse of the right of petition'. The power to determine that petitions were ill-founded allowed the Commission summarily to dismiss cases that were not procedurally inadmissible but that would clearly fail if taken to the merits phase. It allowed the Commission to weed out weak and hopeless cases at an early stage in order to expedite proceedings and avoid wasting time on cases with little or no merit.

If the Commission determined that a case was admissible it then attempted to reach a friendly settlement between the two parties,[35] and this was achieved in a number of freedom of religion cases.[36] If a solution was not reached, the Commission drew up a report that outlined the facts and stated its opinion as to whether there had been a breach of the Convention provisions.[37] As the Commission was not a judicial body, States were not bound by the report of the Commission but within three months the matter had either to be referred to the Committee of Ministers or to the Court.[38] The decision of the Committee of Ministers as to whether there had been a breach of the Convention was binding on parties,[39] but as the Committee is primarily a political body and as it did not overrule the Commission in relation to any Article 9 complaints, it is largely irrelevant for the purposes of the interpretation of Article 9. The role of the Committee will thus not be considered further.

1.3.2 Procedure of the Court

Originally, only the Commission or relevant States could bring a case to the Court,[40] leaving victims who were dissatisfied with the decision reliant on the Commission itself or their national State (if it was a Contracting Party) to take the case to the Court.[41] Under Protocol 9, it became possible for the original petitioner to bring a case to the Court, although a panel

---

[33] Art. 27.

[34] For a detailed overview of the Commission's procedure see VAN DIJK AND VAN HOOF, above, note 25, at chapter III.

[35] Art. 28(b) and 30.

[36] e.g. *Pentidis and Others v. Greece*, 39 Eur. Ct. H.R. (ser. A) 983 at 990 (1997-III); *Hazar, Hazar and Açik v. Turkey* (friendly settlement), App. Nos. 16311, 16312, 16313/90 (joined), 73 Eur. Comm'n H.R. Dec. & Rep. 111 (1992).

[37] Art. 31.   [38] Art. 32.   [39] Art. 32(4).   [40] Art. 48 (original text)

[41] As the Commission's decision technically was not judicial, it was not strictly speaking an appeal but it effectively acted as such.

of the Court was given power to scrutinize these applications to ensure that they raised a 'serious question involving the interpretation or application of the Convention'.[42] The Court then had the power to make a final decision[43] as to whether a State had acted in breach of its obligations under the Convention and to award 'just satisfaction' to the injured party when that was appropriate.[44] The decision of the Court was binding on Contracting Parties[45] and compliance with these decisions seems to be of a generally high level, especially as compared to other human rights treaties, although some authors have queried whether the Convention was as effective as it could be.[46]

1.3.3 Changes Under Protocol 11

While the original system set up under the Convention was arguably the most successful international regime for the protection of human rights it became, in some ways, a victim of its own success.[47] The number of petitions grew so great that it often took many years for cases to come before the Commission. In order to try to expedite matters and to create a more judicial and less political system, Protocol 11 was drafted.[48] The basic reasons for introducing Protocol 11 were to abolish the Commission, to limit the role of the Committee of Ministers, and to set up a new Court which is able to sit in smaller chambers to deal with a greater number of matters.

Under Protocol 11, the Plenary Court, which is constituted by a number of judges equal to the number of member States, only sits for administrative matters, such as the election of the President and Vice-Presidents and the adoption of the rules of the Court.[49] Cases are thus heard by smaller

---

[42] Art. 48 (as amended by Protocol 9).
[43] Art. 52.   [44] Art. 50.   [45] Art. 53.
[46] Council of Europe and Hanna Suchocka (eds.), *General Report of the European Regional Colloquy: The Effectiveness of Human Rights Protection 50 Years after the Universal Declaration*, 5 ODUDH(98)10 at 14 (4 Sept. 1998) questions the ability of the Convention bodies to deal with 'serious or systematic violations of human rights'. See also Council of Europe (ed.), *Monitoring of Compliance with Commitments Entered into by Council of Europe Member States: An Overview*, MONITOR/INF(97)1 at 13; D. GOMIEN AND L. ZWACK, LAW AND PRACTICE OF THE ECHR AND THE EUROPEAN SOCIAL CHARTER (1996); R. R. Churchill and J. R. Young, *Compliance with the Judgments of the European Court of Human Rights and Decisions of the Committee of Ministers: The Experience of the United Kingdom 1975–1983*, 62 BRIT. Y.B. OF INT'L L. 283 (1992).
[47] HARRIS, O'BOYLE, AND WARBRICK, above, note 7, at 35–6; JANIS, KAY, AND BRADLEY, above, note 25, at 89–97.
[48] Council of Europe (ed.), *Reform of the Central System of the European Convention on Human Rights*, doc. H(92) 14, reprinted in 14 HUM. RTS L.J. 31 (1993); Andrew Drzemczewski and Jan Meyer-Ladewig, *Principal Characteristics of the New European Convention on Human Rights Mechanism, as Established by Protocol 11, signed on 11 May 1994*, 15 HUM. RTS L.J. 81 (1994); HARRIS, O'BOYLE, AND WARBRICK, above, note 7, at chapter 26.
[49] Art. 21 (as amended).

subdivisions of the Court. Committees, made up of three judges, have the power to declare unanimously that a case is inadmissible.[50] If no such decision is made, admissibility decisions are made by Chambers, consisting of seven judges, who also hear the merits of cases.[51] Where the Chamber believes that the matter raised in a case before it involves serious questions about the interpretation of the Convention, it may refer the case to a Grand Chamber of seventeen judges.[52] The Grand Chamber may also hear cases that have already been heard by Chambers at the request of one of the parties if the Grand Chamber considers that the case raises sufficiently serious questions of interpretation.[53]

1.4 ADMISSIBILITY

One of the important jobs of the Commission was to deal with the admissibility of claims under the Convention. Even when these claims were made in relation to Article 9 breaches, this book does not deal with a number of types of admissibility claims. For example, the Commission could dismiss a claim on the basis that the applicant did not present sufficient evidence supporting his or her claim[54] or did not exhaust domestic remedies.[55] There were also a number of such cases where the person claiming a breach of Article 9 could not show that he or she ever asked the authorities for facilities to practise his or her religious obligations[56] or could not show that the authorities did anything to interfere with the right to religious freedom. In one case, a Jewish prisoner complained that he was not given kosher food but the prison authorities gave evidence that appropriate food was available and that the prison had gone to some trouble to consult with representatives of the Jewish community about the diet of Jewish prisoners.[57] In another case the applicant did not respond to several requests by the Commission for further information regarding his case and thus had it declared inadmissible.[58] Such cases are appropriately dealt with by the Commission in summary fashion and are too general in nature to assist in developing an understanding of the approach of the Commission and Court to Article 9.

[50] Art. 28 (as amended).   [51] Art. 29 (as amended).
[52] Art. 30 (as amended).   [53] Art. 43 (as amended).
[54] Some such cases will be considered, as they raise important issues of the evidential rules in Art. 9, but cases where the applicant has presented little or no evidence to support his or her claim raise no issues of particular relevance to religious freedom.
[55] *D.S and E.S v. the United Kingdom*, App. No. 13669/88, 65 Eur. Comm'n H.R. Dec. & Rep. 245 (1990).
[56] *X v. the United Kingdom*, App. No. 8231/78, 28 Eur. Comm'n H.R. Dec. & Rep. (1982).
[57] *X v. the United Kingdom*, App. No. 5947/72, 15 Eur. Comm'n H.R. Dec. & Rep. 8 (1976).
[58] *Shields v. the United Kingdom*, App. No. 7442/76, Eur. Comm'n H.R., 4 Dec. 1984, unreported.

Some cases that have been summarily dismissed, however, do require analysis. In particular, cases that are found to be inadmissible on the basis that they are manifestly ill-founded are of particular interest because often the failure of the Commission to deal seriously with these cases demonstrates its conservative approach to Article 9. Also, some members of the Court have suggested that sometimes the technical provisions that can be used to deem a case inadmissible (such as failure to exhaust domestic remedies) have been used by the Court to avoid looking into difficult or controversial areas.[59] Where there is evidence that these provisions are being used by the Court or Commission for such purposes, this is discussed. As a general rule, however, the use of the technical provisions to deem cases inadmissible is beyond the scope of this work.

1.5 STANDING

One technical area of admissibility in which issues particular to religious freedom have arisen is that of standing.[60] Under Article 39 of the Convention, a Committee of the Court may receive petitions from 'any person, non-governmental organization or group of individuals claiming to be the victim of a violation . . . of one of the rights set forth in this Convention'.[61] Thus the Commission regularly heard Article 9 claims from individuals and groups of individuals.

1.5.1 Churches and Other Religious Organizations

A difficult question arose for the Commission in relation to the standing of Churches. The Commission originally held that Churches or religious organizations had no right to bring a claim under either Article 9 or Article 2 of the First Protocol. It was the adherents of the Church who had a right to freedom of religion, not the Churches themselves. In the case of *Church of X v. the United Kingdom*,[62] the United Kingdom government made a determination that a particular group or 'cult' was dangerous to society. The government took a number of fairly wide-sweeping measures to check the activities of the Church, including de-registering its institutions as

---

[59] *Ahmet Sadik v. Greece*, 20 Eur. Ct. H.R. (ser. A) 1638, 1660 (1996-V), dissenting judgment by Judge Martens, joined by Judge Foighel, who commented that 'it is scarcely surprising that learned authors have time and again suggested that the real grounds for such decisions . . . are to be found elsewhere, namely in the Court's wish to avoid a decision on the merits'.

[60] See generally, JACOBS AND WHITE, above, note 7, at 211–13; EVANS, above, note 2, at 286–9; VAN DIJK AND VAN HOOF, above, note 25, at 552–3.

[61] The Commission had the same power under what was Art. 25(1) of the Convention.

[62] *Church of X v. the United Kingdom*, App. No. 3798/68, 13 Y.B. Eur. Conv. on H.R. 306 (Eur. Comm'n on H.R.) (1968).

educational institutions, refusing entry into Britain for people wishing to study or work with the Church, refusing entry for some eight hundred delegates who had come to an international conference of the Church, and other acts aimed at limiting the operations of the group. The Church, which was a corporation, brought the action on its own behalf and on behalf of its members. No natural person, however, was named as a party to the action. The Commission simply dismissed the case in relation to alleged breaches of Article 9 and Article 2 of the First Protocol, on the grounds that 'a corporation being a legal and not a natural person, is incapable of having or exercising the rights mentioned in Article 9, paragraph 1 of the Convention and Article 2 of the First Protocol'.[63] It did not consider the fact that a Church is in a somewhat different position to an ordinary commercial corporation and may be an appropriate and effective body to enforce the provisions relating to freedom of religion, especially in cases where the government has undertaken an explicit campaign to limit the effectiveness of a religious group rather than to restrict the rights of individual members.[64] The decision was reiterated by the Commission and extended to Article 2 of Protocol 1, in the decision of *X v. Sweden*[65] where the right of the Evangelical-Lutheran Church of Sweden to bring an action regarding religious education in schools was denied for 'the same reasoning' that applied in the earlier case.[66]

Later, however, the Commission revised its decision to refuse to grant standing to Churches. In the case of *X and the Church of Scientology v. Sweden*[67] a case was brought against Sweden in relation to the prohibition of advertisements of the 'E-meter', a device which the Church of Scientology claimed in the advertisement was for measuring the mental well-being of an individual. The claims (under Articles 9 and 10 of the Convention) were brought jointly by a minister of the Church and by the Church as representative of its members. While the Commission had rejected such 'representative' status for Churches before, in this case it overruled its previous decisions.

[The Commission] is now of the opinion that the . . . distinction between the Church and its members under Article 9(1) is essentially artificial. When a church body lodges an application under the Convention, it does so in reality, on behalf of its members. It should therefore be accepted that a church body is capable of possessing

---

[63] *Id.* at 314.

[64] Individual members of the Church also suffered as a result of the government's actions but for any one of them to bring an action would have been merely in a representative capacity for the broader Church.

[65] *Karnell and Hardt v. Sweden*, App. No. 4733/71, 14 Y.B. Convention on H.R. 676 (Eur. Comm'n on H.R.) (1971).

[66] *Id.* at 679.

[67] *X v. Church of Scientology*, App. 7805/77, 16 Eur. Comm'n H.R. Dec. & Rep. 68 (1979).

and exercising the rights contained in Article 9(1) in its own capacity as representative of its members.[68]

The Commission has also recognized that some Churches may be nongovernmental organizations and thus entitled to standing under Article 25.[69] This seems to be a more satisfactory approach, as in many of these cases the nomination of a person or persons as the applicant is essentially artificial and the Church is the most appropriate body to bring a claim. The right of a Church to bring a claim is derivative, however, based on aggregating of the rights of its members. It cannot claim a breach of its own rights.[70] The Commission has also extended its ruling to 'an association with religious and philosophical objectives'.[71]

1.5.2 Legal Persons

While the Commission has decided that the legal person of a Church can have a standing to bring a freedom of religion case, freedom of conscience is not exercisable by a legal person.[72] The Commission has consistently denied that a profit-making corporation could have any claim (either as to conscience or religion) under Article 9. In 1979 it dismissed a claim by a company that being forced to pay ecclesiastical taxes was a breach of its freedom of religion.[73] The Commission simply held that 'a limited liability company given the fact that it concerns a profit-making corporate body, can neither enjoy nor rely on the rights referred to in Article 9, paragraph 1, of the Convention'.[74] It also held that an organization, which was set up for the purpose of rehabilitating drug addicts, did not have a right to Article 9 protection. In a later case, however, the Commission did 'not exclude'[75] the possibility that a profit-making organization that was established for the purposes of exercising philosophical beliefs in community

---

[68] *Id.* at 70.

[69] *Holy Monasteries v. Greece*, 301 Eur. Ct. H.R. (ser. A) at 28 (1995); *Finska Forsamlingen I Stockholm and Hautaniemi v. Sweden*, App. No. 24019/94, 85-A Eur. Comm'n H.R. Dec. & Rep. 94, 96 (1996).

[70] *X. and the Church of Scientology v. Sweden*, App. 7805/77, 16 Eur. Comm'n H.R. Dec. & Rep. 68, 70 (1979). But see VAN DIJK AND VAN HOOF, above, note 25, at 552 for a criticism of this position.

[71] *Omkarananda and the Divine Light Zentrum v. Switzerland*, App. No. 8118/77, 25 Eur. Comm'n H.R. Dec. & Rep. 105, 117 (1981).

[72] *Kontakt-Information-Therapie and Hagen v. Austria*, App. No. 11921/86, 57 Eur. Comm'n H.R. Dec. & Rep. 81, 88 (1988). In this case the legal person in question was a drug rehabilitation centre and not a Church but the Commission seemed to be making the point as a general rule and specifically mentions the right of Churches to freedom of religion.

[73] *Company X v. Switzerland*, App. No. 7865/77, 16 Eur. Comm'n H.R. Dec. & Rep. 85 (1979).

[74] *Id.* at 87.

[75] *Kustannus Oy Vapaa Ajattelija AB and Others v. Finland*, App. No. 20471/92, 85-A Eur. Comm'n H.R. Dec. & Rep. 29, 43 (1996).

with others could have rights under Article 9(1). The extent to which the organization had to be philosophical or religious rather than profit-making was not addressed by the Commission, which decided the case on other grounds.

The change in approach to the issue of standing over time is welcome. The dismissal of cases on the grounds that they were brought by Churches rather than individuals allowed the Commission to refuse to deal with cases of widespread government action against particular religious groups on largely technical grounds.[76] In cases of widespread discrimination or government persecution of a religious group, a Church or other religious body may be in a better position to bring a representative case before the Court, and the recognition granted to such organizations to bring these cases does strengthen the position of vulnerable groups. While the Commission has not tended to use the standing it has granted to religious bodies to enter into questions of these wider issues of systemic discrim-ination or persecution, this type of claim is perhaps more likely to succeed than a 'representative' claim by a single applicant.[77] The potential for such group claims can be seen in a claim in which the Commission dismissed (for failure to exhaust domestic remedies) a case brought by the Church of Scientology claiming systemic persecution by Germany against its members. The Commission noted that such claims could give rise to an issue as to whether the State had failed in its positive obligation to protect individuals under Article 9.[78]

1.6 CONCLUSION

The work-load of the Court has increased dramatically over time and, particularly with the addition of new member States from Eastern Europe, it is likely that it will continue to increase in the coming years. In the first ten years in which applications could be made to the Commission (1955–64), 2,088 applications were made.[79] During 1999, however, 8,396

---

[76] Although in *Church of X v. the United Kingdom*, App. No. 3798/68, 29 Collection 70, 77–8 (1968) the Commission held that, even if the case had been brought by individuals, it would have failed as none of the actions taken by the United Kingdom amounted to an inter-ference with a Convention right.

[77] In a number of cases brought by individuals against Greece, for example, the applicant has sought to challenge the law itself or its discriminatory application, but the Court has only dealt with the specific issues raised by the case and not the broader issues raised by the appli-cant. e.g. *Kokkinakis v. Greece*, 260-A Eur. Ct. H.R. (ser. A) (1993).

[78] *Scientology Kirche Deutschland e.V v. Germany*, App. No. 34614/97, 89-A Eur. Comm'n H.R. Dec. & Rep. 163 (1997). On the general reluctance of the Court to deal with issues in the abstract see J. G. MERRILLS, THE DEVELOPMENT OF INTERNATIONAL LAW BY THE EUROPEAN COURT OF HUMAN RIGHTS 36–8 (1993); Dickson, above, note 7, at 215–18.

[79] COUNCIL OF EUROPE, SURVEY OF ACTIVITIES AND STATISTICS (1996).

applications were made to the Court.[80] Even if the hoped-for efficiencies under Protocol 11 eventuate, the work-load of dealing with admissibility decisions will be significant. This puts some pressure on the Court to dismiss a large percentage of claims at the admissibility stage, as it does not have the resources to deal with thousands of cases at the level of detail required by a full investigation into the merits.[81] As will be discussed, in the Article 9 context this can lead to admissibility claims that are dismissed as manifestly ill-founded by the routine application of sections of earlier Court decisions without real consideration of subtle differences in facts or review of whether the original decision was appropriate or remains appropriate in the current climate.

This makes it all the more important that, when cases are deemed admissible, the Court develops clear principles for dealing with them that will provide useful guidance in making admissibility decisions. In considering the merits of cases, however, the Court also has limitations, in particular the need to come to a consensual majority decision within a reasonable period of time. This can lead to lowest common denominator decisions that give little insight into the reasons behind the decision and tend to repeat large sections of previous judgments. Professor Merrills has described this as a tendency on the part of the Court to 'repeat talismanic words, often verbatim in later cases' and notes that this means that the majority decisions 'rarely display either the forcefulness or the depth of judicial analysis characteristic of the best individual opinions'.[82] Separate and dissenting opinions can, for this reason, be illuminating but by definition they do not reflect the thinking of the Court as a whole. Professor Merrills likewise stresses the importance of decisions on the merits demonstrating through thorough legal reasoning and analysis an understanding of the issues at stake, as otherwise the Court's judgments 'appear ill-informed or arbitrary, neither of which is conducive to confidence in the Court'.[83] While he notes that the Court generally tries to give full reasons for its decisions within the constraints of a consensual judgment system, there are times when the judgments of the Court are not all that they might be in terms of reasoned justification.[84]

These problems are systemic and do not only apply to Article 9 cases, although, as it is a highly controversial area, it may be harder to achieve consensus among the judges in religious freedom cases than in less controversial areas. Yet freedom of religion and belief is an important right, explicitly protected by the Convention. While practical difficulties

---

[80] Council of Europe, Survey of Activities and Statistics (1999 provisional version).
[81] Dickson, above, note 7, at 217 is critical of the way in which admissibility decisions that find cases are manifestly ill-founded are used inappropriately to deal with substantive legal issues.
[82] Merrills, above, note 78, at 28–9.   [83] *Id.* at 34.   [84] *Id.* at 36.

in developing a clear, consistent, and principled approach to cases raising issues of religious freedom do exist, such problems do not lessen the obligation on the judges of the Court to protect the freedom of religion or belief of all people within the jurisdiction of Contracting States. As the following chapters argue, they have not adequately fulfilled this obligation.[85]

[85] Shaw, above, note 8, at 463 concludes that 'the role of article 9 has not really fulfilled its potential'.

2

Towards a Theory of Freedom of Religion or Belief

Article 9 of the Convention explicitly protects freedom of religion or belief. Yet there are a wide variety of conceptions as to what this freedom entails. These conceptions vary between different States, religions, and individuals. Even if a group of States agrees to the general principle of freedom of religion or belief in an international treaty, for example, it is quite possible that they do not share an understanding of what values are at stake in making such an agreement. This conceptual disagreement is not merely of theoretical importance. As this chapter discusses, it can lead to very different results when the broad concept of religious freedom is applied in specific circumstances.

This is precisely the problem that faces the Court and Commission in the interpretation of Article 9. A variety of States agreed to a principle of freedom of religion or belief but the Convention gives little guidance as to the reasoning behind this decision or any detailed explanation of what the freedom entailed. It has been left to the Court and Commission to flesh out an understanding of how this principle applies to concrete cases. There is always a danger in attempting to apply a concept as complex and controversial as religious freedom, that those charged with applying it will simply draw on their own experiences or notions of 'common sense' and thus give deference to systems of belief with which they are familiar or comfortable, but fail to adequately protect that which seems foreign or strange. A sophisticated conception of the rationale for freedom of religion or belief can help to cut through the biases and presumptions of the arbiter and create a framework for assisting in ensuring that cases are dealt on the basis of the same values, rather than in an *ad hoc* manner.

The appropriate conception to be applied by bodies such as the Court and Commission is not universal or timeless. This chapter explores the theoretical rationale for religious freedom in modern European States. Other models might better describe the value of freedom of religion or belief in other cultures or at other points in European history. For present purposes, however, it is necessary to understand the role that religion plays in European constitutional systems in order to develop a theory of freedom of religion or belief that can be of assistance in the interpretation of the Convention.

2.2 RELIGION AND THE STATE IN EUROPE

World-wide there are a huge variety of religions, sects, cults, philosophies, and other forms of belief. There are also a significant variety of relationships between these religions or beliefs and the State. At one extreme, there are States in which there is no meaningful division between religion and the State. The State dedicates itself to religious ends and State officials and religious officials have overlapping roles. Other religions may be restricted in their rights to practise or prohibited from exercising their freedom of religion at all.[1] At the other extreme, a State may dedicate itself to secular ends and persecute all religions and beliefs that do not conform to a State ideology.[2] No member of the Council of Europe has adopted either extreme position, but nevertheless a wide variety of relationships exist between religions and States in the region.

At one end of the European spectrum, a number of States emphasize the secular role of the State and the division between Church and State. Turkey has a strongly secularist constitution, which its armed forces have gone to some lengths to defend.[3] The constitutional preamble includes a paragraph that says 'as required by the principle of secularism, sacred religious feelings shall in no way be permitted to interfere with state affairs and politics'.[4] Article 24 of the Constitution of the Republic of Turkey (1982/1987) grants all people freedom of religion but prohibits the 'exploit[ation] or abuse of religion or religious feelings . . . for the purpose of personal or political influence, or for even partially basing the fundamental social, economic, political, and legal order of the State on religious tenets'. Political parties are prohibited from adopting programmes that conflict with the 'principles of the democratic and secular Republic'.[5]

While most other States do not have provisions that so vigorously promote secularism, a number do require the separation of Church and State. The Constitution of the Republic of France (1958) in its preamble describes France as 'a Republic, indivisible, secular, democratic and social'.[6]

---

[1] e.g. the CONSTITUTION OF THE REPUBLIC OF IRAN, 1980, which describes Iran as an Islamic State and which is permeated with references to Islam. Officials involved in the various arms of government have to be learned in Muslim law and practices. The only minority religions that are permitted are Zoroastrian, Christian, and Jewish.

[2] Albania under Communist rule is probably the best example of such a regime. KEVIN BOYLE AND JULIET SHEEN, FREEDOM OF RELIGION OR BELIEF: A WORLD REPORT 261–2 (1997).

[3] Ömer Faruk, *Towards a Civilian Constitution: Recent Constitutional Amendments by Turkey, in* CONSTITUTIONS OF THE COUNTRIES OF THE WORLD (Gisbert Flanz ed.).

[4] CONSTITUTION OF THE REPUBLIC OF TURKEY, Law No. 2709 of 7 Nov. 1982 as amended by Law No. 3361 of 17 May 1987. Art. 2 describes the Republic of Turkey as a 'democratic, secular and social state' and Art. 4 makes these basic principles irrevocable.

[5] *Id.* at Art. 68.

[6] CONSTITUTION OF THE REPUBLIC OF FRANCE, promulgated on 4 Oct. 1958, preamble.

The German Basic Law (1949) states that there 'shall be no state church',[7] although its preamble refers to the 'responsibility before God and humankind' of the German people.[8] Similarly, while the Constitution of Ukraine (1996) speaks of 'responsibility before God, our own conscience and past, present and future generations',[9] it also states that the Church and religious organizations are to be separate from the State and the school.[10]

At the other end of the spectrum, some constitutions reveal strong links between the State and a Church or religion. The Constitution of Greece (1975/1986), for example, begins 'In the Name of the Holy, Consubstantial Indivisible Trinity'. It goes on to state that the 'prevailing religion in Greece is that of the Eastern Orthodox Church of Jesus Christ. The Orthodox Church of Greece, acknowledging our Lord Jesus Christ as its head, is inseparably united in doctrine with the Great Church of Christ in Constantinople and with every other Church of Christ of the same doctrine, observing unwaveringly, as they do, the holy apostolic and synodal canons and sacred traditions.'[11] The Orthodox Church is autocephalous, and the European Court noted that 'according to Greek conceptions, it represents *de jure* and *de facto* the religion of the State itself'.[12] As can be seen from the case law that has come before the Court, the Greek government maintains very close ties with the Orthodox Church and has arguably become too active at times to protect it from 'intrusions' by minority religions.[13]

Other States explicitly adopt an established Church. The Constitution of Iceland (1944), for example, states that the 'Evangelical Lutheran Church shall be the National Church in Iceland and shall, as such, be supported and protected by the State'.[14] The Catholic Church lost its status as the 'State religion' of Italy only in 1984[15] and the Constitution of the Republic of Italy (1947) still recognizes that the 'State and the Catholic Church are, each within its own ambit, independent and sovereign'.[16] The United Kingdom has established the Church of England to the extent that the monarch must be the head of the Church of England, the House of Lords

---

[7] BASIC LAW OF GERMANY, 23 May 1949, as amended. This article was incorporated into the Basic Law from Art. 137 of the WEIMAR CONSTITUTION of 11 Aug. 1919.

[8] BASIC LAW OF GERMANY, 23 May 1949, preamble.

[9] CONSTITUTION OF UKRAINE, 28 June 1996, preamble.

[10] *Id.* at Art. 35. See also *inter alia* the CONSTITUTION OF THE REPUBLIC OF SLOVENIA, 29 Dec. 1978, Art. 7, which states that the 'State and religious communities are separated'.

[11] THE CONSTITUTION OF GREECE, 7 June 1975 (as amended), Art. 3.

[12] *Kokkinakis v. Greece*, 260-A Eur. Ct. H.R. (ser. A) at 7 (1993).

[13] See discussion at Chapter 5.4.

[14] CONSTITUTION OF THE REPUBLIC OF ICELAND, No. 33, 17 June 1944 (as amended), Art. 62.

[15] Concordat between the Republic of Italy and the Vatican, signed 18 Feb. 1984 and ratified by the Chamber of Deputies on 20 Mar. 1984.

[16] CONSTITUTION OF THE REPUBLIC OF ITALY, 22 Dec. 1947 (as amended), Art. 7.

includes bishops from the Church of England and no other Church, and certain public ceremonies (such as the coronation of the monarch) take place as part of the ceremonies of the Church.[17]

Other States fall between active secularism and establishment. The Spanish constitution, for example, says that no religion shall have a State character. Spain has, however, entered into a Concordat with the Catholic Church which extends to that Church a number of financial and other privileges not available to all religions in the State,[18] although there is nothing in the Concordat that would prevent this extension. The Constitution of the Republic of Ireland (1937) incorporates a number of elements from the dominant Catholic religion, including a statement that the 'State acknowledges that the homage of public worship is due to Almighty God. It shall hold his name in reverence and shall respect and honour religion.'[19] The influence of the Catholic Church's teachings can also be seen in the provisions dealing with the right to life of the unborn, the importance of motherhood, and the express mention of blasphemy as a grounds for limiting free expression.[20] Yet the Constitution also says that the State 'shall not endow any religion'.

Thus there are a wide variety of relationships between Church and State in members of the Council of Europe. There is also a variety of religious demographics. While, with the exception of Turkey and Albania, the States share a largely Christian heritage, the majority Christian denominations in the various States range from Catholic, to Eastern Orthodox, to a variety of Protestant Churches. Despite their shared Christianity, the bloody history of religious conflict in Europe shows that these denominations cannot be assumed to necessarily share values or to extend respect to one another. There are also minority, non-Christian religions even in the relatively religiously homogenous States of Europe such as Greece.[21]

Despite this variety in both religious demographics and the perception of the proper relationship between Church and State, almost all member States have adopted constitutional or statutory provisions prohibiting

---

[17] e.g. The Act of Settlement, 1701 (U.K.). Art. 1 requires that the monarchy descend only to Protestants; Art. 2 expressly excludes Catholics from the monarchy; and Art. 3 requires that those who come into possession of the Crown 'shall join in commission with the Church of England as by law established'. See generally, BOYLE AND SHEEN, above, note 2, at 316–17.

[18] *Iglesia Bautista "El Salvador" and Ortega Moratilla v. Spain*, App. No. 17522/90, 72 Eur. Comm'n H.R. Dec. & Rep. 256, 260 (1992).

[19] CONSTITUTION OF THE REPUBLIC OF IRELAND, enacted 1 July 1937, in operation from 29 Dec. 1937, Art. 44(1).

[20] *Id.* at Arts. 40(3), 41(2), and 40(1) respectively.

[21] While reliable statistics are difficult to find, members of the Greek Orthodox Church are said to constitute approximately 97–98% of the Greek population, yet this still leaves 2–3% of the population that does not share the Orthodox religion. BOYLE AND SHEEN, above, note 2, at 331 note that minority religions present in Greece include 'Muslims, Jews, Catholics, various Protestant denominations, Orthodox, Old Calendarist, Jehovah's Witnesses, Mormons, Krishna Consciousness and Baha'is'.

discrimination on the basis of religion and allowing for freedom of religion.[22] The provisions take different forms but demonstrate a reasonably strong level of consensus that freedom of religion is an important, European-wide principle. All of the States that have signed the Convention have also committed themselves to freedom of religion or belief under the provisions of Article 9. Thus there appears to be a European commitment to the principle of religious freedom.

It is also clear, however, that there is no such consensus that this commitment requires the separation of Church and State or necessarily leads to disestablishment. While some States have travelled that path, others have not. Thus the large and sophisticated literature that has developed around religious freedom in the United States is of limited use when considering why religious freedom is important in Europe and what values underlie its adoption by so many States with different religious backgrounds. The notions of strict State 'neutrality' and the 'wall of separation' between Church and State that play such a large role in United States jurisprudence can only have a limited role in developing an understanding of what values are being protected in Article 9 of the Convention. In order to develop a theory that is more relevant in the European context, and thus an appropriate interpretative aid for the Convention, it is necessary to consider arguments in favour of freedom of religion or belief that do not rely on strict separation between Church and State.

2.3 INSTRUMENTAL ARGUMENTS

There are a number of instrumental arguments for tolerance in religious matters and for some degree of religious freedom. Such instrumental arguments tend to emphasize the importance of tolerance (which includes some degree of free practice) as a means of achieving another important end. The notion of tolerance presupposes that what one is tolerating is to some extent undesirable, improper, misguided, or wrong, but that there are nevertheless reasons for permitting the objectionable behaviour to continue.[23] Unless a person is him- or herself misguided or mistaken, he or she does not tolerate things that are beneficial or good. Thus instrumental reasons for tolerance may be acceptable to people who are committed to a variety of religious positions, as well as those who have no religion or no strong belief.

---

[22] e.g. CONSTITUTION OF THE REPUBLIC OF IRELAND (1937), Art. 44(2)(i); CONSTITUTION OF THE REPUBLIC OF ITALY (1947), Arts. 3, 8, and 19; CONSTITUTION OF THE REPUBLIC OF SLOVENIA (1991), Art. 7; CONSTITUTION OF THE REPUBLIC OF ICELAND (1944), Arts. 63–5; SWEDISH INSTRUMENT OF GOVERNMENT, chapter 2, Art. 1(6).

[23] JOSEPH RAZ, THE MORALITY OF FREEDOM 401–2 (1986); Steve D. Smith, *The Restoration of Tolerance*, 78 CAL. L. REV. 305, 306 (1990).

Even if some people perceive that the best society of all is one where all people accept the same, true religion (or no religion at all), they might understand that religious diversity is a fact of life that must be accommodated. Thus they might wish to avert the suffering that religious intolerance and persecution brings, recognizing that it causes social problems without necessarily bringing a religiously cohesive society any closer.

This type of pragmatic argument is now familiar and commonly used in international discussions on religious tolerance. The social problems caused by religious intolerance can be used as a justification for religious tolerance for those with a commitment to a particular religious tradition and those who have no such commitment, which makes it attractive to bodies such as the United Nations which are trying to appeal to a wide constituency. The United Nations Declaration on the Elimination of All Forms of Intolerance and of Discrimination Based on Religion and Belief[24] illustrates this approach when, in its preamble, it refers to the fact that 'the disregard and infringement of human rights and fundamental freedoms, in particular of the right to freedom of thought, conscience, religion or whatever belief, have brought directly or indirectly, wars and great suffering to mankind', and that religious freedom can contribute to the attainment of the goals of 'world peace, social justice and friendship among people'. Thus religious freedom is seen, at least in part, as a means to other desirable ends.

While these pragmatic arguments may have significant force in convincing individuals (especially those who would not be convinced by the more subjective/sceptical approaches to religion) and States of the benefits of adopting a policy of religious tolerance, they are of limited value. First, the arguments suggest that freedom of religion is valuable only in so far as it helps to achieve another end, such as social harmony or the promotion or protection of one's own religion. If there are pragmatic reasons for ceasing to practise religious tolerance, then the argument in favour of it is significantly weakened. In a relatively religiously homogenous society, for example, where the overwhelming majority hate a religious minority and cause significant social disruption in their attempts to oppress this minority, the State may find it easier to simply institutionalize the oppression than to deal with the religious hatred. Thus the pragmatic arguments do not allow for the independent value of religious freedom or for the importance of human rights. They do not, for these reasons, give much in the way of guidance to the Court when it comes to interpreting the role of Article 9 in the Convention.

[24] Declaration on the Elimination of All Forms of Intolerance and Discrimination Based on Religion or Belief, G.A. Res. 36/55, U.N. GAOR, Supp. (No. 51) 171, U.N. Doc. A/36/684 (1981) [hereinafter the 'Declaration on Religious Intolerance and Discrimination'].

2.4 THE HISTORICAL JUSTIFICATION

Another argument that is raised as a rationale for religious freedom looks to the history of persecution on the basis of religion or belief in Europe. This is allied to the social conflict argument as it seeks to protect religious freedom in order to prevent the undesirable outcomes of intolerance, such as torture, imprisonment on the basis of belief, exile, and all of the other horrors that were once visited on religious dissenters. This argument can be construed so as to claim that there is nothing particularly important about freedom of religion as such except for the fact that historically religion has been used as a basis to justify persecution and repression. This persecution generally took the form of breaches of other rights in the Convention, such as the right to freedom of assembly, freedom of speech, and—in more extreme but not uncommon cases—the right to life and the prohibition on torture.[25] Given the widespread nature of general human rights abuses it was necessary to make absolutely clear in the Convention that the exercise of somebody's religion did not justify the denial of their rights. If there had not been such historical persecution, then it may not have been necessary to specifically include freedom of religion. Similarly it might be said that it has been necessary to protect people from violations of their rights on the basis of race, as this had long been a basis for discrimination, but that it was not considered necessary to protect people from discrimination on the basis of height or eye colour for the simple reason that these had not historically been a cause for mistreatment. If they had been, then they too would probably have merited special protection in the Convention.

This argument has some force in explaining why religion has been included in all the major human rights treaties. It also serves as a salutary reminder that religion and belief have been used to justify the most appalling treatment of human beings and that vigilance is required to ensure that European societies do not fall back into habits of hysteria, misinformation, and prejudice in relation to religions that seem strange or alien to majority sentiment. While the historical basis for the protection of freedom of religion is important, however, it is not a satisfactory answer to the question of why freedom of religion or belief is valuable. It may be a partial explanation of why discrimination on the basis of religion and belief is specifically prohibited in Article 14 of the Convention, along with discrimination on other bases which have historically given rise to prejudice, but it does not explain why it is that people should not only have the right to be free from torture, execution, and so forth on the basis of religion but

---

[25] See, e.g. the history of religious freedom in Europe given in MALCOLM EVANS, RELIGIOUS LIBERTY AND INTERNATIONAL LAW IN EUROPE chapters 1–2 (1997); Myres S. McDougal, Harold D. Lasswell, and Lung-chu Chen, *The Right to Religious Freedom and World Public Order: The Emerging Norm of Non-Discrimination*, 74 MICH. L. REV. 865, 866–72 (1976).

should also have a positive right to freedom of religion or belief. Neither does it explain why the exercise of one's religious freedom was considered an inappropriate basis on which to discriminate against a person. Clearly, the State has a right to 'discriminate' against those who engage in anti-social behaviour, such as crime, and religious dissidence was once considered anti-social. It is necessary to go further than the mere history of persecution to explain why religious liberty came to be seen as a positive idea and worthy of protection.

2.5 RELIGIOUS ARGUMENTS

There are a number of pragmatic reasons why a person who believes in the truth of his or her own religious beliefs may nevertheless be prepared to tolerate those of other people and to accept freedom of religion. One such ground might be that the believer's own religion is a minority religion in either all or some of the States in which its adherents exist. Believers may then see the importance of promoting religious freedom where they are in a minority in all States, or of recognizing the right to religious freedom in States where they are in a majority in order to promote reciprocal respect in States where they are in a minority.[26] This type of reciprocity may help to convince some religions to adopt teachings that are supportive of religious tolerance but it is not a principle from which the scope of religious freedom can be derived.

Another religious argument in favour of religious freedom is that it might be easiest to convince people to believe in the 'true religion' in an environment of religious freedom. Coercion in religious matters may affect the quality of belief by encouraging hypocrisy and deceit. Both Locke and Mill, for example, argued from Christian premises and thought that true religion would benefit from allowing some degree of religious freedom. Locke argued that 'I may be cured by remedies I have not faith in; but I cannot be saved by a religion I distrust.'[27] Mill also argued that there were good reasons for those who belonged to the true faith to tolerate religious debate and dissent, in part on grounds that it would be good for the true religion itself. [28]

---

[26] GENE BURNS, THE FRONTIERS OF CATHOLICISM, THE POLITICS OF IDEOLOGY IN A LIBERAL WORLD chapter 4 (1994), argues that American Catholics played a strong role in promoting the change in Church doctrine to an acceptance of religious freedom because of their experiences as a minority religion.

[27] JOHN LOCKE, *Letters on Toleration* in the WORKS OF JOHN LOCKE, Vol. VI, at 28 (1823).

[28] JOHN STUART MILL, ON LIBERTY (Wordsworth Classic edition, 1996), notes *inter alia* that it is always possible that truth would not prevail over error and that it would be the true religion that was persecuted (at 30), that religious controversy can help to keep religion a 'living truth' rather than a 'dead dogma' (at 36) and that religious debate would assist people in developing a full understanding and appreciation of their faith (at 37).

This is one type of religious argument that is common in some Christian denominations. However, one trend in human rights and some religious discussion of religious freedom is an attempt to extract from *all* religions some core commitment to religious freedom. All of the texts of the major world religions contain some teachings that can be used to support freedom of religion and belief, and these can be drawn to argue that *properly understood* all religions are or should be supportive of the right to religious freedom as a good in and of itself. Religious tolerance, however, may be part of the teaching of some religions but it is not common to all religions, and even religious groups that share some commitment to a notion of freedom of religion may disagree fundamentally as to the meaning of and limits to that freedom.[29] To attempt to conflate these complex arguments into a simple statement that freedom of religion or belief is good for and supported by all religions does not reflect the reality of diverse religious opinion.[30]

To give only two examples of the problems with taking religious arguments as the basis for the jurisprudence of the Court in Article 9 cases, the Catholic Church until very recently was completely opposed to the notion of religious freedom. It reacted strongly against the growth of liberalism in Europe, and the idea that the 'Church ought to be separated from the State, and the State from the Church' was one of the beliefs condemned by Pope Pius IX in his *Syllabus of Errors* in 1864.[31] Likewise, the notion that 'liberty of conscience and worship is each man's personal right' was condemned by Pope Gregory XVI as 'an insanity' and by Pius IX as an 'erroneous opinion, most fatal in its effects on the Catholic Church and the salvation of souls'.[32] In 1965, the Second Vatican Council broke with the traditional approach of the Catholic Church and for the first time recognized religious freedom as the right of all people. In its *Declaration on Religious Freedom 1965*, the Council declared that,

The truth cannot impose itself except by virtue of its own truth, as it makes its entrance into the mind at once quietly and with power. Religious freedom, in turn, which men demand as necessary to fulfil their duty to worship God, has to do with immunity from coercion in civil society. Therefore, it leaves untouched traditional Catholic doctrine on the moral duty of men and societies toward the true religion and toward the one Church of Christ.[33]

[29] Robert Traer, Faith and Human Rights 3–6 (1994).

[30] On the way in which the predominant 'rights talk' has come to hijack many religious organizations' approaches to freedom of religion see Malcolm Evans, *Religion, Law and Human Rights: Locating the Debate,* unpublished paper delivered at a meeting of the British Institute of International and Comparative Law, at Charles Clore House on 2 Mar. 1999.

[31] Pius IX, *Syllabus of Errors* 1864, *in* The Sources of Catholic Dogma 440 (Henry Denzinger ed., 1957).

[32] Pius IX, *Quanta Cura* 1864, *in* The Papal Encyclicals, Vol. 1 1740–1878, at 382 (Carlen ed.), which encyclical also cites the views of Pope Gregory XVI.

[33] Vatican II, *Declaration on Religious Freedom, in* The Documents of Vatican II, at 677 (Walter M. Abbott ed., 1966).

Yet even this new approach, which is far more compatible with liberal human rights than the traditional condemnation of religious freedom, is premissed on the absolute truth of the teaching of the Catholic Church and, as can be seen from the final sentence of the Council's declaration, it has a far narrower scope than many liberals may find appropriate.

This conflict between religious teaching and human rights can be seen even more strongly in certain Islamic teachings.[34] Unlike the Christian Churches, the idea of free will is a weak one in Islam, which rather emphasizes that the object of human life is submission to God and that the State (in so far as this is a meaningful concept in Islam[35]) and individuals should dedicate themselves to this purpose.[36] Those who emphasize the compatibility of Islam with religious freedom tend to point to the statement in the Qur'ān that 'there should be no compulsion in religion'.[37] In practice, however, in many Islamic States, this injunction has been interpreted in a very limited manner and has not given rise to a general right to religious freedom in Islamic law.[38] The liberality of this quotation must also be set against the traditional hostility of Islam toward conversion from Islam to another religion.[39] The Prophet was believed to have said that 'he who changes his religion, must be killed', although the authenticity of this statement is questioned by some Muslim writers.[40] Apostasy is likewise a serious offence, for which the death penalty has sometimes been invoked.[41] There is a tradition of some degree of religious freedom for 'People of the Book' in Muslim countries, but this freedom does not extend to all religions and does not give equal rights to Muslims and non-Muslims.

[34] See generally, Donna E. Arzt, *The Application of International Human Rights Law in Islamic States*, 12 Hum. Rts Q. 202 (1990); Abdullahi A. An-Na'im, *Religious Minorities under Islamic Law and the Limits of Cultural Relativism*, 9 Hum. Rts Q. 1 (1987). An-Na'im represents a new generation of Islamic thinking which has sought to reinterpret Islamic traditions compatibly with notions of human rights, including the idea of religious freedom. The traditional view, however, still holds sway in many Muslim States, particularly in the Middle East.

[35] M. Cherif Bassiouni, *Sources of Islamic Law and the Protection of Human Rights in the Islamic Criminal Justice System, in* The Islamic Criminal Justice System 23 (M. Cherif Bassiouni ed., 1982) notes that, 'Unlike western philosophical and political perceptions of the separability of the individual and the state, Islamic social concepts do not make such a distinction.'

[36] M. Khadduri, The Islamic Concept of Justice 236–7 (1984) discusses the difficulty of relating the idea of individual freedom as understood in the West with the Islamic notion. The word 'Muslim' literally means 'one who submits'.

[37] *Quran* 2: 256.

[38] Artz, above, note 34, at 209.

[39] Saudi Arabia, for example, objected to the inclusion of the right to change religion in Art. 18 of the Universal Declaration, because Islam prohibits changing religion and because it would encourage proselytism. See 3 U.N. GAOR C.3 (127 mtg) at 391–2; U.N. Doc. A/C.3/SR. 127 (1948).

[40] Khadduri, above, note 36, at 177, 195–8.

[41] Most famously in the West in relation to Salman Rushdie for the publication of Satanic Verses. Comments of panellists, *Speech, Religious Discrimination, and Blasphemy*, in 83 A.S.I.L. Proc. 434–5 (1989).

As with the Catholic Church, and indeed most religions that claim exclusive access to the truth, religious freedom is valuable in Islam only to the extent that it can be accommodated within the teachings of the religion. In a religiously pluralistic Europe, the Court should thus be wary of drawing too heavily on religious models as a basis for freedom of religion or belief. While some individuals may respect religious freedom because of their religious beliefs, others may have to be forced to respect the freedom of others despite their religion or belief. Some religious arguments acknowledge the intrinsic good of freedom of religion or belief, but not all do. Even those religions that have acknowledged the importance of such freedom will often limit it more severely than allowed for in human rights treaties.

2.6 RELIGIOUS FREEDOM AND RELIGIOUS TRUTH

The theological arguments in favour of religious freedom often begin with the assumption that their religion is the true religion and any arguments in favour of religious freedom must be compatible with the teachings of the religion more generally. The truth of any particular religion is, however, a matter of considerable debate and contention. One liberal argument in favour of freedom of religion—or at least freedom of debate on religious matters—is that it is important to ensure that religious truth is not suppressed. This argument was made by John Stuart Mill, in his famous essay *On Liberty* as the first of a series of arguments in favour of freedom of speech:

First: the opinion which it is attempted to suppress by authority may possibly be true. Those who desire to suppress it, of course, deny its truth; but they are not infallible. They have no authority to decide the question for all mankind, and to exclude every other person from the means of judging. To refuse a hearing to an opinion, because they are sure that it is false, is to assume that *their* certainty is the same thing as *absolute* certainty. All silencing of discussion is an assumption of infallibility.[42]

This argument was expressly said by Mill to extend to issues of religion and conscience and used by him to argue against those who claimed that freedom of speech should only be allowed in certain areas, which did not include the basic truths of Christian doctrine.[43] This argument has force in modern, pluralistic, and increasingly secular societies. Greater contact with other races and cultures has illustrated that there are a huge variety of religious beliefs, in the face of which the self-evidence of one's own religion became more difficult to argue.

[42] MILL, above, note 28, at 20.   [43] *Id.* at 25–6.

2.7 AUTONOMY AND PLURALISM

Linked to Mill's theory is another liberal theory to explain the importance of religious freedom. This theory argues that freedom of religion or belief is an essential and independent component of treating human beings as autonomous persons deserving of dignity and respect.[44] If society does so treat people it will commit itself to at least a weak notion of value pluralism,[45] which will allow for a choice between a variety of religious beliefs, practices, and communities to exist and to be given some protection in that society.[46] Thus respect for individual autonomy will also promote the notion of tolerance and pluralism in a society.

The picture of human nature that is painted by proponents of autonomy varies somewhat from author to author. Professor Raz notes that the

[R]uling idea behind the ideal of personal autonomy is that people should make their own lives. The autonomous person is a (part) author of this life. The ideal of personal autonomy is the vision of people controlling, to some degree, their own destiny, fashioning it through successive decisions throughout their lives.[47]

This he contrasts with a life of coerced choices, no choices (or no awareness of choices), or simply drifting through life without exercising the capacity to choose.[48] While he does not discuss religion as part of the autonomous life in any detail, it is clear from his discussion that choice in matters of religion and conscience, at least to some degree, must be an

---

[44] This is not to enter into the controversy over the detailed implications of these theories in practice. In particular the way in which this justification affects the relationship between the State and religions within the State is a controversial one. In the USA a significant debate has arisen over whether freedom of religion requires the State to be 'neutral' in relation to religion and whether this concept of 'neutrality' is a meaningful one. The debate often gets caught up in the particulars of the USA constitutional system, which does not merely give a right of freedom of religion but also requires that the State not establish a religion. Some of the implications of these analyses will be discussed later in the book, but for now all that is sought to be established is the particular, predominantly liberal view of human nature that justifies religious freedom. For further discussion of the neutrality issue see Smith, above, note 23, at 305; Douglas Laycock, *Formal, Substantive and Disaggregated Neutrality Toward Religion*, 39 DePaul L. Rev. 993 (1990); Stephen L. Carter, *Evolutionism, Creationism and Treating Religion as a Hobby*, 6 Duke LJ 977 (1987); Stanley Fish, *Liberalism Doesn't Exist*, 6 Duke LJ 997 (1987).

[45] This notion is taken from Raz, above, note 23, at 396, where he defines moral or value pluralism as the claim 'not merely that incompatible forms of life are morally acceptable but that they display distinct virtues, each capable of being pursued for its own sake'. At 398 he demonstrates the link between autonomy and weak value pluralism, as the exercise of autonomy requires that the autonomous individual has an adequate range of valuable choices among which to make his or her decisions about the way in which to construct his or her life.

[46] Though Raz has some hesitations about religious cults or communities that create a separate culture that is not supportive of autonomy. In some circumstances it might be best to assimilate such communities into the dominant liberal one, though there are real dangers in doing this. *Id.* at 423–4.

[47] *Id.* at 369.   [48] *Id.* at 371.

essential component of autonomy. Coercion in matters of fundamental importance, such as a belief in the existence of God, or an afterlife, or a religiously based set of morals or obligations towards others, would deny people the ability to be authors of their own lives. The fullest personal autonomy will exist in a society in which a person sees the availability of a range of good choices in regard to religion or belief and is able to make meaningful decisions about which, if any, of these choices he or she wishes to adopt.

Ronald Dworkin expresses a similar political ideal in somewhat different terms,[49] beginning from the notion of equality as the primary political value.

> Government must treat those whom it governs with concern, that is, as human beings who are capable of suffering and frustration, and with respect, that is, as human beings who are capable of forming and acting on intelligent conceptions of how their lives should be lived. Government must not only treat people with concern and respect, but with equal concern and respect. It must not distribute goods or opportunities unequally on the ground that some citizens are entitled to more because they are worthy of more concern. It must not constrain liberty on the ground that one citizen's conception of the good life of one group is nobler or superior to another's.[50]

Dworkin does not spend much time on the specific issue of religion, but again it can be seen that his notion of 'equal concern and respect', and particularly the idea that all people are entitled to develop their ideas of the good life, gives rise to a strong claim for religious freedom. Inherent in the idea of equal concern and respect is the notion that individuals are in the best position to determine their own concept of the good life and should, within certain constraints, be free to pursue their ideal without government interference. In so far as freedom of religion is a right in Dworkian terms it 'trumps' all but the most serious social reasons for restricting it. Mere convenience, or the dislike of the majority for a certain religious practice, or other utilitarian considerations are insufficient to justify interfering in a person's right to freedom of religion or conscience, though conflicts with the rights of others or with strong social/utilitarian reasons would be sufficient in some circumstances.[51] The State that interferes with someone's religious freedom without strong reason does not show appropriate concern and respect for that person.

---

[49] The differences between the viewpoints are important at some points, such as whether a government should have a perfectionist approach to notions of the good, but they do not affect the issues under discussion at any significant level.

[50] RONALD DWORKIN, TAKING RIGHTS SERIOUSLY 272–3 (1977).

[51] *Id.* at 199–200, where Dworkin deals generally with the circumstances in which the State can legitimately interfere with a right. Freedom of religion or belief is not specifically mentioned in the book, although the importance of the right to act in accordance with conscience is discussed in some detail in Chapter 8 (Civil Disobedience).

Other authors have more specifically discussed the issue of religious freedom as a fundamental aspect of human life and self-definition. In *A Theory of Justice*, Professor Rawls develops a notion of justice based on the principles that would be chosen by people in 'the original position', a position in which they are ignorant of all their personal characteristics and beliefs and have to make decisions about the way in which their society is run based on practical rationality.[52] In relation to freedom of conscience he comments that

[I]t seems that equal liberty of conscience is the only principle that the persons in the original position can acknowledge. They cannot take chances with their liberty by permitting the dominant religious or moral doctrine to persecute or to suppress others if it wishes. Even granting (what may be questioned) that it is more probable than not that one will turn out to belong to the majority (if a majority exists), to gamble in this way would show that one did not take one's religious or moral convictions seriously, or highly value the liberty to examine one's belief.[53]

He uses this analysis to conclude that the State cannot favour or penalize membership in any religion, that a confessional State is incompatible with justice, and that all should be free to create, join, and leave religious or moral associations (although the State may have to play a role in protecting the ability to leave).[54]

The importance of religion or belief to the protection of rational choice and autonomy is reiterated by McDougal, Lasswell, and Chen who argue that

In a community genuinely committed to the goal of human dignity, one paramount policy should be to honour and defend the freedom of the individual to choose a fundamental orientation toward the world. One of the most distinctive acts available to man as a rational being is the continual redefinition of the self in relation to others and to the cosmos. Thus, each individual must be free to search for the basic postulates in a perspective that will unify the experiences of life.[55]

Attempts by the State to coerce such decisions or to restrict the individual's freedom to act in light of his or her beliefs have serious implications for the moral well-being of that individual and his or her autonomy.

None of these authors would claim that freedom of religion is an absolute value. While some religious arguments may claim that, because their adherents are acting in accordance with the highest truth, there is no ground on which the State can legitimately limit the practice of their religion, autonomy arguments are more limited. They certainly do not begin with the assumption that one religion has a monopoly on truth or that all religious practices are permissible, and to this extent they will conflict with

[52] JOHN RAWLS, A THEORY OF JUSTICE 17–22 (1972).
[53] *Id.* at 207.   [54] *Id.* at 212.
[55] McDougall, Laswell, and Chen, above, note 25, at 873.

some other, theological understandings of human nature and the place of religion. Religious freedom is one important aspect of autonomy or individual dignity, but there are other important aspects of autonomy that sometimes conflict with religious freedom. The conflict between one person's religious duty to punish apostasy with death and the right to life of the apostate is one clear example of a case when the State should use autonomy arguments to defeat claims of religious freedom.

Yet the autonomy argument at least develops a basis for freedom of religion that is not dependent on any particular religious viewpoint[56] and situates it as part of a broader moral and political philosophy. However complicated its implications may be in practice, it at the very least reminds those in the State who formulate laws that interfere with freedom of religion that, however bizarre, inappropriate, or irrational they may consider a religion or belief, that religion or belief may be part of the deepest self-definition of its adherents and their fullest expression of their commitment to living in compliance with their conception of the good.

2.8 CONCLUSION: IMPLICATIONS FOR INTERPRETATION

Article 9 is expressed, as are many articles in the Convention, in fairly general terms. It is open to a range of interpretations. Using the concept/conception idea developed by Dworkin,[57] freedom of religion and belief is a broad concept of which different people will have different conceptions. As the above discussion demonstrates, there are a number of different rationales for freedom of religion and belief and the conception that is adopted will lead to different interpretations of the scope and importance of the freedom. Thus while many people may agree that the concept of freedom of religion and belief is beneficial, their conceptions may be so divergent that the way in which they envisage religious freedom working in practice will differ significantly. If freedom of religion is important because everyone has different and wholly subjective religious ideas, for example, then beliefs about religion may be no more significant than beliefs about the best flavour of ice-cream, so little reason may be needed to justify State interference. If religious freedom is important only to limit social conflict then constraints on the freedom that do not cause conflict may be acceptable. If questions about religion and belief are, however, perceived as an essential component of self-identity and if interference with them is seen to be an attack on the autonomy of the individual, then religious freedom is likely to be given a wide scope and limitations on it will require serious justification.

---

[56] This is not to suggest that it is religiously neutral. It is, for example, more favourable to religions which are themselves relatively liberal in character.

[57] Dworkin, above, note 50, at 134–6.

This book argues that one of the reasons that the Court and Commission have not developed an adequate jurisprudence on religious freedom is that they have not taken seriously the importance of understanding the rationale for religious freedom. The Court has spoken vaguely of pluralism and the importance of religion to the individual believer,[58] but has not reflected on the way in which these concepts affect their interpretation and application of Article 9. Unless a coherent philosophical justification underlies all the cases dealing with Article 9, then the result is likely to be inconsistency and unfairness as the judges move from one rationale to another to justify their intuitions about the right outcome for a particular factual situation.

The argument from autonomy seems to be the best approach for the Court to take to interpreting Article 9. It is broadly consistent with the ideas of pluralism, tolerance, and the importance of religion to believers that the Court has already adopted.[59] It allows for an integrated approach to Article 9 and other important autonomy rights in the Convention, such as freedom of speech, freedom of association, and the right to family life, which recognize the importance of allowing a person to be the 'author of his or her own life'. Finally it acknowledges the importance of religion and belief to the individual and the danger of trivializing that importance by unwarranted or unjustified State interference. This approach emphasizes the dignity of all human beings and the importance of allowing them to make and live out decisions about the issues that are most important to them. It is thus consistent with the ideals of the Convention as a whole and allows for an integrated and sophisticated approach to the many complex questions to which the application of the Convention gives rise.

---

[58] *Kokkinakis v. Greece*, 260-A Eur. Ct. H.R. (ser. A) at 13 (1993).

[59] The autonomy theory proposed by this chapter, while it will tend to promote a pluralistic society, is based more on the importance of religious freedom to individuals than to society. This difference in emphasis can be important, as discussed by Peter W. Edge, *Current Problems in Article 9 of the European Convention on Human Rights*, 1996 JURID. REV. 42, 47–50.

3

Historical Background

Chapter 2 illustrates that conceptions of freedom of religion and belief differ significantly, so it is likely that ambiguities will arise in interpretations of Article 9 that rely simply on a good faith interpretation of its words in their context. In these circumstances it is appropriate to look to the drafting history of the Convention to see if it can shed light on the way in which the drafters intended Article 9 to be interpreted.

The Convention was intended to build upon the work undertaken in the United Nations[1] and aims at 'securing the universal and effective recognition and observance of the rights'[2] contained in the Universal Declaration of Human Rights.[3] Thus, particularly as the protection of religious freedom was more controversial and therefore more debated in the Universal Declaration than the Convention context, it is necessary to look first at the Universal Declaration's drafting history for any light that it can shed on the appropriate interpretation of the Convention.

3.1 THE UNIVERSAL DECLARATION OF HUMAN RIGHTS

Although the Charter of the United Nations set out a number of general provisions relating to human rights,[4] it was left to the Universal Declaration to begin the process of detailing an international scheme for the protection

---

[1] Of course, the work carried out by the United Nations was itself part of an ongoing process of the development of religious freedom in Europe. For a discussion of developments prior to the establishment of the United Nations see MALCOLM D. EVANS, RELIGIOUS LIBERTY AND INTERNATIONAL LAW IN EUROPE chapters 1–6 (1997); Myres S. McDougal, Harold D. Lasswell, and Lung-chu Chen, *The Right to Religious Freedom and World Public Order: The Emerging Norm of Non-Discrimination*, 74 MICH. L. REV. 865, 876–84 (1976); PATRICK THORNBERRY, INTERNATIONAL LAW AND THE RIGHTS OF MINORITIES 26–37 (1991); JOHN FISCHER WILLIAMS, SOME ASPECTS OF THE COVENANT OF THE LEAGUE OF NATIONS 190–210 (1943); MANOUCHEHR GANJI, INTERNATIONAL PROTECTION OF HUMAN RIGHTS 46–8 (1962).

[2] Preamble to the Convention, first paragraph.

[3] Universal Declaration of Human Rights, G.A. Res. 217, 3(1) U.N. GAOR Res. 71, U.N. Doc. A/811 (1948) [hereinafter 'the Universal Declaration'].

[4] Art. 1(3) states that one of the purposes of the United Nations is to achieve international cooperation 'in promoting and encouraging respect for human rights ... without distinction as to race, sex, language or religion'. Art. 55 reinforces this by stating that the United Nations shall promote respect for human rights 'without distinction as to race, sex, language or religion'. It does not, however, attempt to list, or set up mechanisms for the protection of, these human rights and fundamental freedoms. See EVANS, above, note 1.

of human rights, including freedom of religion. Article 18 of the Universal Declaration is the primary article dealing with freedom of religion.[5] It reads:

Everyone has the right to freedom of thought, conscience and religion; this right includes freedom to change his religion or belief, and freedom, either alone or in community with others and in public or private, to manifest his religion or belief in teaching, practice, worship and observance.

In addition to this protection, Article 2 of the Universal Declaration reiterates the Charter protection of the rights of all people without distinction as to 'race, colour, sex, language, religion, political or other opinion, national or social origin, property, birth or other status'. Article 16 protects the right of 'men and women of full age, without any limitation due to race, nationality or religion . . . to marry and found a family'. Article 19 protects 'the right to freedom of opinion and expression', which presumably extends to freedom to communicate in regard to religious issues. Article 26(2), which is an important article with no equivalent in the Convention, urges that education should be used to 'promote understanding, tolerance and friendship among all nations, racial and religious groups'.

The rights contained in the Universal Declaration are subject to the general limitation contained in Article 29(2), which provides that

In the exercise of his rights and freedoms, everyone shall be subject only to such limitations as are determined by law solely for the purpose of securing due recognition and respect for the rights and freedoms of others and of meeting the just requirements of morality, public order and the general welfare in a democratic society.

The fundamental nature of the right to free belief was stressed by participants from a variety of cultural backgrounds and it was implied by them that only *manifestations* of belief (as compared to matters of internal conscience) could be subject to the limitation in Article 29(2).[6]

The two major controversies that arose during the drafting of Article 18 of the Universal Declaration related to the right to change religion and to the wording of appropriate limitations on freedom of religious practice.[7] The Universal Declaration is the only United Nations instrument to explicitly recognize the right to change religion. It did so in the face of challenges

---

[5] For a view as to the scope of Art. 18 see Phillip Halpern, *Preliminary Report of the Proposed Study on Discrimination in the Matter of Religious Rights and Practices*, para 11, U.N. Doc. E/CN.4/Sub.2/162 (1954).

[6] U.N. Doc. E/CN.4/SR.60 (1948); Martin Scheinin, *Article 18*, *in* THE UNIVERSAL DECLARATION OF HUMAN RIGHTS: A COMMENTARY 266 (Asbjorn Eide *et al.* eds., 1992).

[7] BAHIYYIH G. TAHZIB, FREEDOM OF RELIGION AND BELIEF: ENSURING EFFECTIVE INTERNATIONAL PROTECTION 73–8 (1996); Roger S. Clark, *The United Nations and Religious Freedom*, 11 N.Y.U.J. INT'L L. & POL. 197, 200 (1978); Desmond M. Clarke, *Freedom of Thought in the UN Declaration and Covenants*, 28 IRISH JURIST 121, 121–3 (1993–5).

from a number of Middle Eastern states,[8] which were concerned that this right gave too much scope to missionaries, who had often been involved in the colonization of developing states.[9] Some Islamic State representatives also noted that it was contrary to Islamic law for a Muslim to convert to another religion.[10] Despite this controversy, the right to change religion was included in the final draft and may explain why Saudi Arabia abstained from the final vote on the Universal Declaration.[11]

The other main controversy was as to whether freedom of worship should be subject to special limitations as well as the general limitations provided in Article 29(2). The USSR delegate, for example, unsuccessfully proposed that the conduct of religious services should be 'in accordance with the laws of the country concerned and the requirements of public morality'.[12] A Swedish amendment allowing for freedom of worship 'provided that this does not interfere unduly with the personal liberty of anybody else' was also defeated.[13] Thus, most States rejected the notion that religious freedom should be subject to specific limitations rather than being subject to the type of general limitation used in relation to other human rights.

It was in this context that the Council of Europe, which relied heavily on the wording of the Universal Declaration, began its drafting exercise. The United Nations continued to develop the right to freedom of religion

---

[8] Clark, above, note 7, at 200. A Saudi Arabian proposal to amend the Universal Declaration to remove the words 'freedom to change his religion or belief' was defeated 22 to 12 with 8 abstentions: U.N. Doc. A/C.3/247/Rev.1 (1948).

[9] For the comments of the Saudi Arabian delegate see 3(1) U.N. GAOR C.3 (127th mtg) 391, 392, U.N. Doc. A/C.3/SR. 127 (1948).

[10] 3 U.N. GAOR C.3 (127th mtg) at 391–2, U.N. Doc. A/C.3/SR. 127 (1948); Abdullahi A. An-Na'im, *Religious Minorities Under Islamic Law and the Limits of Cultural Relativism*, 9 Hum. Rts. Q. 1 (1987); Donna E. Arzt, *The Application of International Human Rights Law in Islamic States*, 12 Hum. Rts. Q. 202, 209 (1990); M. Cherif Bassiouni, *Paper to Panel on Religious Discrimination and Blasphemy*, 83 Am. Soc. Int'l L. 432, 433–4 (1989).

[11] This issue is still a cause of serious controversy at the international level and the texts of United Nations treaties have, over time, excluded any express reference to the right to change religion or belief. Most authors, however, conclude that there is such a right under the United Nations human rights instruments that deal with religious freedom. See Odio Benito, U.N. Doc. E/CN.4/Sub.2/1987/26 at paras 20–1; K. J. Partsch, *Freedom of Conscience and Expression and Political Freedoms*, in The International Bill of Human Rights: The Covenant on Civil and Political Rights 209, 211 (L. Henkin ed., 1981); Brice Dickson, *The United Nations and Freedom of Religion*, 44 Int'l & Comp. L.Q. 327, 346 (1995); Natan Lerner, *The Final Text of the U.N. Declaration Against Intolerance and Discrimination Based on Religion and Belief*, 12 Isr. Y.B on H.R. 187, 187–9 (1992); Donna Sullivan, *Advancing the Freedom of Religion and Belief through the United Nations Declaration on the Elimination of Religious Intolerance and Discrimination*, 82 Am. J. Int'l L. 487, 496 (1988).

[12] U.N. Doc. E/800 at 33 (1948). The proposal was defeated in the Third Committee, 3(1) U.N. GAOR, C.3 (128th mtg) 405, U.N. Doc. A/C.3/SR. 128 (1948).

[13] The text of the proposed amendment is at U.N. Doc. A/C.3/SR. 128 (1948). The amendment was defeated in the Third Committee, 3(1) GAOR C.3 (128th mtg) 405, U.N. Doc. A/C.3/SR. 128 (1948).

and belief in a number of other international instruments, [14] most notably Article 18 of the International Covenant on Civil and Political Rights[15] and the more detailed Declaration on Religious Intolerance and Discrimination. No specific treaty dealing with freedom of religion and belief has been concluded by the United Nations because of the ongoing controversies surrounding the content of such a treaty.[16]

A number of other regional treaties that refer to religious freedom have also been concluded in addition to the Convention. These include Article 12 of the American Convention on Human Rights,[17] Article 8 of the African Charter of Human and Peoples' Rights,[18] and Part VI of the Final Act of the Helsinki Conference.[19]

[14] For greater detail on the way in which the United Nations has dealt with the issue of freedom of religion and belief see TAHZIB, above, note 7; Dickson, above, note 11; S. Liskofsky, *The UN Declaration on the Elimination of Religious Intolerance and Discrimination: Historical and Legal Perspectives*, *in* RELIGION AND STATE: ESSAYS IN HONOUR OF LEO PFEFFER 441 (J. Woods ed., 1985); Clark, above, note 7; Natan Lerner, *Toward a Draft Declaration Against Religious Intolerance and Discrimination*, 11 ISR. Y.B ON H.R. 84 (1981); Lerner, above, note 11; Sullivan, above, note 11.

[15] International Covenant on Civil and Political Rights, G.A. Res. 2200 A, 21 U.N. GAOR, Supp. (No. 16) 52, U.N. Doc. A/6316 (1966) [hereinafter the 'I.C.C.P.R.'].

[16] Even commentators who are supportive of the development of an international right of religious freedom are divided over the desirability of a treaty at this point in time. See Theo van Boven, Working Paper Pursuant to Commission Resolution 1988/55 and Sub-Commission Decision 1988/11, U.N. Doc. E/CN.4/Sub.2/1989/32, para 20 (1989); Odio Benito, No. 2 Human Rights Studies Series, United Nations (1989); TAHZIB, above, note 7, at chapter 5; Sullivan, above, note 11, at 519.

[17] American Convention on Human Rights, No. 22, 1969, O.A.S. Treaty Series No. 36, at 1, O.A.S. Off. Rec. OEA/Ser.L./V/II. 23 doc. rev. 2.
Art. 12: Freedom of Conscience and Religion
1. Everyone has the right to freedom of conscience and religion. This right includes the freedom to maintain or to change one's religion or beliefs, and the freedom to profess or disseminate one's religion or beliefs, either individually or together with others, in public or in private.
2. No one shall be subject to restrictions that might impair his freedom to maintain or to change his religion or beliefs.
3. Freedom to manifest one's religion or beliefs may be subject only to the limitations prescribed by law that are necessary to protect public safety, order, health or morals, or the rights and freedoms of others.
4. Parents or guardians, as the case may be, have the right to provide for the religious and moral education of their children or wards that is in accord with their own convictions.

[18] African Charter on Human and Peoples' Rights, 26 June 1981, O.A.U. Doc. CAB/LEG/67/3 Rev. 5, Art. 8 'Freedom of conscience, the profession and free practice of religion shall be guaranteed. No one may, subject to law and order, be submitted to measures restricting the exercise of these freedoms.'

[19] Final Act of the Conference on Security and Co-operation in Europe, 1 Aug. 1975, reprinted in 1975 14 I.L.M. 1292 (1975). Part VII is entitled 'Respect for Human Rights and Fundamental Freedoms, including Freedom of Thought, Conscience, Religion or Belief' and it begins 'The participating States will respect human rights and fundamental freedoms, including freedom of thought, conscience, religion or belief, for all without distinction as to race, sex, language or religion.' The third paragraph of the part recognizes the right of the individual 'to profess or practise, alone or in community with others, religion or belief acting in accordance with the dictates of his own conscience'.

3.2 DEVELOPMENTS IN THE COUNCIL OF EUROPE

3.2.1 The Limitations of the *Travaux Préparatoires*

While reference to the *travaux préparatoires* is generally accepted as a subsidiary interpretative device in cases where a treaty is ambiguous,[20] and is also a way of gaining insight into the views of treaty drafters, a note of caution should be sounded about the use of the *travaux préparatoires* of the Convention. The *travaux préparatoires* are neither complete nor particularly revealing as regards the reasons for the development of the various drafts of the Convention. Originally, the *travaux préparatoires* were confidential and available only to States.[21] They were published in 1975 but, although some debates are included in addition to the drafts, many of the critical debates were not recorded.[22] As few of the people who were involved in the drafting of the Convention have written about their experiences,[23] a certain amount of guesswork is involved in piecing together the reasons why Article 9 developed as it did.[24]

The process of drafting was a complex one, in part initiated by the draft Convention prepared by M. Pierre-Henri Teitgen, Sir David Maxwell-Fyfe, and Professor Fernand Dehousse under the auspices of the European Movement.[25] The official drafting process by the Council of Europe included participation by a Consultative Assembly, a Committee of Experts, a Conference of Senior Officials, a Committee on Legal and Administrative Questions, and the Committee of Ministers of the European Council. Each of these bodies had some input into the drafting of the Convention, although it was the Committee of Ministers that made the ultimate decision about the adoption of a final draft. Not all of these bodies kept minutes and not all the minutes that were kept have been published. Thus it is often

---

[20] See the V.C.L.T., Art. 32.

[21] *Travaux Préparatoires*, vol. 1, at xxviii–xxx, introduction by A. H. Robertson.

[22] *Id.* at xxx.

[23] G. Marston, *The United Kingdom's Part in Preparation of the European Convention on Human Rights*, 42 INT'L & COMP. L.Q. 766 (1993); THE EUROPEAN MOVEMENT, THE EUROPEAN MOVEMENT AND THE COUNCIL OF EUROPE (1949); P. H. Teitgen, *Introduction to the European Convention on Human Rights, in* THE EUROPEAN SYSTEM FOR THE PROTECTION OF HUMAN RIGHTS (R. StJ. Macdonald, F. Matscher, and H. Petzold eds., 1993); J. E. S. FAWCETT, *Reform of the European Convention on Human Rights*, 1983 PUB. L. 468; A.H. ROBERTSON AND J. G. MERRILLS, HUMAN RIGHTS IN EUROPE 1–14 (1993); FRANCIS G. JACOBS AND ROBIN C. A. WHITE, THE EUROPEAN CONVENTION ON HUMAN RIGHTS 3–6 (2nd edn. 1996); MARK JANIS, RICHARD KAY, AND ANTHONY BRADLEY, EUROPEAN HUMAN RIGHTS LAW: TEXT AND MATERIALS 18–25 (1995).

[24] Hurst Hannum, *Collected Travaux Préparatoires of the European Convention on Human Rights*, 82 AM. J. INT'L L. 680, 682 (1988) (book review) warns that the usefulness of such material in assisting with the interpretation of ambiguous articles does not 'obviate the need for sound legal reasoning and good faith when one seeks to implement human rights treaties'.

[25] *Travaux Préparatoires*, vol. 1, at xxii–xxviii, introduction by A. H. Robertson. The draft was presented to the Committee of Ministers of the Council of Europe on 12 July 1949.

difficult to draw conclusions about why action was taken. Professor A. H. Robertson, the editor of the Collected Edition of the *Travaux Préparatoires*, notes that they 'do not constitute an instrument providing an authoritative interpretation of the text of the Convention and the First Protocol, although they may be of such a nature as to facilitate the application of their provisions'.[26] With these considerations in mind, some conclusions can still be drawn from the *travaux préparatoires* of the Convention about the intention of the drafters regarding the right to freedom of religion. [27] Such conclusions, however, are necessarily of a more general nature and more tentative than might have been possible if a better record of proceedings had been kept.

3.2.2 The Drafting of Article 9(1): Freedom of Religion or Belief

There was no doubt, from the earliest drafts, that freedom of religion was to be included in the rights and freedoms protected in the Convention. M. Teitgen, in his opening address to the Consultative Assembly, included 'freedom of religious belief' in a list of 'fundamental, undisputed freedoms'.[28] M. Cinglani, of Italy, used the same opening debate to condemn 'suppression of the most sacred right of all—that of religious belief and the works through which religious faith is manifested'.[29] Mr Everett, representative of the religiously divided Republic of Ireland, referred to civil and religious freedom as 'two of the fundamental rights of man' and concluded that 'if the Council of Europe achieves no other end than the guarantee of those two rights, it will have justified its existence'.[30] The fundamental nature of religious freedom was reiterated by speaker after speaker in this debate,[31] many referring to the importance of their own religious beliefs or experiences and the importance of religion to their countries.[32]

Many of the delegates were indeed explicit about the role they saw for the *Christian* religion in assisting with the development of human rights. Reflecting his perception of the Christian/liberal homogeneity of Europe, Sir David Maxwell-Fyfe concluded his speech by calling on 'those nations who belong to and revere the great family of Western Europe and Christian civilisation'[33] to ensure the promotion and protection of human rights.

[26] *Id.* at xxx–xxxii.

[27] See generally, EVANS, above, note 1, at chapter 10.

[28] *Travaux Préparatoires*, vol. 1, at 46, First Session of the Consultative Assembly.

[29] *Travaux Préparatoires*, vol. 1, at 62, First Session of the Consultative Assembly.

[30] *Travaux Préparatoires*, vol. 1, at 102–4, First Session of the Consultative Assembly.

[31] *Travaux Préparatoires*, vol. 1, First Session of the Consultative Assembly, speeches by Fayat (Belgium) at 86, Everett (Ireland) at 102, Perisco (Italy) at 112.

[32] *Travaux Préparatoires*, vol. 1, First Session of the Consultative Assembly, speeches by Ungoed-Thomas (United Kingdom—Wales) at 78, Maccas (Greece) at 106, Norton (Ireland) at 128, MacEntee (Ireland) at 140.

[33] *Travaux Préparatoires*, vol. 1, at 124, First Session of the Consultative Assembly, speech by Maxwell-Fyfe (United Kingdom).

While speaking about torture, Mr Cocks declared that torture is 'a crime against high heaven and the holy spirit of man. I say that it is a sin against the Holy Ghost for which there is no forgiveness.'[34] In similar mode, Mr Everett finished his address with the words '[m]ay God direct us in our work and deliberations'.[35] With this degree of personal importance of religion to many delegates and the place of religious freedom in the Universal Declaration, it was not surprising that the Consultative Assembly recommended that the Convention include a right to freedom of religion.

The wording used by the Consultative Assembly in its recommendation to the Council of Ministers was that the Convention include a right to '[f]reedom of thought, conscience and religion as laid down in Article 18 of the Declaration of the United Nations'.[36] This was an amendment of the earlier proposal recommending '[t]he freedom of religious practice and teaching, as laid down in Article 18 of the Declaration of the United Nations'[37] be included. The amendment, which was accepted unanimously,[38] was presumably aimed at recognizing the importance of religious belief (as compared to practice) and the fact that non-religious beliefs, such as atheism, were to be covered in the scope of the article on religious freedom. The draft prepared by the Consultative Assembly for presentation to the Ministers included, as Article 10, a right to freedom of religion in identical terms to those set out in the Universal Declaration.[39] The ultimate wording of Article 9(1) was identical in every important respect to that set out in the equivalent provision of the Universal Declaration. The Article went through little recorded debate and almost no amendments during the drafting of the Convention. Perhaps the most that can be said in regard to the drafting of Article 9(1) is that delegates considered the issue of freedom of religion to be of great importance and that they accepted that the Universal Declaration provided an appropriate model for its protection. There is no evidence of debate over the issues, such as the definition of religion or belief and the right to change religion, [40] that were so controversial during the drafting of various United Nations instruments.

---

[34] *Travaux Préparatoires*, vol. 2, at 40, First Session of the Consultative Assembly, speech by Cocks (United Kingdom).

[35] *Travaux Préparatoires*, vol. 1, at 106, First Session of the Consultative Assembly, speech by Everett (Ireland). See also Norton (Ireland) at 130.

[36] *Travaux Préparatoires*, vol. 1, at 174, First Session of the Consultative Assembly.

[37] *Travaux Préparatoires*, vol. 1, at 168, First Session of the Consultative Assembly.

[38] *Travaux Préparatoires*, vol. 1, at 174, First Session of the Consultative Assembly.

[39] *Travaux Préparatoires*, vol. 1, at 196, First Session of the Consultative Assembly.

[40] Although Turkey, a member State of the Council of Europe, spoke against the inclusion of a right to proselytize in the drafting debates over the Declaration on Religious Intolerance and Discrimination at 22 U.N. GAOR, C.3 (1487th mtg) 120, U.N. Doc. A/C.3/SR.1487 (1967).

3.2.3 The Drafting of Article 9(2): Limitations on Freedom of Religion

3.2.3.1 *Formulations of Article 9(2)*

If the scope of the protection of freedom of religion was relatively uncontroversial, this was not the case in relation to the limitation clause for what was to become Article 9(2). A number of different formulations of this clause were mooted. Some were specific and linked only to freedom of religion, while others were more general and applied to all rights (in a similar fashion to the Universal Declaration). Ultimately, it was decided to adopt the first approach,[41] although Article 9(2) is still rather general in nature and does little to assist with any specific problems arising with freedom of religion. Unfortunately, the debates on the limitations clause are not well recorded and, while it is possible to trace which States supported which clause, it is not clear from the *travaux préparatoires* why such approaches were taken or why the ultimate decision was made in the way it was.[42]

The draft Convention initially used a general limitation clause similar to the clause used in the Universal Declaration.[43] The first suggested amendment, to shift from a general limitation clause to specific limitations for each right, was made by the United Kingdom.[44] It proposed that freedom of religion be subject 'only to such limitations as are pursuant to law and are reasonable and necessary to protect public safety, order, health, or morals or the fundamental rights and freedoms of others'.[45] This formulation, which is similar though not identical to the final provision, was not taken up by the Committee in its draft produced at the sitting of 7 February 1950. This draft continued to use a general limitation clause, which stated:

In the exercise of these rights, and the enjoyment of these freedoms guaranteed by the Convention, no limitations shall be imposed except those established by law, with the sole object of ensuring the recognition and respect for the rights and freedoms of others, or with the purpose of satisfying the just requirements of morality, public order, security, and national unity, or of the operation of administration and justice in a democratic society.[46]

[41] *Travaux Préparatoires*, vol. 7, at 56, Final Text of the European Convention, Doc. A290.

[42] Evans, above, note 1, at 267–72.

[43] *Travaux Préparatoires*, vol. 1, at 178, First Session of the Consultative Assembly, proposal by the Consultative Assembly to the Committee of Ministers.

[44] The United Kingdom argued that it was of great importance to define precisely the limitations on rights in a legally binding human rights treaty, as compared to the more aspirational Universal Declaration. See *Travaux Préparatoires*, vol. 3, at 252–8, Preliminary Draft Report to the Committee of Ministers by the Committee of Experts, Doc. CM/WP I (50) 1, A847, 24 Feb. 1950; *Travaux Préparatoires*, vol. 4, at 8–14, Report of the Committee of Experts to the Committee of Ministers, Doc. CM/WP I(50) 15, A924, 16 Mar. 1950.

[45] *Travaux Préparatoires*, vol. 3, at 206, Meeting of the Committee of Experts, sitting of 6 Feb. 1950, Doc. A798.

[46] *Travaux Préparatoires*, vol. 3, at 224, Meeting of the Committee of Experts, Draft Text of a draft convention based on the work of the Consultative Assembly, Doc. A809, 7 Feb. 1950. See a similar, though differently worded, provision in the Preliminary Draft Convention

This wide-sweeping provision was also ultimately rejected. It is, perhaps, a good example of the dangers of general limitation provisions. The mention of 'national unity' as a ground for limitation, for example, could have serious implications for groups such as the Jehovah's Witnesses who often resist participation in national unity activities such as saluting the flag. A similar, though slightly less wide-sweeping provision was suggested in later drafts.[47] The United Kingdom then proposed an amended draft Convention, which included a limitation provision for freedom of religion that was almost identical to that used in the final text.[48] The only distinction was that the clause proposed by the United Kingdom did not include the proviso that the limitation be necessary 'in a democratic society'. Similar provisions, some including the limitation regarding pre-existing laws requested by Turkey and Sweden (discussed below), continued to circulate after this amendment.[49]

The limitation clause finally appeared in its current form in the draft Convention produced by the Conference of Senior Officials. It follows directly after the religious freedom clause and it reads:

Freedom to manifest one's religion or beliefs shall be subject only to such limitations as are prescribed by law and are necessary in a democratic society in the interests of public safety, for the protection of public health or morals, or for the protection of the rights and freedoms of others. [50]

This wording gained currency and was used in drafts after this point.[51]

3.2.3.2 *The Proposed Turkish/Swedish Amendments*

While the proposed clauses discussed above were variations on the type of limitation clause that has become common in human rights instruments,[52] the Turkish and Swedish governments suggested a different type of limitation clause. The Turkish members of the Committee were concerned

for the Maintenance and Further Realisation of Human Rights and Fundamental Freedoms, *Travaux Préparatoires*, vol. 3, at 238, Doc. A 833, 15 Feb. 1950, which includes 'national security and integrity (and solidarity)' as grounds for limitation.

[47] *Travaux Préparatoires*, vol. 3, at 238, Preliminary Draft for the Maintenance and Further Realisation of Human Rights and Fundamental Freedoms, 15 Feb. 1950, Doc. A833; and vol. 3, at 322, Preliminary Draft Convention, Doc. CM/WP 1(50) 14; A932, Option B.

[48] *Travaux Préparatoires*, vol. 3, at 286, Meeting of the Committee of Experts, Doc. CM/WP1 (50) 2, A915, 6 Mar. 1950.

[49] See e.g. *Travaux Préparatoires*, vol. 3, at 292 and 318.

[50] *Travaux Préparatoires*, vol. 3, at 218, Draft Convention appended to the draft report; Doc. CM/WP 4 (50) 16, appendix; A 1445.

[51] e.g. *Travaux Préparatoires*, vol. 5, at 82, Doc. CM (50) 52 of 7 Aug. 1950; A1884; vol. 5, at 126, Draft Convention Adopted by the Committee of Ministers, Doc. A 1937, 7 Aug. 1950; vol. 5, at 152, draft sent by the Committee of Ministers to the Consultative Assembly, Doc. Consultative Assembly, No. 11, 8 Aug. 1950, at 600–19.

[52] See e.g. I.C.C.P.R., Art. 18(3); American Convention on Human Rights, Art. 12(3). The African Charter on Human and Peoples' Rights, Art. 8, simply guarantees religious freedom 'subject to law and order'.

about a resurgence of Islamic fundamentalism in their State and wished to ensure that a wide provision for freedom of religion or belief did not undermine Turkey's attempts to 'reform and modernise' and to ensure that these efforts were not put in jeopardy by 'the Moslem orders and their archaic institutions'.[53] The representatives of Turkey stressed that the legislative measures were in 'no way intended to place restrictions on freedom of religion' but were rather to prevent attempts to frustrate reform by 'certain groups of persons who wish to keep the population in ignorance for their own ends'.[54]

Turkey's experts thus proposed an amendment to the Committee of Experts' recommendation to the Council of Ministers. The experts agreed that freedom of thought, conscience, and religion should be protected in accordance with Article 18 of the Universal Declaration. Turkey wished to add to that recommendation the rider that the freedom be 'subject to reservations concerning legislative measures to prevent attempts being made once again to suppress these freedoms'.[55] It recommended an amendment to the substantive provision dealing with the protection so that it included the sentence, 'This provision does not effect [sic] existing national laws as regards rules relating to religious practice and membership of certain faiths.'[56]

Sweden was also concerned that the provisions on religious freedom could undermine its domestic religious arrangements, in particular the prominent role of the Lutheran Church in the Swedish State. It argued that the long tradition of the Lutheran Church in Sweden, combined with the right of all people to join other religions, justified the maintenance of the status quo. The high degree of religious homogeneity rendered 'the inconvenience of this situation [the role of the Lutheran Church in the State] almost negligible' compared to the serious 'constitutional and other difficulties' in changing it.[57] The Swedish experts therefore proposed an amendment to the limitations clause that read, 'This provision does not affect existing national laws as regards rules relating to religious practice and membership of certain faiths.'[58]

While the Turkish delegates were concerned to limit the role of religious groups in the State and the Swedish delegates were concerned to maintain

[53] *Travaux Préparatoires*, vol. 4, at 80; Addendum 2 to Doc. CM/WP 1 (50) 15; A 1280, 27 May 1950.
[54] *Id.*
[55] *Travaux Préparatoires*, vol. 3, at 182, Meeting of Committee of Experts, Doc. A775, sitting of 2 Feb. 1950.
[56] *Travaux Préparatoires*, vol. 3, at 184, Meeting of the Committee of Experts, sitting of 4 Feb. 1950. A slightly different amendment was later negotiated, see *Travaux Préparatoires*, vol. 3, at 200, Meeting of the Committee of Experts, sitting of 5 Feb. 1950.
[57] *Travaux Préparatoires*, vol. 4, at 28, Meeting of the Committee of Experts, Report to the Committee of Ministers, Doc. CM/WP I (50) 15, A929, 16 Mar. 1950.
[58] *Travaux Préparatoires*, vol. 3, at 184, Meeting of the Committee of Experts, Doc. A776, sitting of 4 Feb. 1950.

the role of the State Church, both proposals sought some limitation on religious freedom in order to maintain the existing legislative arrangements in their States. They thus were persuaded to withdraw their separate proposals and to submit a joint suggested amendment that read, 'This provision does not affect existing national laws which contain restrictive regulations concerning religious institutions and endowments or membership to certain faiths.'[59] Despite the potentially significant role that such an amendment could play in limiting religious freedom, the draft text of the Convention for some time included the provision that nothing in the Convention 'may be considered as derogating from the already existing national rules as regards religious institutions and foundations, or membership of certain confessions'.[60]

The Committee of Experts thus seemed content with the amendment, although the representatives of the Netherlands and the United Kingdom argued that it was unnecessary as any truly exceptional needs of a State to continue with laws that limited religious freedom could be adequately dealt with under the general limitations clause.[61] The Conference of Senior Officials and the Committee of Ministers, however, adopted the version of the Convention that did not include the suggested amendment. There is little recorded debate as to why this happened, but the United Kingdom representative in the Conference of Senior Officials continued to argue that the amendment was inappropriate. Instead the United Kingdom suggested that the new version of the Convention allow for reservations[62] and this may have satisfied Sweden that there was no need to pursue its desired amendment.[63]

3.2.3.3 Scope of the Final Limitations Clause

With the exception of the limitation suggested by Turkey and Sweden there was almost no consideration (at least which is reflected in the record) given to the particular issues raised by freedom of religion. The only sign that freedom of religion has some peculiar characteristics is that the freedom

---

[59] *Travaux Préparatoires*, vol. 3, at 200, Meeting of Committee of Experts, joint proposed amendment by Ustun (Turkey) and Salen (Sweden), sitting of 5 Feb. 1950.

[60] e.g. *Travaux Préparatoires*, vol. 4, at 188, Conference of Senior Officials, New Draft Alternative B and B/2, Doc. CM/WP 4 (50) 9, A 1372 (based on the recommendations of the Committee of Experts). However, the Single Text of the Conference of Senior Officials, *Travaux Préparatoires*, vol. 4, at 224, Doc. CM/WP 4 (50) 16, appendix, A 1445, did not include this additional limitation.

[61] *Travaux Préparatoires*, vol. 3, at 208, Meeting of the Committee of Experts, sitting of 5 Feb. 1950 and vol. 4 at 26–8, Report to the Committee of Ministers, Doc. CM/WP 1 (50) 15, A 924, 16 Mar. 1950. The report was based on the comments of the representative of the Netherlands, *Travaux Préparatoires*, vol. 4, at 26–8. See also J. E. S. FAWCETT, THE APPLICATION OF THE EUROPEAN CONVENTION ON HUMAN RIGHTS 236–7 (1987).

[62] *Travaux Préparatoires*, vol. 4, at 258, Report of the Conference of Senior Officials.

[63] EVANS, above, note 1, at 270–1.

to have or change religious belief does not seem to be subject to the same limitations as the right to 'manifest' that belief.[64] It is unfortunate that there is not more information available about the process that went into choosing the final text or whether any thought was given to distinguishing between the right to have a religion or belief and the right to manifest that belief.

What is suggested by the *travaux préparatoires*, however, is that the drafters preferred a narrower, tighter approach to limitations than a broader one, presumably to protect the integrity of the right to freedom of religion or belief. The final draft does not include the right of a government to limit the rights granted under Article 9(1) on the grounds of 'national unity' or 'the operation and administration of justice' as was suggested by an early draft of a general limitation clause. The notion that the restrictions had to be necessary 'in a democratic society' was added to the original United Kingdom draft, limiting the circumstances in which necessity can be claimed. The drafters also refused to include a specific provision protecting existing legislative provisions, suggesting that historic arrangements can only be maintained if current need is clearly demonstrated.

The limitation clause for Article 9 is one of the least permissive in the Convention. If compared to those for similar rights, such as freedom of expression,[65] it can be seen that there are many more circumstances in which freedom of expression can be circumscribed than freedom to manifest a religion or belief. For example, the right of the State to restrict freedom of speech for reasons of national security, to protect territorial integrity, and for the prevention of disorder or crime is set out in Article 10(2) but not mentioned in Article 9(2). This reiterates the importance of the right of freedom of religion and belief to the drafters and demonstrates that the drafters were only prepared to see the right to manifest a religion or belief limited in a small number of circumstances. The State was not permitted to interfere in any circumstances with the right to have or to change a religion.

3.2.4 The Drafting of Article 2, First Protocol: Belief and Education

While it was clear that freedom of religion or belief was to be included in the Convention, there was some controversy over the scope of the rights that should be covered, especially as to whether social and economic rights should be included.[66] The three areas that caused the most controversy in

---

[64] Convention, Art. 9(1).

[65] Convention, Art. 10(2). See also the second clauses of Arts. 8–11.

[66] The exclusion of these rights was only justified as a temporary measure. See *Travaux Préparatoires*, vol. 1, at 218, Report of the Consultative Assembly, which states that social rights 'have in themselves a fundamental value [and] must also, in the future, be defined and protected'. See also *Travaux Préparatoires*, vol. 5, at 8–12, Working papers prepared by the Secretariat-General for the Committee of Ministers.

relation to their inclusion and wording were the right to own property, the right to universal suffrage, and the right to education.[67] While the first two are largely irrelevant to freedom of religion, the third was fought predominantly on that ground.

In continental Europe at least, the issue of the right of parents to choose private education for their children was linked closely with freedom of religion.[68] It was argued that one of the most dangerous ways in which a totalitarian government can reinforce its power is to take over the education system and exclude parents from decisions about the moral and religious/philosophical education of their children.[69] The right of parents to choose their children's religious and philosophical education was said by certain delegates to be essential in any treaty claiming to outline fundamental human rights.[70]

Other delegates were more cautious. One concern that was shared by a number of representatives was that requiring the State to respect parents' religion or belief in education could be used by parents to force the provision of education in anti-democratic philosophies, particularly communism.[71] These fears seem to have been largely laid to rest by proponents of the inclusion of a right to education, who pointed out that Article 17 of the Draft Convention made clear that the rights in the Convention did not extend to protect those who sought to undermine those rights and freedoms for others.[72]

Some States were also concerned that the proposal might cause problems with their funding of both secular and religious education.[73] This fear was

[67] *Travaux Préparatoires*, vol. 1, at xxviii, Introduction by A. H. Robertson.

[68] Sir David Maxwell-Fyfe expressed his concern at the way in which totalitarian States could use education for their own ends. *Travaux Préparatoires*, vol. 5, at 162. Much of the debate in the *Travaux Préparatoires*, vol. 2, at 16–124, First Sitting of the Consultative Assembly, 5–8 Sept. 1949, dealt with the dangers in allowing totalitarian States to interfere with moral and religious education and also with the 'natural' right of fathers (or sometimes parents) to choose the manner in which their children should be educated. See also ROBERTSON AND MERRILLS, above, note 23, at 11–12.

[69] *Travaux Préparatoires*, vol. 6, Second Session of the Consultative Assembly, speech of Pernot (France) at 104; speech of Maxwell-Fyfe (United Kingdom) at 162.

[70] e.g. *Travaux Préparatoires*, vol. 5, at 250, Second Session of the Consultative Assembly, speech of Schmal (Netherlands); *Travaux Préparatoires*, vol. 6, at 108–10, Second Session of the Consultative Assembly, speech by Pernot (France); *Travaux Préparatoires*, vol. 7, at 142–8, Memorandum and Letters from the Secretariat-General.

[71] e.g. *Travaux Préparatoires*, vol. 7, at 148, Memorandum and Letters from the Secretariat-General, question by Mollet (France).

[72] *Travaux Préparatoires*, vol. 8, at 92, Third Session of the Consultative Assembly, speech by Teitgen (France).

[73] *Travaux Préparatoires*, vol. 6, at 152–4; 156–60; Second Session of the Consultative Assembly, *Travaux Préparatoires*, vol. 7, at 128, Memorandum and Letters from the Secretariat-General, Doc. CM(50) 90, A 3034, 14 Nov. 1950; *Travaux Préparatoires*, vol. 8, at 10, Commentary by the Secretariat-General on the Draft Protocol, Doc. AS/JA (3) 131 A5904, 18 Sept. 1951. Reassurance on this issue was given by Bastid at the Meeting of the Committee of Experts, vol. 7, at 208–10.

also dismissed as baseless, as the Convention merely required the State to respect the right of parents to determine religious and moral education and not to provide funding for such education.[74] Mr de Valera, however, while ultimately supporting the inclusion of the right to education, noted his concern that it was 'simply an expression of secularist opinion' that had the potential to interfere in the provision of State-funded religious education.[75] Other delegates were concerned that requiring respect for parental beliefs could turn children into 'moral and spiritual ghetto[s]', although very few delegates voiced concern that the rights of the child to a full education could be undermined by giving too great a role to parents' rights.[76]

Other arguments against the inclusion of this type of provision in the Convention included the notion that the right of parents to determine the moral and religious/philosophical upbringing of their children was already covered in the article dealing with freedom of religion[77] or that it (and the right to property) was essentially a social right and therefore not appropriately dealt with in the Convention.[78] Mr Rolin raised a number of concerns about the practical problems that such a clause could give rise to that proved to be quite prescient but which were dismissed as groundless by the other delegates.[79]

Ultimately, however, the Consultative Assembly came down strongly in favour of the inclusion of a right to education.[80] The Committee of Ministers, for reasons that were never made clear (much to the annoyance of the Assembly[81]), was not convinced and referred the matter to the Committee of Experts. The debate could not be resolved before the signing of the Convention.[82] The sense of urgency and public expectation which the drafting had produced encouraged the Ministers to complete the signing

---

[74] *Travaux Préparatoires*, vol. 7, at 208–10, Meeting of the Committee of Experts.

[75] *Travaux Préparatoires*, vol. 6, at 152, Second Session of the Consultative Assembly, 25 Aug. 1950.

[76] *Travaux Préparatoires*, vol. 2, at 76, First Session of the Consultative Assembly, Sundt (Norway) and Philip (France) at 74–5; *Travaux Préparatoires*, vol. 6, at 156, Second Session of the Consultative Assembly, Mollet (France).

[77] *Travaux Préparatoires*, vol. 6, at 88, Second Session of the Consultative Assembly, speech of Roberts (United Kingdom).

[78] *Travaux Préparatoires*, vol. 6, at 44–6, Second Session of the Consultative Assembly, Draft Recommendation, Doc. AS/JA (2) 20, 23 Aug. 1950.

[79] His concerns about the potential breadth of the notion of belief have proved to be far more of a sticking point than the other delegates recognized. *Travaux Préparatoires*, vol. 6, at 124, Second Session of the Consultative Assembly.

[80] See *Travaux Préparatoires*, vol. 6, at 248, Text of the Draft Convention by the Consultative Assembly. The Assembly urged the Committee of Ministers to adopt the draft. Art. 12 contained a right to education, including the right of parents to ensure that their children's education was in 'conformity with their own religious and philosophical convictions'.

[81] *Travaux Préparatoires*, vol. 7, at 82–4, Sixth Session of the Standing Committee of the Consultative Committee; vol. 8, at 94–102, Third Session of the Consultative Assembly, speeches by Teitgen (France) at 94, Schmal (Netherlands) at 96, and van Cauweiaert (Belgium) at 102.

[82] *Travaux Préparatoires*, vol. 7, at 4, Sixth Session of the Committee of Ministers.

on 4 November 1950, despite the fact that the issues regarding property, elections, and education were not resolved.[83] It was agreed to leave these controversial issues aside and return to them after the signing, this time with a view to including them in a protocol.[84]

The main debate after this delay was the type of belief that should be protected. The Committee of Experts proposed that States should only be required to 'respect the liberty of parents to ensure the religious education of their children in conformity with their own convictions'.[85] Similarly, there was a debate over whether States should be required to respect the 'convictions' of parents (the preferred term of the Assembly) or only the 'creed' (preferred by the Experts).[86] The Experts justified replacing 'philosophical convictions' with 'creed' by arguing that philosophical convictions that were fundamentally opposed to democracy should not be given the same protection as religion, and that one State required children whose parents did not subscribe to any creed to be educated in the State religion.[87] These justifications were criticized by the Committee on Legal and Administrative Questions, which deemed them to be an insufficient basis to exclude non-religious philosophies.[88] Members of the Consultative Assembly were also critical of this change, considering that treating religion and philosophy unequally in education was not appropriate in a liberal Europe.[89]

The Committee of Ministers (again for reasons that do not appear on the record) decided to adopt the draft that referred to convictions rather than creeds and not to limit the role of parents to religious education.[90] The right to education was included as Article 2 of the First Protocol.

3.3 RATIFICATION OF AND RESERVATIONS TO THE CONVENTION

The Convention has enjoyed a high rate of participation in Western Europe and, since the break-up of the Soviet Union, has extended its reach to

---

[83] This is clear from the discussion at the Sixth Session of the Committee of Ministers, which emphasized the need to compromise certain articles rather than delay the signing: *Travaux Préparatoires*, vol. 7, at 22–34.

[84] *Travaux Préparatoires*, vol. 7, at 34, Sixth Session of the Committee of Ministers.

[85] *Travaux Préparatoires*, vol. 7, at 202, Meeting of the Committee of Experts, 22 Feb. 1951.

[86] *Travaux Préparatoires*, vol. 7, at 246, Meeting of the Committee of Experts, 19 Apr. 1951.

[87] *Travaux Préparatoires*, vol. 8, at 12, Commentary by the Secretariat-General on the Draft Protocol, Doc. AS/JA (3) 13, A 5904, 18 Sept. 1951.

[88] *Travaux Préparatoires*, vol. 8, at 22–6, Committee on Legal and Administrative Questions.

[89] *Travaux Préparatoires*, vol. 8, Third Session of the Consultative Assembly, speech of Stanford (Ireland), at 124; speech by Pernot (France), at 134; speech of Boggiano Pico (Italy), at 140; speech by Teitgen (France), at 154–6.

[90] *Travaux Préparatoires*, vol. 7, at 336–8, Ninth Session of the Committee of Ministers.

Eastern Europe. There are now 41 States that are parties.[91] There has only been one reservation to Article 9 of the Convention and that reservation only stood for a brief period. Norway, on ratifying the Convention, stated that

Whereas Article 2 of the Norwegian Constitution of 17 May 1814 contains a provision under which Jesuits are not tolerated, a corresponding reservation is made with regard to the application of Article 9 of the Convention.[92]

Norway withdrew this reservation on 4 December 1956 after amending Article 2 of its Constitution.[93] This amendment, together with the absence of broader reservations to Article 9, suggests that the article commanded support and agreement at the time when States were ratifying the Convention. Despite Turkey's earlier concerns that Article 9 might interfere with its legislation aimed at preventing the rise of an Islamic government, it did not make a reservation to the religious freedom article. Interestingly, none of the many Contracting Parties with a State religion entered a reservation to Article 9 either, presumably indicating a consensus that freedom of religion does not require a separation of Church and State. This implicit consensus became important in cases involving State Churches.[94]

3.4 CONCLUSION

As noted at the beginning of this chapter, the *travaux préparatoires* are of limited use in assisting in understanding what the drafters intended to protect in Article 9 of the Convention and Article 2 of the First Protocol. The brevity and selectivity of the materials recorded make it necessary to exercise caution when drawing any but the most general conclusions. The *travaux préparatoires* do, however, usefully illustrate a number of points. The first point is that freedom of religion was an important priority for those involved in the drafting of the Convention. They spoke about the right passionately and treated it as fundamental from the beginning of the drafting process. As the inclusion of the right to freedom of religion in

[91] As of 25 May 2000 the States that have ratified the Convention are: Albania, Andorra, Austria, Belgium, Bulgaria, Croatia, Cyprus, the Czech Republic, Denmark, Estonia, Finland, France, Georgia, Germany, Greece, Hungary, Iceland, Ireland, Italy, Latvia, Liechtenstein, Lithuania, Luxembourg, Malta, Moldova, the Netherlands, Norway, Poland, Portugal, Romania, Russia, San Marino, Slovak Republic, Slovenia, Spain, Sweden, Switzerland, TFYR Macedonia, Turkey, Ukraine, and the United Kingdom. An updated list of member States can be found on the website of the European Court of Human Rights, http://www.echr.coe.int

[92] Reservation contained in the instrument of ratification deposited on 15 Jan. 1952. See the website of the European Court of Human Rights, http://www.echr.coe.int

[93] *Id.*

[94] See discussion at Chapter 5.4.

the Convention seemed axiomatic to the drafters, they did not spend much time in consideration of the meaning of that right or its scope. The wording of Article 9(1), however, reflects almost exactly the wording of the Universal Declaration. One of the express purposes of the drafting of the Convention was to build on the project of the international protection of the human rights set out in the Universal Declaration.[95] It is thus relevant to keep in mind the debates and decisions made in drafting the earlier instrument when interpreting the latter.

The second point is that the limitations which governments would be permitted to place on freedom of religion were the subject of some consideration and thought was given to the precise wording to be used. While the reasons for the rejection of some drafts and the acceptance of the wording that was ultimately used remain obscure, the result of the negotiations was that the draft allowed for States to limit freedom of religion and belief only in fairly restricted circumstances. Article 9(2) certainly did not hand a *carte blanche* to States to restrict religious freedom—it created a series of specified and express circumstances in which limitations would be permissible. That the exact nature of these circumstances is important can be seen by the fact that other articles, such as Article 10, set down a different, if sometimes overlapping, series of circumstances in which rights may be restricted. Thus, the drafting history of Article 9(2) reiterates the importance attached to freedom of religion or belief by the drafters and suggests that the limitation clause should not be read expansively.

Finally, the long pattern of acceptance of Article 9 of the Convention without any significant reservations indicates acceptance by the participating States of the right to freedom of religion and belief as set out there. This agreement is probably predicated on the belief that Article 9 does not prohibit a State religion as long as the freedom of others to have or change their religion is still respected. Thus, looking at the terms of Article 9, the drafting history of the Convention, and the pattern of acceptance of Article 9 without reservation, it would be easy to conclude that the protection of freedom of religion and belief had a high priority in the Council of Europe and that the Contracting Parties had a commitment to making that protection effective. This has not, however, continued to be the case. As the rest of the book argues, the principal organs of the Council of Europe with the responsibility for interpreting the Convention and applying it in particular circumstances have taken an inappropriately limited and conservative approach to their interpretation of Article 9(1) and an expansive view of government power under Article 9(2).

[95] Convention, Preamble.

4

Defining Religion or Belief

4.1 INTRODUCTION

It might be thought that a definition of religion or belief would be essential to the development of Article 9 case law, yet the issue has proved so controversial that it has been difficult to achieve any consensus as to the meaning of the term. No human rights treaty, including the Convention, has ever defined religion or belief. The level of controversy that the issue has generated in the United Nations makes it difficult to claim that the drafters of United Nations treaties had a common intention in their use of the words. For example, the issue of whether atheism and agnosticism were included within the definition of 'religion or belief' has been a vexed and much debated one in the United Nations. The debate has never been conclusively resolved[1] and Partsch has pointed to the deliberately 'diplomatic wording' of the term 'thought, conscience and religion', which he claims was carefully chosen for the I.C.C.P.R. to mean different things to different people.[2] In contrast, as was discussed in the previous chapter, the drafters of the Convention do not seem to have given the issue much thought. This has left the main task of definition to the Court and Commission.

Before looking at the specific case law on Article 9, it is worth briefly considering the general approach of the Court and Commission to the interpretation of the Convention.[3] The Court has accepted that Articles 31–3 of the Vienna Convention on the Law of Treaties represent customary international law and that they are thus applicable to interpreting the Convention.[4] This means that the Court will interpret the words of the Convention in good faith, in light of its objects and purposes, and that

---

[1] The controversy over the definition of religion or belief has continued, as can be seen by the debates over the wording of the Declaration on Religious Intolerance and Discrimination. See Natan Lerner, *Toward a Draft Declaration against Religious Intolerance and Discrimination*, 11 Isr. Y.B on H.R. 82 (1981); Bahiyyih G. Tahzib, Freedom of Religion or Belief: Ensuring Effective International Protection 165–90 (1996).

[2] K. J. Partsch, *Freedom of Conscience and Expression and Political Freedoms, in* The International Bill of Human Rights: The Covenant on Civil and Political Rights 209, 211 (L. Henkin ed., 1981).

[3] For a more detailed discussion of the Court's approach to interpretation see D. J. Harris, M. O'Boyle, and C. Warbrick, The Law of the European Convention on Human Rights 6–9 (1995); P. van Dijk and G. J. H. van Hoof, Theory and Practice of the European Convention on Human Rights 72–81 (3rd edn. 1997); Francis G. Jacobs and Robin C. A. White, The European Convention on Human Rights chapter 3 (2nd edn. 1995).

[4] *Golder v. the United Kingdom*, 18 Eur. Ct. H.R. (ser. A) at 14 (1975). The majority held that 'Articles 31–34 enunciate in essence generally accepted principles of international law'.

it will be prepared to use the *travaux préparatoires* as a supplementary means of interpretation. Yet in some cases the Court can be seen to emphasize the importance of fulfilling the objects and purposes of the Convention, even if that at times requires a very broad approach to the meaning of the words themselves.[5] The Court has held that it should seek an interpretation of articles that 'is most appropriate in order to realise the aim and achieve the object of the treaty, and not that which would restrict to the greatest possible degree the obligations undertaken by the parties'.[6] It has also recognized the importance of applying the Convention in such a way as to ensure that the rights granted in it are 'practical and effective' and not merely 'theoretical and illusory'.[7]

4.2 THE TEXT OF ARTICLE 9

The first part of Article 9 protects the 'right to freedom of thought, conscience and religion' without mentioning belief, but refers also to the right to change 'religion or belief'. The second part refers to the right of a person to 'manifest his religion or belief, in worship, teaching, practice and observance', without mentioning thought or conscience. Thus 'thought and conscience' must be distinct in some way from 'religion or belief', as there is a non-derogable obligation to protect the right to freedom of thought and conscience, but there is no right to manifest them.[8] Yet the words thought and conscience are—perhaps even to a greater extent than religion and belief—vague and difficult to convincingly define. Thus there is a legally important distinction between two complex and similar ideas ('thought and conscience' and 'religion or belief'). The text tells us no more than that such a distinction exists, but it could be assumed that the Court would have to consider the scope of one set of ideas when defining the other. It should not, for example, define religion or belief so widely that they also incorporate all that would be more appropriately described as thought or conscience. Such a distinction is, of course, far from easy to make in a principled manner, especially given the way in which the ideas are interrelated. Many people come to their religious

---

[5] *Id.* at 53, dissent of Judge Fitzmaurice who argued that the application of the Convention made significant inroads into State sovereignty and therefore demanded 'a cautious and conservative interpretation'.

[6] *Wemhoff v. Germany*, 7 Eur. Ct. H.R. (ser. A) at 23 (1968).

[7] *Artico v. Italy*, 37 Eur. Ct. H.R. (ser. A) at 16 (1980); *Airey v. Ireland*, 32 Eur. Ct. H.R. (ser. A) at 13, 15–16 (1979–80).

[8] Cf. Peter W. Edge, *Current Problems in Article 9 of the European Convention on Human Rights*, 1996 JURID. REV. 42, 43, who claims that the distinction between thought or conscience and belief is irrelevant. Such an interpretation, however, would open the right to manifest a religion or belief to a general right to manifest conscience. Most authors have concluded that there is no such general right. See VAN DIJK AND VAN HOOF, above, note 3, at 542–4; MALCOLM EVANS, RELIGIOUS LIBERTY AND INTERNATIONAL LAW IN EUROPE 284–5 (1997).

beliefs by following their conscience and their conscience is, in turn, shaped by the nature of those religious beliefs. The individual believer may not find the distinction a meaningful one. Yet the distinction has been made in the wording of Article 9 and should inform the decision-making of the Court.

Another, more minor, difficulty in the wording of Article 9 is the introduction of the word 'belief' in the second part of Article 9(1). It seems to cover conveniently groups such as atheists and agnostics and possibly members of groups that have some religious elements but do not necessarily fall into the category of a religion. Yet, if this is correct, the exclusion of belief from the first part of Article 9 seems to suggest the strange outcome that an atheist has the right to manifest his or her belief (and in ways, such as 'worship', that are linked more closely to religious practice than atheism) but his or her right to hold this belief is not protected. Probably the best way around this apparent anomaly would be to assume that beliefs are a subset of the broader category of thought and conscience. The Court and Commission have worked under the assumption that there is a right both to have and to manifest beliefs without making their reasoning on this issue clear, but such an approach makes sense in the context of the article as a whole.

In approaching the definition of belief the Court could also be assisted by the French version of the text. In the drafting of the Universal Declaration the term *croyance* was originally used as a counterpart to the English term 'belief'. The use of *croyance* indicated a close relationship with religious beliefs. This was changed in latter drafts to *conviction* (the term that is also used in the Convention), which is less religiously oriented and suggests a broader scope for non-religious beliefs than does the word *croyance*.[9] Neither term is, however, much clearer than beliefs, and the use of *convictions*, while perhaps showing a greater inclusiveness than *croyance*, has not sufficiently clarified the issue to resolve the difficult issues of definition that arise under Article 9.

4.3 THE CASE LAW

4.3.1 A Generally Liberal Approach

The task of defining religion or belief in the context of Article 9 has generally been performed by·the Commission.[10] In many domestic systems that

---

[9] 3(1) U.N. GAOR, C.3 (128th mtg) 405, U.N. Doc. A/C.3/SR 128 (1948). See also Roger S. Clark, *The United Nations and Religious Freedom*, 11 N.Y.U.J. INT'L L. & POL. 197, 201 (1978); DESMOND M. CLARKE, *Freedom of Thought in the UN Declaration and Covenants*, 28 IRISH JURIST 121, 130 (1993–5).

[10] EVANS, above, note 8, at 290–3; HARRIS, O'BOYLE, AND WARBRICK, above, note 3, at 357–8; Malcolm Shaw, *Freedom of Thought, Conscience and Religion*, in THE EUROPEAN SYSTEM FOR THE PROTECTION OF HUMAN RIGHTS 445, 447–50 (R. StJ. Mcdonald, F. Matscher, and H. Petzold eds., 1993).

protect freedom of religion (and sometimes belief) in constitutional or legislative regimes, the issue of what constitutes a religion has been a source of great controversy.[11] The Commission has, by and large, not entered into that controversy as it has rarely determined that something that is alleged to be a religion or belief is not.[12] There are a few exceptions. In a case concerning a man who did not want to be buried in a cemetery that contained many graves with Christian symbols and writings and who wished rather to be cremated and have his ashes spread over his land,[13] the Commission acknowledged that the desired action had a 'strong personal motivation' but concluded that it was not protected under Article 9 as his wish did not express some 'coherent view on fundamental problems'.[14] This suggests that some basic level of intellectual or moral coherence is required before something can be considered a religion or belief: vague notions are not enough.

This approach was reiterated by the Court in *Campbell and Cossans v. the United Kingdom*[15] where the Court held that a 'conviction' under Article 2, Protocol 1 of the Convention is not synonymous with 'opinion' or 'ideas' as used in Article 10 but is rather akin to the term 'beliefs' in Article 9. To amount to a conviction under Article 2 of Protocol 1, the belief in question had to 'attain a certain level of cogency, seriousness, cohesion and importance'.[16] Thus, in that case, the philosophical opposition of the parents to corporal punishment was characterized by the Court as relating to 'a weighty and substantial aspect of human behaviour' and it was this, in combination with the opposition to corporal punishment reaching the required level of cogency, seriousness, and cohesion, that distinguished it from mere ideas or opinions.[17] In contrast, a parent whose opposition to the corporal punishment of her child seemed to be based on the grounds that such punishment was not justified in relation to his behaviour in the particular circumstances was held not to have attained the

---

[11] Kent Greenawalt, *Religion as a Concept in Constitutional Law*, 72 Cal. L. Rev. 753 (1984); Note, *Defining 'Religion' in the First Amendment: A Functional Approach*, 84 Cornell L. Rev. 532 (1986); Richard O'Frame, *Belief in a Non-Material Reality—A Proposed First Amendment Definition of Religion*, U. Ill. L. Rev. 819 (1992); Jesse H. Choper, *Defining 'Religion' in the First Amendment*, U. Ill. L. Rev. 579 (1982); Dmitry N. Feoanov, *Defining Religion: An Immodest Proposal*, 23 Hofstra L. Rev. 309 (1994); Val. D. Ricks, *To God God's, to Caesar Caesar's, and to both the Defining of Religion*, 26 Creighton L. Rev. 1053 (1993); Wojciech Sadurski, *On Legal Definitions of 'Religion'*, 63 Austl. L.J. 834 (1989); Joshua Puls, *The Wall of Separation: Section 116, the First Amendment and Constitutional Religious Guarantees*, 26 Fed. L. Rev. 139 (1998).

[12] Harris, O'Boyle, and Warbrick, above, note 3, at 357–8.

[13] *X. v. Germany*, App. No. 8741/79, 24 Eur. Comm'n H.R. Dec. & Rep. 137 (1981).

[14] *Id.* at 138.

[15] *Campbell and Cossans v. the United Kingdom*, 48 Eur. Ct. H.R. (ser. A) (1982).

[16] *Id.* at 16.

[17] *Id.* at 16–17.

required level of cogency, seriousness, cohesion, and importance to gain the protection of the Convention.[18]

Generally, however, the Court and Commission have taken a generous approach to defining religion or belief. The Church of Scientology was accepted as falling under the protection of Article 9 with no discussion of the issues that have concerned domestic courts.[19] Pacifism has been accepted as a belief even when it is not linked to a particular religion.[20] Traditional religions and beliefs such as a variety of Christian denominations,[21] Islam,[22] Hinduism,[23] Buddhism,[24] Judaism,[25] and atheism[26] have all been recognized as falling within Article 9(1). Even the Druids[27] and the Divine Light Zentrum[28] were presumed by the Commission to be religions or beliefs, although the Commission made it clear that it was not making a determination on that issue as both cases were decided under Article 9(2).

4.3.2 Political and Philosophical Beliefs

Thus, other than the requirement of some ill-defined level of cogency and seriousness, the Commission has given little consideration to creating a

[18] *X, Y and Z v. the United Kingdom*, App. No. 8566/79, 31 Eur. Comm'n H.R. Dec. & Rep. 50, 53 (1982).

[19] Indeed the Church of Scientology was the first organized religion to benefit from the Commission's reversal of earlier decisions to refuse to hear cases from Churches complaining of a breach of their religious freedom. The Commission held that the Church of Scientology had a right to pursue an action in its own right in *X and Church of Scientology v. Sweden*, App. No. 7805/77, 16 Eur. Comm'n H.R. Dec. & Rep. 68, 70 (1978), revising the earlier opinion of the Commission in *Church of X v. the United Kingdom*, App. No. 3798/68, 13 Y.B. Eur. Conv. on H.R. 306 (Eur. Comm'n on H.R.) (1968). However, in a recent admissibility application the Court merely referred to the Church of Scientology as an 'association', probably because one of the issues raised in the case was the refusal of Germany to recognize Scientology as a religion. There was no indication, however, that this meant that the members of the association did not at least have a belief under Art. 9: *Scientology Kirche Deutschland e.V. v. Germany*, App. No. 34614/97, 89-A Eur. Comm'n H.R. Dec. & Rep. 163 (1997); cf. *The Church of the New Faith v. The Commissioner of Pay-Roll Tax (Victoria)*, 154 C.L.R. 120 (1983).

[20] *Arrowsmith v. the United Kingdom*, App. No. 7050/75, 19 Eur. Comm'n H.R. Dec. & Rep. 5, 19 (1978); *Le Cour Grandmaison and Fritz v. France*, App. Nos. 11567/85 and 11568/85 (joined), 53 Eur. Comm'n H.R. Dec. & Rep. 150 (1987).

[21] *Knudsen v. Norway*, App. No. 11045/84, 42 Eur. Comm'n H.R. Dec. & Rep. 247 (1985).

[22] *Ahmed v. the United Kingdom*, App. No. 8160/78, 22 Eur. Comm'n H.R. Dec. & Rep. 27 (1981); *Karaduman v. Turkey*, App. No. 16278/90, 74 Eur. Comm'n H.R. Dec. & Rep. 93 (1993).

[23] *ISKCON and others v. the United Kingdom*, App. No. 20490/92, 76-A Eur. Comm'n H.R. Dec. & Rep. 41 (1994).

[24] *X. v. the United Kingdom*, App. No. 5442/72, 1 Eur. Comm'n H.R. Dec. & Rep. 41 (1974).

[25] *D v. France*, App. No. 10180/82, 35 Eur. Comm'n H.R. Dec. & Rep. 199 (1983).

[26] *Angeleni v. Sweden*, App. No. 10491/83, 51 Eur. Comm'n H.R. Dec. & Rep. 41 (1986).

[27] *A.R.M. Chappell v. the United Kingdom*, App. No. 12587/86, 53 Eur. Comm'n H.R. Dec. & Rep. 241, 246 (1987).

[28] *Omkarananda and the Divine Light Zentrum v. Switzerland*, App. No. 8118/77, 25 Eur. Comm'n H.R. Dec. & Rep. 105 (1981).

formal definition of religion or belief. Often the Commission tried to simply ignore the issue by dealing with controversial cases on different grounds.

Early in the life of the Convention one difficult type of case arose in the context of people claiming persecution for their fascist or Nazi beliefs. In the first such recorded case, *X v. Austria*,[29] the applicant had been convicted on charges of promoting neo-Nazi behaviour (the Commission dealt in almost identical fashion with a later case of a man convicted of fascist activities).[30] His application primarily related to the fairness of his trial and the vagueness of the definition of neo-Nazi behaviour. It also, however, raised issues of whether his conviction was in breach of Article 9. The Commission assumed (without making an explicit finding) that the conviction was in breach of Article 9(1), but held that the Austrian government was permitted under the Convention to determine that laws suppressing neo-Nazism were necessary in a democratic society under Article 9(2).[31]

This seems to be the type of case that required the Commission to consider whether Nazism was a belief or whether it merely fell into thought or conscience (or indeed outside the scope of Article 9 altogether). The Commission avoided any such discussion by moving directly to issues raised under Article 9(2). Yet this strategy could be said to imply that Nazism was a belief that was capable of manifestation. This is because Article 9(2) only applies to manifestations of religion or belief—it does not apply to the right to freedom of thought and conscience. Thus, by moving to Article 9(2), the Commission at least implied that Nazism is a belief, because otherwise the issue of whether it can be restricted in a democratic society was irrelevant. It is likely that the Commission did not intend this result but merely used Article 9(2) as a relatively simple way of dismissing a case that the Commissioners thought was wholly lacking in merit. Nevertheless, in a later case the Commission was prepared to hold that applicants claiming that they had a right to manifest their belief in Communism could not have their application dismissed at the admissibility stage, although they did not go into the issue in any detail.[32] Again there was no explicit discussion of the definition of belief or the distinction between belief and thought or conscience, and the case was settled before it reached the merits. It is thus unclear whether some political beliefs fall within the term 'religion or belief' under Article 9 and it is possible that even a set of beliefs as repugnant to human rights values as Nazism and fascism are entitled to protection as beliefs under the Commission's Article 9 jurisprudence. The acceptance by the Commission of politically/ethically motivated pacifism as a belief

---

[29] *X v. Austria*, App. No. 1747/62, 13 Collections 42 (1963).
[30] *X v. Italy*, App. No. 6741/74, 5 Eur. Comm'n H.R. Dec. & Rep. 83 (1976).
[31] *X v. Austria*, App. No. 1747/62, 13 Collections 42, 53–4 (1963).
[32] *Hazar, Hazar and Açik v. Turkey*, App. No. 16311, 16312, 16313/90 (joined), 72 Eur. Comm'n H.R. Dec. & Rep. 200, 212 (1991).

suggests that there is some scope for the incorporation of a wide range of philosophical and possibly political beliefs into the definition of belief in Article 9. [33]

4.3.3 Individualized Religions or Beliefs

Another type of case that has raised difficult definitional issues for the Commission has been in relation to individuals who claim to be adherents of a religion or belief the existence of which the Commission has reason to doubt.[34] The two leading cases in this area dealt with prisoners claiming that their right to the free exercise of their religion had been hampered by prison officials. In order to determine whether these claims were justified, the Commission had to decide whether there was a religion that could be manifested. In the first case, the applicant claimed to be a light worshipper but gave insufficient details as to what this entailed or how the prison authorities had prevented him from manifesting his belief. [35] The Commission did not actually determine that being a light worshipper fell outside Article 9, but rather held that it had insufficient evidence to substantiate the applicant's claim.[36]

In the second case, the applicant claimed that he was a member of the Wicca religion and he protested at the failure of the prison authorities to enter him into the prison records as such. [37] In this case the Commission noted that there was no evidence as to the ways in which the prison was denying the applicant the right to practise the Wicca religion as there was no evidence that he had ever asked the prison authorities for facilities to manifest his beliefs. (The mere refusal to register him as Wicca was not sufficient basis for a claim as it was merely an administrative act.) The Commission, however, added that 'in the present case the applicant has not mentioned any facts making it possible to establish the existence of the Wicca religion'.[38]

---

[33] *Arrowsmith v. the United Kingdom*, App. No. 7050/75, 19 Eur. Comm'n H.R. Dec. & Rep. 5, 19 (1978).

[34] HARRIS, O'BOYLE, AND WARBRICK, above, note 3, at 358 suggest that it should be easier for someone with an individualistic belief to make a claim under Art. 9 than it would be for a member of an organized religion or belief, as there may be a difficulty for someone within a religion or belief who comes into conflict with the teaching of their organization. While the latter has caused problems, applicants with individualistic beliefs do not seem to have found it easier to make claims under Art. 9.

[35] *X v. the Federal Republic of Germany*, App. No. 4445/70, 37 Collection 119, 122 (1970).

[36] *Id.* at 122. The Commission noted that the applicant 'did not explain in what manner he wished to practice (*sic*) his religious belief and in what way the prison authorities refused him the right to do so'.

[37] *X v. the United Kingdom*, App. No. 7291/75, 11 Eur. Comm'n H.R. Dec. & Rep. 55 (1977).

[38] *Id.* at 56.

This dictum raises some interesting questions, not least being what evidence of the Wicca belief the Commission would have found satisfactory. Clearly no adherent of an established religion is going to be required to prove the existence of, for example, Catholicism or Hinduism. It is thus in cases involving new or more individualistic religions or beliefs that evidence would be required. The Commission gives no indication of how many members a 'religion' has to have, what length of time it has to have been in existence, how developed its rules need to be, or what other criteria it would consider relevant to the determination of whether or not a religion or belief exist. One author has suggested that, while the burden to prove the existence of a religion or belief is on the applicant, it can be discharged fairly easily, but he does not give any details as to how that could be done.[39] In the absence of a definition of religion or belief, it is not clear what type of evidence would be relevant. Different definitions would require different types of proof, even if the evidential burden would then be fairly easy to discharge.

The issues that arise here are complicated further by the fact that the term 'belief' could include relatively individualistic beliefs that are not part of a structured religion or organization of believers. Many atheists fall into this category and the Court has explicitly recognized that the protection of the Convention extends to 'free-thinkers' and the 'unconcerned'.[40] There is legitimate concern that Article 9 could be abused by, for example, prisoners who invent a 'religion' or 'belief' simply as a way of getting privileges to which they would not otherwise be entitled. It is likely in the prison cases outlined above, that the Commission was concerned with the strong possibility that the religions were just a façade of this kind.[41]

Such fear of abuse, however, could be dealt with more directly. The Texas District Court in a similar case to the two discussed above, was prepared to hold that the 'religion' of which the prisoner claimed to be the founder was 'a masquerade designed to obtain First Amendment protection'.[42] While the issue of assessing someone as having a fraudulent belief is a fraught and complex one,[43] developing a test that requires too much by way of 'evidence' of the existence of a belief can place perfectly sincerely and committed people with individualistic beliefs beyond the protection of

---

[39] EVANS, above, note 8, at 291.

[40] *Kokkinakis v. Greece*, 260-A, Eur. Ct. H.R. (ser. A) at 13 (1993).

[41] Similar concerns probably motivated the Commission in the 'prisoners of conscience' case of *McFeeley and Others v. the United Kingdom*, App. No. 8317/78, 20 Eur. Comm'n H.R. Dec. & Rep. 44 (1980).

[42] *Theriault v. Silber*, 453 F. Supp. 254 (CWD Tex, 1978).

[43] Care needs to be taken, however, to ensure that a sincerity test does not become a *de facto* test of religious truth. This point was made in *U.S. v. Ballard*, 322 U.S. 78, 92–3 (1944), in the dissent of Judge Jackson. See also John H. Mansfield, *The Religion Clauses of the First Amendment—the Philosophy of the Constitution*, 72 CAL. L. REV. 847, 872–7 (1984).

Article 9. In cases where fraud may be suspected the precise nature of the evidence that would be required to demonstrate insincerity would differ from case to case, but the burden of proof should be on the State to show some reason to think that the person is using religious or other belief fraudulently in order to obtain an advantage to which he or she would not otherwise be entitled.

This would be a more satisfactory response to the problems of individualistic beliefs than simply finding that they are not within the scope of Article 9. The case of the man who wished to have his ashes scattered rather than being buried in the public cemetery[44] is a case in which the Commission was arguably less ready to find for a person on the basis of the individualistic nature of their belief than it might have been if the applicant had belonged to a more structured religious organization. The reason that the applicant wished to be cremated rather than buried was that he did not want to lie in a graveyard full of Christian symbolism.[45] If he had objected to such burial on the basis that he belonged to a non-Christian religion (especially one with specified rites for disposal of the dead), he might not have faced the same hurdle of proving that his concern was motivated by a 'religion or belief'.[46] While the Commission has not been too ready to rule out cases because the applicant's beliefs, while sincerely held, are not sufficiently coherent to amount to a belief under the terms of Article 9, the case law has the potential to exclude some more individualistic and personal beliefs.

4.4 A BRIEF COMPARISON WITH ALTERNATIVE APPROACHES

Many courts and other legal institutions have had to deal with the definition of either 'religion' or 'religion or belief' in interpreting constitutional or statutory provisions, treaties, or other international instruments. The task is a complicated one and no universally accepted definition has been developed. No international treaty that deals with religious freedom has included a definition of the key terms, and even the most detailed international instrument in the area, the Declaration on Religious Intolerance and Discrimination, gives no indication of the scope of the religion or belief. Some authors have even suggested that any attempt at definition would be

---

[44] *X v. the Federal Republic of Germany*, App. No. 8741/79, 24 Eur. Comm'n H.R. Dec. & Rep. 137 (1981).

[45] *Id.* at 138.

[46] The Krishnaswami study, at 34–5, notes that rites for burial of the dead are of great significance to many religions and beliefs and that, where possible, their preferences for burial (including burial in an area that is free of the symbols of other religions if that is considered necessary) should be respected.

counter-productive, as it would be likely to generate conflict and controversy and, if a definition could be agreed, it could have the potential to be
used in a mechanical or restrictive manner to exclude beliefs that should
appropriately fall within the scope of the protection.[47] Yet courts have the
job of applying the broad terms to specific cases, and for such applications
to be consistent and clear some type of definition is required.[48]

4.4.1 International Law Definitions

At an international level, there does seem to be a broad consensus that the
term 'religion or belief' includes 'theistic, non-theistic and atheistic beliefs'[49]
and this formulation was used in the Draft Convention on the Elimination
of all Forms of Religious Intolerance.[50] The ongoing controversy that this
issue generates, however, can be seen in the fact that even this minimal
definition was not included in the Declaration on Religious Intolerance and
Discrimination, over the protests of some Eastern European States that
this exclusion meant that the Declaration did not give adequate protection
to non-religious beliefs.[51] There were a number of proposals for including
a clearer definition in the Declaration, including some that sought to
explicitly exclude some beliefs such as racism, Nazism, and apartheid,[52]
but it was decided that the term religion or belief did not require further
elaboration.

Thus none of the United Nations or regional treaties give a definition of
religion or belief and, while the *travaux préparatoires* of the various United
Nations treaties do suggest a broad consensus on the inclusion of non-
theistic beliefs in the term belief, they give little insight into what the terms

[47] Donna Sullivan, *Advancing the Freedom of Religion or Belief Through the UN
Declaration on the Elimination of Religious Intolerance and Discrimination*, 82 Am. J. Int'l
L. 487, 491–2 (1988). In the USA, it is argued by some that the Supreme Court has to exercise caution in defining the term 'religion' in the First Amendment, because too restrictive or
permissive a definition may in itself be an impermissible interference with religious freedom
by an organ of the State. The Supreme Court referred to defining religion as a 'delicate question' but one that could not be completely avoided in *Wisconsin v. Yoder*, 406 U.S. 203, 215
(1972). Phillip E. Johnson, *Concepts and Compromise in First Amendment Religious Doctrine*,
72 Cal. L. Rev. 817, 832 (1984) concludes that 'no definition of religion for constitutional
purposes exists and no satisfactory definition is likely to be conceived'.
[48] While Sullivan, above, note 47, at 492 does not think that it would be helpful to have
a definition in an international treaty on religious freedom, she does recognize that the issue
would have to be fleshed out in the application of the treaty to particular cases.
[49] *Id.* at 491; Clark, above, note 9, at 208–9.
[50] Note by the Secretary-General, Annex III, U.N. Docs. A/7930 (1970) and A/8330 (1971)
reprinted in 1967 U.N.Y.B. 491–4.
[51] See the statements of the representative of East Germany at U.N. Doc. A/C.3/36/SR.32,
(1981) and the USSR at U.N. Doc. A/C.3/36/SR.36 at 8 (1981). The USA argued that the
term 'belief' offered sufficient protection for those such as 'materialists, atheists or agnostics'
at U.N. Doc. A/C.3/36/SR.36 at 5 (1981).
[52] U.N. Doc. A/C.3/L.2033 (1973).

mean beyond this. The application of these treaties by the relevant bodies has also tended toward broad and inclusive definitions that lack precision. In this way the approach of the Court and Commission is in line with the thinking in the United Nations Human Rights Committee. In its General Comment on Article 18 of the I.C.C.P.R. the Committee observed that

Article 18 protects theistic, non-theistic and atheistic beliefs, as well as the right not to profess any religion or belief. The terms belief and religion are to be broadly construed. Article 18 is not limited in its application to traditional religions or to religions and beliefs with institutional characteristics or practices analogous to those of traditional religions.[53]

While this is helpful in clarifying that religion and belief extends to atheism,[54] it is a definition that focuses on not being exclusionary. Such a definition, while supporting a generally liberal approach to questions of inclusion, is still of little use when deciding what is included and what falls outside the scope of the term. It is clear that there must be some boundaries, and the Committee has itself refused to recognize that a group claiming to be a religion was entitled to the protection of Article 18, when the beliefs and practices of the group were almost exclusively linked to the cultivation, distribution, and use of marijuana (or 'God's tree of life', as the group referred to it).[55] Yet the decision of the Committee was highly specific and merely stated that 'a belief consisting primarily or exclusively in the worship and distribution of a narcotic drug cannot conceivably be brought within the scope of article 18 of the Covenant'.[56] While this allows for the possibility of a genuine religion which uses a narcotic as a part of a religion or form of worship,[57] it does not make clear the more general reason for excluding the group in question from the definition of a religion. It may have been simply because the religion was thought to be a sham for evading the law but, if not, the lack of delimitation in the definition

[53] United Nations Human Rights Committee, General Comment No. 22(48) on Article 18, Freedom of Thought, Conscience and Religion, U.N. Doc. CCPR/C/21/Rev.1/Add.4, para 2 (1993); see reprint in 15 HUM. RTS L.J. 233 (1994) [hereinafter General Comment on Article 18].

[54] As most commentators are agreed that the inclusion of the word 'belief' includes beliefs such as atheism and agnosticism, care must be taken in drawing on the jurisprudence of courts that have to interpret religious freedom clauses (such as the First Amendment of the US Constitution) that only mention religion and not belief. The views of those who use this exclusive term 'religion' to argue that the freedom only applies to religious/spiritual beliefs can be of little relevance in the international context. O'Frame, above, note 11, for example, takes this exclusively religious approach.

[55] *M.A.B., W.A.T. and J.A.Y.T v. Canada* (Communication No. 570/1993, Inadmissibility Decision of 8 Apr. 1994, para 2.1, U.N. Doc. CCPR/C/51/D/570/1993 (1994); U.N. GAOR, 49th Sess., Supp. No. 40, Vol. II, Annex IX, U.N. Doc. A/49/40 (1994).

[56] *Id.* at para. 4.2.

[57] Such as some American First Nation religions that have traditionally used peyote in their ceremonies. See *Employment Division, Department of Human Resources of Oregon v. Smith*, 494 U.S. 872 (1990).

given by the Committee does not allow any principled explanation of their refusal to accept that a group that 'worshipped' narcotics is not a religion.

Another definition was given by Odio Benito, a Special Rapporteur of the Sub-Commission on Prevention of Discrimination and Protection of Minorities, who suggested that a religion was 'an explanation of the meaning of life and how to live accordingly. Every religion has at least a creed, a code of action and a cult', although she says that this is not a definition as the 'meaning of the words is generally understood by all'.[58] In his study, Krishnaswami merely referred to the fact that religion and belief must be understood to include non-theistic, atheistic, and agnostic beliefs.[59] Such definitions are not authoritative, however, and are not particularly illuminating in defining the boundaries of religion or belief.

4.4.2 Domestic Courts

Domestic courts have been forced to be a little more precise, although they too have been wary of developing an unduly restrictive or conservative definition of religion or belief. The Supreme Court of the United States has been more willing than the international bodies to exclude certain types of belief from the scope of the religion clauses of the First Amendment of the United States Constitution. Beliefs with a 'secular basis' or that are 'philosophical and personal rather than religious' are not included within the term religion.[60] However, it is clear that it is not only traditional religious beliefs that fall within the definition of religion. While the First Amendment does not specifically mention 'beliefs', the Supreme Court has held that the requirement of a belief in a 'Supreme Being' as one of the criteria for the avoidance of military service on conscientious grounds, included a 'belief that is sincere and meaningful occupies a place in the life of its possessor parallel to that filled by the orthodox belief in God'.[61] Compared to the European Court's emphasis on the coherence of a belief, the Supreme Court has expressly recognized that religious beliefs need not be 'acceptable, logical, consistent or comprehensible' to qualify for protection under the First Amendment.[62]

[58] Odio Benito, Special Rapporteur, Sub-Commission on the Prevention of Discrimination and Protection of Minorities, Elimination of All Forms of Intolerance and Discrimination Based on Religion or Belief, at 4 (1989), originally published as U.N. Doc. E/CN.4/Sub.2/1987/26; see also Angelo Vidal d'Almeida Ribeiro, *Implementation on the Declaration on the Elimination of Discrimination and Intolerance on the Basis of Religion or Belief*, UN Doc. E/CN.4/1990/46, para 110.

[59] Krishnaswami study, at 1.

[60] *Wisconsin v. Yoder*, 406 U.S. 203, 215–16 (1972).

[61] See *U.S. v. Seeger*, 380 U.S. 163 (1965), where the right to conscientiously object was extended to a man who claimed opposition to military service based on 'a belief in and devotion to goodness and virtue for their own sakes, and a religious faith in a purely ethical creed'.

[62] *Thomas v. Review Board of the Indiana Employment Security Division*, 450 U.S. 707, 714 (1981).

In developing a positive definition, the Supreme Court drew on the works of theologians, particularly Paul Tillich, to hold that religious beliefs incorporate all sincere beliefs that occupy a parallel role to religion.[63] Tillich's work draws on the notion of 'ultimate concern' as the touchstone of religious experience. Every person, by this test, has an ultimate concern that gives meaning and orientation to their lives.[64] Thus, to fall within the meaning of religion, it is necessary for a person to show that they have a concern (i.e. a deep motivation) that is ultimate (i.e. fundamental and unable to be compromised).

This test has been defended as an appropriate legal definition of religion as it is functional rather than content oriented, it is not hopelessly open-ended, it avoids as far as possible the dangers of religious chauvinism, and it is appropriate to the preferred status given to religion in the First Amendment.[65] It has, however, also been criticized as reducing a complex notion to a single 'definition' that is vague and capable of producing counter-intuitive results.[66] For example, a Jewish prisoner's religion may allow him to eat non-kosher food in extreme cases, suggesting that his dietary requirements are not 'ultimate' because they are capable of compromise, whereas a desperate drug addict may be prepared to forsake all else and compromise all other values in order to obtain a drug hit. Yet it seems absurd to suggest that the first is not a case of religion and that the second is.

In a suggested substitute for this approach, Kent Greenawalt suggests an analogical concept (rather than definition) of religion. This approach draws out several key features that are present in the clear cases of religion and then tests other beliefs by analogy to these features.[67] A claimant for protection would have to show sufficient shared features with the 'indisputably religious' in a similar way that Wittgenstein showed that the term 'games' had no common definition but rather a series of family resemblances. Greenawalt's list of resemblances[68] focuses on the religious/spiritual aspects, probably in part because the First Amendment refers only to 'religion' and also because he perceives a serious difficulty in distinguishing religion from philosophy or belief 'if no ideas about higher reality are involved'.[69]

---

[63] *U.S. v. Seegar*, 380 U.S. 163, 180–1 (1965).

[64] PAUL TILLICH, THE DYNAMICS OF FAITH 1–2 (1958); PAUL TILLICH, THE PROTESTANT ERA 58, 87 (1948); PAUL TILLICH, THE SHAKING OF THE FOUNDATIONS 63–4 (1972).

[65] Note, *Toward a Constitutional Definition of Religion*, 91 HARV. L. REV. 1056, 1073–5 (1978).

[66] Greenawalt, above, note 11, at 806–11. The example of the Jewish prisoner and the drug addict is taken from the same work, at 808 and 810.

[67] *Id.* at 763.

[68] *Id.* at 767. His list includes 'a belief in God; a comprehensive view of the world and human purposes; a belief in some form of afterlife; communion with God through ritual acts of worship and through corporate and individual prayer; a particular perspective on moral obligation'.

[69] *Id.* at 779.

However, a somewhat more inclusive approach to the concept of religion *or belief* could make use of the analogical approach.

A similar approach was taken by two Australian judges dealing with section 116 of the Australian Constitution.[70] They held that

There is no single characteristic which can be laid down as constituting a formu-larized legal criterion, whether of inclusion or exclusion, of whether a particular system of ideas and practices constitutes a religion ... The most that can be done is to formulate the more important of the indicia or guidelines by reference to which that question falls to be answered. Those indicia must, in the view we take, be derived from empirical observation of accepted religions. They are liable to vary with changing social conditions and the relative importance of any particular one of them will differ from case to case.[71]

They listed some of the more important indicia of religion such as a belief in the supernatural, a concept of man's nature and place in the universe, adherence to a certain code of conduct and other similar factors, and an identifiable (even if loose-knit) group of adherents.[72] These criteria were to be used to determine that the Church of Scientology was a religion for constitutional purposes.

4.5 CONCLUSION: A DEFINITION OF RELIGION AND BELIEF

Defining religion is a complex and controversial question and one that has proved problematic in both domestic courts and the international sphere. The addition of the term 'or belief' to religion in Article 9 of the Convention may clarify some issues (particularly whether atheists are entitled to the protection of religious freedom) and does suggest that marginal cases, such as so-called 'New Religions', should be presumed to be included in the wider scope of the term 'religion or belief', even though some States refuse to acknowledge them as religions *per se*. At another level, however, the term belief has increased the conceptual confusion in this area and the approach that the Commission has taken to the cases has only magnified this confusion.

While the terms thought, conscience, religion, and belief are all of uncer-tain scope, they are used distinctly in the Convention. In particular, by

[70] CONSTITUTION OF THE COMMONWEALTH OF AUSTRALIA (1901). Section 116 reads, 'The Commonwealth shall not make any law for establishing any religion, or for imposing any religious observance, or for prohibiting the free exercise of any religion, and no religious test shall be required as a qualification for any office or public trust under the Commonwealth.'
[71] Wilson and Deane JJ, in *Church of the New Faith v. Commissioner for Pay-Roll Tax (Vic.)*, 154 C.L.R. 120, 173 (1983).
[72] *Id.* at 174. See also Puls, above, note 11.

referring to the freedom of 'thought, conscience and religion' but only the right to manifest 'religion or belief', Article 9 distinguishes one type of personal philosophy for a greater degree of protection than others. Some argue that it is neither appropriate nor possible to make these kinds of distinctions,[73] but the wording of Article 9 and some of the cases decided by the Court suggest that such distinctions are legally necessary.[74]

Yet by choosing a test that looks only at some degree of intellectual coherence and importance in defining religion or belief, the Commission has not acknowledged that such a test could equally apply to a range of things that might be better described as thought or conscience. This problem has been compounded by the tendency of the Commission to look at the term 'belief' in isolation from its context. Linking the notion of belief to a similar function to the role of religion would include groups such as atheists and agnostics, and also borderline groups such as the new religions and some Eastern philosophies (such as Taoism and Buddhism) that sit somewhat uneasily within traditional definitions of religion. The link with religion in the case of an atheist or an agnostic is clear, as these beliefs are both responses to the same basic questions of ultimate meaning, the existence of god, and the role of the supernatural in human affairs. The rejection of the notion of god can be as fundamental to self-identity as the acceptance of the existence of god. The inclusion of the other quasi-religious beliefs ensures that the definition does not become too historically rooted and rigid or too influenced by Judaeo-Christian assumptions about the nature of religion.

The Commission has, however, tended to look at the word 'belief' in a rather abstract way and has not recognized that it is part of the phrase 'religion or belief' in Article 9. This leads to questions over the inclusion as a 'belief' of things such as political membership or broad ethical positions. Part of this conceptual confusion could be avoided if belief were to be given a more restricted meaning, linked to it playing essentially the same role in the life of the individual as religion. The particular formulation that could be used to define this role need not be a simple definition, such as 'the ultimate concern' used at times by the United States Supreme Court, but could look at a range of factors. This more conceptual approach to religion or belief could help to ensure that the term does not become unduly restrictive or exclusionary of new religious groups, but does not become so open-ended that it is rendered essentially meaningless. It could also allow the Court to move away from the relatively unsophisticated notion that religion or belief is an important and coherent set of beliefs. As many of the more sophisticated approaches to this issue note, religion is not merely

---

[73] VAN DIJK AND VAN HOOF, above, note 3, at 397.
[74] HARRIS, O'BOYLE, AND WARBRICK, above, note 3, at 357.

a set of intellectual propositions but may have a moral, ethical, supernatural, communal, or symbolic role in people's lives.

This is not to deny the importance of issues such as political orientation or philosophical positions in human affairs, but rather to suggest that they are protected in the Convention without any need to give them the broader scope that would allow those who hold them to have a right to 'manifest' them. The right to freedom of thought and conscience is protected in Article 9(1) and is not subject to limitation. Thus all people are free to develop their intellectual and ethical positions without interference by the State. They are also free to express their views according to Article 10, to join associations of other like-minded people under Article 11, and entitled to the privacy in which to develop their ideas under Article 8. These are more appropriate ways of ensuring that all people have the freedom to pursue a range of ideas and are given a degree of protection from the State or from the intolerance of others who disagree with their views.

Yet, possibly in an attempt to treat all philosophies equally and fairly, and also because of its reluctance to develop a theory of religious freedom, the Commission has stretched the idea of belief so that there is an extra protection given to many ideas that would be better dealt with as simply thought or conscience. Even the types of manifestation outlined in the second part of Article 9(1) suggest that belief is not intended to have a very general and broad scope, as the protected manifestations are connected to relatively traditional religious practices (particularly worship and observance). This leads the Commission into a dilemma when dealing with cases involving the meaning of freedom of religion or belief and the scope of the notion of manifestation. Having failed to use the definitional stage as a way of filtering out any but a very limited number of 'beliefs', it is then necessary for it to define the rights under Article 9 narrowly in order to ensure that the scope of the Article does not become so wide that it is impracticable. If everyone has a fairly broad right to manifest their beliefs (be they political, ethical, philosophical, or personal) then this would cut across a huge range of State activity and render many of the other Articles in the Convention virtually meaningless, as almost everything that could be protected by more specific Articles would fall under the scope of an expanded Article 9.

Thus, as the next two chapters explore, the Commission and Court have moved from a very liberal definition of 'religion or belief' to a very restrictive view of what freedom of religion and belief entail. In developing a conception of freedom of religion or belief and in limiting the right to manifest a religion or belief, they must deal in a roundabout way with the question of the definition or religion or belief, and they have in fact developed a conservative conception of these notions that belies the expansive approach taken at the definitional stage.

5

Freedom of Religion or Belief

Article 9(1) states that 'everyone has the right to freedom of thought, conscience and religion' but, just as the terms 'thought, conscience and religion' are not defined, neither is the term 'freedom' given any clear definition under Article 9. As Partsch has noted in the United Nations context, 'It is striking that despite the variety of State attitudes towards religion there was no substantial discussion of the fundamental principle that "everyone shall have the right to freedom of thought, conscience and religion" in the drafting of the International Covenant on Civil and Political Rights.'[1] The same could be said for that fundamental principle in the Convention.

Freedom of religion or belief is said in the text of Article 9 to *include* freedom to change religion or belief and a freedom to manifest one's religion or belief in certain ways. Yet it is clear both from the text (particularly the use of the non-exclusive term 'includes') and from the decisions of the Court and Commission that these two elements are only part of a broader notion of freedom of religion. This chapter explores the concept of freedom of religion or belief to the extent that it operates independently from the right to manifest a religion or belief. The next chapter considers the issues that arise from the manifestation of those religions or beliefs.

5.1 THE IMPORTANCE OF THE FREEDOM

The Court has made clear that freedom of religion and belief is an important Convention right and, in *Kokkinakis v. Greece*,[2] it set out what it termed the 'general principles' that underlie Article 9. It stated that

As enshrined in Article 9, freedom of thought, conscience and religion is one of the foundations of a 'democratic society' within the meaning of the Convention. It is, in its religious dimension, one of the most vital elements which go to make up the identity of believers and their conception of life, but it is also a precious asset to atheists, agnostics, sceptics and the unconcerned. The pluralism indissociable from a democratic society, which has been dearly won over the centuries, depends on it.[3]

---

[1] K. J. Partsch, *Freedom of Conscience and Expression and Political Freedoms, in* THE INTERNATIONAL BILL OF HUMAN RIGHTS: THE COVENANT ON CIVIL AND POLITICAL RIGHTS 209, 210 (L. Henkin ed., 1981).

[2] *Kokkinakis v. Greece*, 260-A Eur. Ct. H.R. (ser. A) (1993).

[3] *Id.* at 13.

These general principles seem to draw on a similar understanding of the importance of freedom of religion developed in Chapter 2 in noting the importance of religious freedom to the development of both individual self-definition and the promotion of democratic pluralism within a society. The Court emphasized the primacy of the notion of individual conscience, though it noted that this also 'implies' a right to manifest one's religion or belief.[4] The Court said that the importance of the fundamental nature of the right set out in the first part of Article 9(1) was underlined by the fact that no derogation by the government is allowed from the freedom to have or change a religion. In contrast, the right to manifest a religion or belief may be legitimately subject to restrictions set out in Article 9(2).[5]

Thus the Court has emphasized the importance of freedom of religion or belief, in particular at the level of the internal, individual conscience. It has not, however, given much consideration to the content of the freedom. At the most basic level, it could be considered simply the right to hold opinions silently (on religious or other important issues) without interference by the State. At this level the right is almost impossible for the State to breach, except by use of invasive mind-altering techniques, such as brainwashing or systematic indoctrination. This seems to be what Arcot Krishnaswami suggested in his study of religious discrimination when he wrote, 'Freedom to maintain or to change religion or belief falls primarily within the domain of the inner faith and conscience of an individual. Viewed from this angle, one would assume that any intervention from outside is not only illegitimate but impossible.'[6]

If the right to freedom of thought, conscience, and religion is sufficiently protected as long as a person is able to continue to hold those beliefs, no matter how difficult the State makes it for them to do so, the content of the right is minimal. At the time when the Convention was drafted, however, soon after the Second World War and toward the beginning of the Cold War, Europeans could not even be complacent about the State never using its powers to attempt to coerce people into changing the internal aspects of religion or belief. One of the drafters spoke of the first part of Article 9 being a bulwark against the dehumanizing techniques adopted in a police state.[7] Sir David Maxwell-Fyfe argued for the need for Article 2 of the First Protocol by reminding the drafters of 'what we all know was a terrible aspect of totalitarianism, namely, that the youth of the country were brought up so much under the dogmatic teaching of totalitarianism by the agencies or para-agencies of the State that it was impossible for their parents to bring them up in their own religious and philosophic

---

[4] *Id.*   [5] See Chapter 6.   [6] Krishnaswami study, at 16.
[7] *Travaux Préparatoires*, vol. 1, at 200 and 222, Report of the Committee on Legal and Administrative Questions, 5 Sept. 1949, Doc. 77 of the Constitutional Assembly Report, Doc. A290.

beliefs'.[8] It was thus important to ensure that such methods were prohibited by the Convention, but it is not clear where the border lies between forcing people to act in a certain way and forcing them to change their beliefs. This issue has two aspects. The first is whether the State has a positive obligation to create conditions in which the individual can freely exercise his or her freedom of religion or belief or whether it merely has a negative obligation to refrain from interfering with the freedom. The second is at what point burdens on religion or belief imposed by the State infringe the negative obligation of the State to refrain from interfering with freedom of religion or belief.

5.2 A POSITIVE RIGHT TO FREEDOM OF RELIGION OR BELIEF

The Preamble of the Framework Convention for the Protection of National Minorities reflects the developing understanding of the positive role of the State in ensuring that individuals can freely exercise their rights. It provides, in part, that 'a pluralist and genuinely democratic society should not only respect the ethnic, cultural, linguistic and religious identity of each person belonging to a national minority, but also *create appropriate conditions enabling them to express, preserve and develop this identity*'.[9]

This suggests that a State that is committed to minority rights should not simply refrain from harming minorities but should be positively involved in creating conditions in which they can express their identity— an important aspect of which can be their religious identity. The question that arises in the context of Article 9 is whether the State is required to play a similarly positive role. The wording of Article 9 is not determinative of the issue. Every person has a right to freedom of religion but, for a long time, the obligation of the State in securing this extended only to refraining from interfering with the freedom rather than creating conditions in which it could flourish. At times, however, States have acted to limit certain rights in order to protect some element of religious freedom. This has led to claims that the State had an *obligation* in some circumstances to take action to protect freedom of religion or belief.

In an early case raising this issue, a Scientologist wished to bring an action against a professor who had spoken disparagingly of Scientology.[10] He brought a case against the State for failing to create a form of action

---

[8] *Travaux Préparatoires*, vol. 6, at 162, Second Session of the Consultative Assembly, Speech of Maxwell-Fyfe (United Kingdom).
[9] Preamble to the Framework Convention on the Protection of National Minorities (emphasis added).
[10] *Church of Scientology and 128 of its members v. Sweden*, App. No. 8282/78, 21 Eur. Comm'n H.R. Dec. & Rep. 109 (1980).

that would allow him to sue the professor. The Commission, in dismissing the case as manifestly ill-founded, said that it was not of the opinion 'that a particular religion or creed can derive from the concept of freedom of religion a right to be free from criticism',[11] although it did leave open the possibility that agitation against a religion could be so severe that it would engage State responsibility.

Subsequently, in *Otto-Preminger v. Austria*,[12] the Court rejected a claim based on a violation of free speech by a film-maker who was prevented from showing his film (which mocked important Christian figures and doctrines) in Tyrol. The Court accepted the arguments by Austria that it could confiscate a film on the basis that it was likely to cause deep offence to the religious feelings of the predominantly Roman Catholic province in which it was to be shown. The Court reiterated that religions could not expect to be free from criticism, but noted that in extreme cases the methods of opposing a religion or belief 'can be such as to inhibit those who hold such beliefs from exercising their freedom'.[13] This reasoning seems sound and might apply in a situation, for example, in which a group actively sought out and intimidated others for their religious beliefs or blockaded places of worship. Yet, in this case, the Commission went further and discussed the 'respect for the religious feelings of believers as guaranteed in Article 9'[14] despite the fact that nowhere in Article 9 is such respect explicitly guaranteed.

As was to be expected, these *dicta* gave rise to a case in which this expanded notion of the right to religious respect was claimed as a positive right by two applicants. They argued that the State should have intervened to bring criminal charges against a Polish magazine that published a picture of Czestochowa Madonna and Child (a venerated icon of Catholicism and Polish nationalism) wearing a gas mask, in order to illustrate a cover story about growing air pollution.[15] The Polish government investigated complaints made by a number of people who were offended by the image but decided not to bring charges. When the applicants brought a case to the Commission complaining that their right to religious freedom had been denied, the Commission dismissed the case as manifestly ill-founded. The Commission, while acknowledging that the State could be under some positive obligation to protect freedom of religion, emphasized that the applicants were not 'inhibited from exercising their freedom to hold and express their belief'.[16] Yet only a couple of months later, in *Wingrove v.*

[11] *Id.* at 111.

[12] *Otto-Preminger-Institut v. Austria*, 295 Eur. Ct. H.R. (ser. A) (1994).

[13] *Id.* at 18.   [14] *Id.*

[15] *Dubowska v. Poland*, App. No. 33490/96, and *Skup v. Poland*, App. No. 34055/96 (joined), 89-A Eur. Comm'n H.R. Dec. & Rep. 156 (1997).

[16] *Id.* at 161.

the United Kingdom, the Court referred again to the 'right of citizens not to be insulted in their religious feelings'.[17] In that case, the publication of a video portraying a woman playing St Teresa having an ecstatic and erotic fantasy about Christ was certainly likely to offend and insult many Christians, but it is not at all clear that it would have interfered with the ability of the majority Christian community to hold their own beliefs, practise their religion, or express views about their religions (including criticisms of the films).

It is thus arguable that there is a developing right not to have one's religious feelings offended, at least when this is done in a manner which is intentionally and 'gratuitously' insulting.[18] Yet the question of what is likely to be sufficiently offensive to the particular religious community attacked to involve the criminal or civil law is one where the State has a wide discretion. The Court has been reluctant to become involved in second guessing the decision of a State, even when the laws of the State expressly protect only one religion and not others from such attacks.[19] This means that the Court has not so much created a positive right on which many applicants will be able to rely but rather granted States a wide margin of appreciation to take action to protect the religious feelings of members of the society, even if this restricts other rights such as freedom of expression. This can, however, be seen as a mere permission for the State to capitulate to pressure from groups that are intolerant of criticism of their religion. While there are probably still boundaries beyond which State action would not be tolerated (censoring academic criticism of a religion, for example) the judgments in this line of cases do give the State a lot of room to move in responding to popular displeasure, particularly in response to artistic criticisms of religion.

This break from the original principles set down in the Scientology case is particularly unfortunate as it will tend to benefit majority religions or religions that are prepared to respond to criticism or mockery with intolerance or outrage. Where there is widespread social discrimination against a minority religion or belief, or where private parties are advocating religious hatred, discrimination, or persecution, there may be an argument that the State should have an obligation to take steps to remedy the situation. It may be that in some situations it becomes virtually impossible for individuals to freely exercise their religion or belief because of hostility from the population as a whole and perhaps also from parts

[17] *Wingrove v. the United Kingdom*, 23 Eur. Ct. H.R. (ser. A) 1937 (1996-V).

[18] *Id.* at 1954. The Court held that exercise of freedom of speech carries with it the duty to 'avoid as far as possible an expression that is, in regard to objects of veneration, gratuitously offensive to others and profanatory'.

[19] Such as Britain's blasphemy laws, which apply only to Christianity and not to blasphemy against other religious groups. See *Choudhury v. the United Kingdom*, App. No. 17439/90, 12 HUM. RTS L.J. 172 (1991).

of the State.[20] Yet the cases in which the State has limited other rights in the name of religion have involved the religious sensibilities of the majority that can place pressure on the State to ensure that the freedom of others is curtailed when it provokes outrage. The State is given so much discretion under the current case law that minority groups suffering from more serious attacks may have difficulty invoking a positive obligation of religious freedom to ensure protection by the State.

This recent deference to religious sensibilities (as compared with religious freedoms) is particularly problematic given that the bulk of the case law on freedom of religion or belief has allowed States a considerable scope of action before they could be said to breach their clear negative obligation to refrain from interfering with freedom of religion or belief.

5.3 THE NEGATIVE OBLIGATION

5.3.1 The Primacy of the Private Sphere

The approach of the Commission and Court to the nature of freedom of religion or belief, and the extent to which it acts as a restraint on governments, is rather vague, although they have developed some general notions. The most important of these is the so-called *forum internum* (a term that is also used in relation to United Nations treaties dealing with freedom of religion[21]). Neither the Court nor the Commission has explained what is meant by this term in any detail. Both have used the standard recital that 'Article 9 primarily protects the sphere of personal beliefs and religious creeds, i.e. the area which is sometimes called the *forum internum*'.[22]

Thus the emphasis in the interpretation of Article 9 is on the internal: the private thought, conscience, and religion of the individual. Yet little consideration is given to precisely what this entails. If it only entails the right to maintain one's internal beliefs, without any attempt to communicate them or act upon them then, as Professor Malcolm Evans puts it,

there would be little difficulty in its application both because of its simplicity and the rarity of it being breached, since an applicant would have to show that external pressure sufficient to induce a forcible change in inner belief has been applied. In

---

[20] This was the situation alleged to exist in *Scientology Kirche Deutschland e.V. v. Germany*, App. No. 34614/97, 89-A, Eur. Comm'n H.R. Dec. & Rep. 163 (1997). The case was dismissed for failure to exhaust domestic remedies (at 172–3) but the Court noted (at 171–2) that the issues raised by the Scientologists might give rise to a claim about the positive obligation of the State to protect freedom of religion or belief.

[21] BAHIYYIH G. TAHZIB, FREEDOM OF RELIGION OR BELIEF: ENSURING EFFECTIVE INTERNATIONAL PROTECTION 25–7 (1996).

[22] e.g. *C v. the United Kingdom*, App. No. 10358/83, 37 Eur. Comm'n H.R. Dec. & Rep. 142 (1983); *Valsamis v. Greece*, 2 Eur. Ct. H.R. (ser. A) 2312 at para. 48 (1996-VI).

fact the approach adopted is somewhat broader and focuses upon the danger of indoctrination inherent in being obliged to act by the State in away that runs counter to one's inner beliefs.[23]

This analysis seems to be correct if one looks at the outcome of the cases, but the Court and Commission tend to treat the line between the *forum internum* and the *forum externum* (the external manifestation of religion or belief) as self-evident and needing little in the way of explanation. However, the point at which being forced to act in a manner contrary to one's beliefs becomes indoctrination is far from clear. The Commission in *Darby v. Sweden* may have been working toward such a definition when it held that Article 9(1) 'protects everyone from being compelled to be involved in religious activities against his will'.[24] Yet how direct this participation has to be, the means by which a person can be said to be involved 'against his will', and whether this is to be considered the only way in which the State can breach the *forum internum* were not discussed.

The difficulty in consistently applying such a vague conception of the *forum internum* is shown in a recent case in which the Court seemed to ignore the distinction between the two limbs of Article 9(1) altogether. In *Buscarini and others v. San Marino*[25] new members of the General Grand Council (Parliament) of San Marino were required to take an oath swearing 'on the Holy Bible' to perform their duties properly. Several members made the promise but excluded reference to the Holy Bible. They eventually did take the oath but only after it was made clear to them that they would lose their parliamentary seats if they did not comply. The Court held that the obligation to take the oath in this form was contrary to Article 9 as it 'required them to swear allegiance to a particular religion'.[26] This is arguably a case of interference with the *forum internum*,[27] in which case the right should have been non-derogable, but the Court did not even consider this possibility. Instead it considered whether the oath was necessary in a democratic society under Article 9(2).[28] The Court simply assumed that it was dealing with a case

---

[23] See MALCOLM D. EVANS, RELIGIOUS LIBERTY AND INTERNATIONAL LAW IN EUROPE chapter 1 (1997).

[24] *Darby v. Sweden*, 187 Eur. Ct. H.R. (ser. A) (1990) annex to the decision of the Court at para. 51.

[25] *Buscarini and others v. San Marino*, App. No. 24645/94, Eur. Ct. H.R., 18 Feb. 1999, unreported.

[26] *Id.* at para. 34.

[27] Although the Krishnaswami study, at 42–3, dealt with the issue of refusing to take an oath under the heading of manifesting religion and belief. Krishnaswami's discussion of the *forum internum* (at 16) focused more on 'compelling an individual to join or preventing him from leaving the organization or a belief in which he has no faith'.

[28] *Buscarini and others v. San Marino*, App. No. 24645/94, Eur. Ct. H.R., 18 Feb. 1999, unreported, at paras 35–40. The Court held that taking the oath was not necessary in a democratic society.

of manifestation of religion or belief and did not mention the issue of the basic freedom of religion itself. The *Buscarini* case was heard by the Grand Chamber and its facts seemed to provide an ideal opportunity for the members of the newly constituted Court to develop its jurisprudence relating to the first limb of Article 9. The fact that they did not do so suggests that it is unlikely that the Court will develop a more sophisticated idea of the *forum internum* in the near future.

One author who has attempted to draw a more detailed picture of the scope of the *forum internum* is Bahiyyih G. Tahzib. In a book on the protection of freedom of religion at the international level, she outlines a number of ways in which the State could interfere with the *forum internum* short of systematic brainwashing. Her suggestions of unlawful interferences include

discrimination on the basis of having, or not having, a certain religion or belief;

proscription of membership of certain religions or beliefs under law;

coercion to reveal one's religion or belief or to have it revealed without one's consent; and

use of threat of physical force or penal sanctions to compel individuals to adhere to their religious or other beliefs and congregations, to recant their religion or belief or to convert.[29]

As discussed below, a number of the Commission and Court cases arguably have condoned these practices as not interfering with freedom of religion and belief. However, while this list is far clearer than the description developed by the Commission or Court, it still begs the question of the precise line between the internal and the external realm in matters of religion or conscience and it assumes that a reasonably clear line between those two realms can be maintained.

5.3.2 The Internal/External Dichotomy

While there is no acknowledgement of this in the jurisprudence of the Court and Commission,[30] the idea that beliefs and actions are separate and distinguishable notions is controversial.[31] In the United States a similar division between belief and action (the first being inviolable and the second open

---

[29] Tahzib, above, note 21, at 26.

[30] Some writers in the area also make simplistic assumptions about the primacy of belief within a religion. See Brice Dickson, *The United Nations and Freedom of Religion*, 44 Int'l & Comp. L.Q. 327 (1995), who argues that 'A religion first and foremost is a collection of beliefs.'

[31] Gabriel Moens, *The Action–Belief Dichotomy and Freedom of Religion*, 12 Sydney L. Rev. 195 (1989); J. E. S. Fawcett, The Application of the European Convention on Human Rights 238–9 (1987); Donna Sullivan, *Advancing the Freedom of Religion or Belief Through the UN Declaration on the Elimination of Religious Intolerance and Discrimination*, 82 Am. J. Int'l L. 487, 500–10 (1988).

to limitation) has become part of the orthodoxy of First Amendment case law.[32] Yet despite its widespread use, Chief Justice Burger commented that 'belief and action cannot be neatly confined in logic tight compartments'.[33] Philip Kurland, a noted commentator on the religion clauses in the First Amendment, simply dismisses the notion that action and belief can be clearly distinguished, saying 'it is obviously not a line that can provide any assistance in resolving . . . knotty problems'.[34] Many writers point out the extent to which one's religious or other beliefs and actions are intertwined.[35] In this context H. A. Freeman made the point that every 'great religion is not merely a matter of belief; it is a way of life; it is action' and that one of the most 'scathing rebukes in religion is reserved for hypocrites who believe but fail to so act'.[36]

The emphasis given in the case law to the primacy of internal or belief-based systems as the core meaning of religion is also not necessarily consonant with the way in which many religions would define themselves. As Professor Donna Sullivan argues in a similar context, 'Many religious doctrines or beliefs dictate standards of social conduct and responsibility, and require believers to act accordingly. For those who follow such precepts of social responsibility, the distinction between religious and political activity may be artificial.'[37] The eminent theologian Cantwell Smith argues that outside traditional European religions, the whole notion of religion, let alone the primacy of particular beliefs as opposed to a religious way of life, is alien.[38] The notion that religion is primarily a set of particular, coherent beliefs, as some of the Article 9 case law suggests, is therefore not the way in which all religions or religious people perceive the issue. Forcing a person to act in a way which is against the teachings of his or her religion or belief, or penalizing him or her for acting in

---

[32] Beginning with *Reynolds v. U.S.*, 98 U.S. 244, 250 (1878). The most commonly quoted case in this regard is *Cantwell v. Connecticut*, 310 U.S. 296, 303–4 (1940) in which the Supreme Court stated that, 'Thus the Amendment embraces two concepts—freedom to believe and freedom to act. The first is absolute but, in the nature of things, the second cannot be.'

[33] *Wisconsin v. Yoder*, 406 U.S. 203, 220 (1972).

[34] Philip Kurland, Religion and the Law: Of Church and State and the Supreme Court 22 (1961).

[35] Paul Hayden, *Religiously Motivated 'Outrageous' Conduct: Intentional Infliction of Emotional Distress as a Weapon Against 'Other People's Faiths'*, 34 Wm & Mary L. Rev. 579, 611–13 (1993); Desmond M. Clarke, *Freedom of Thought in the UN Declaration and Covenants*, 28 Irish Jurist 121, 121–3 (1993–5).

[36] H. A. Freeman, *A Remonstrance for Conscience*, 106 Pa. L. Rev. 806, 826 (1958).

[37] Sullivan, above, note 31, at 500.

[38] Wilfred Cantwell Smith, The Meaning and End of Religion chapters 2 and 3 (1962). In his study of the roots and usage of the term 'religion(s)', Cantwell Smith describes the way in which the usage of the terms has changed over time and has only relatively recently come to be associated with the idea of a collection of particular beliefs. Earlier usages tended to emphasize more the quality of life (perhaps 'piety' is the closest modern term) or the religious activities of people. Its modern association with a particular orthodoxy is basically a post-Reformation product.

compliance with the teaching of his or her religion, is not irrelevant to the core of many people's religion or belief. As the last chapter discussed, many definitions of religion note the importance of developing and living by an ethical code, adhering to communal patterns of behaviour and involvement in ritual. Only very narrow definitions of religion restrict it to the primarily intellectual sphere of developing a system of ideas/beliefs in one's own mind. More sophisticated definitions take note of how religion may play an important role in the way in which people live their whole lives.

The wording of Article 9 itself does suggest that a distinction must be drawn between the general right to freedom of religion or belief and the right to manifest that religion or belief. Yet it is not clear that the first limb of Article 9 simply becomes irrelevant once some manifestation is in question. At some point, burdening external manifestations of belief must have serious implications for the internal realm. This point was made by Chief Justice Burger for the US Supreme Court in *Wisconsin v. Yoder*,[39] a case that dealt with a law that required all children in Wisconsin to attend compulsory schooling until the age of 16. The Amish wanted an exemption from this rule because they felt that the last two years of education interfered with the children's ability to integrate into the Amish religious and social community. The Court held that they were entitled to that exemption under the First Amendment. The outcome of the case was controversial but, whatever the merits of the decision, the reasoning shows up the extent to which the internal and external realms are intertwined. Religion, for the Amish, was not 'merely a matter of theocratic beliefs' but a 'deep religious conviction' that pervaded their whole way of life. Interfering in the way of life would have the inevitable consequence of interfering with the belief.[40] At some point, placing burdens on manifestations of belief must also be a breach of the basic right to freedom of religion or belief.

5.3.3 Burdens on Belief

As Professor Evans noted in the above quotation, the Commission *has* acknowledged that at some point forcing a person to act in breach of his or her religion or belief has implications not only for the *forum externum* but also for the private, internal conscience. The area in which modern European States have been most often accused of attempting indoctrination is in relation to teaching in schools. Yet at some level, every time the State requires an individual to act against the dictates of his or her religion or penalizes a refusal to act in contravention of conscience,

---

[39] *Wisconsin v. Yoder*, 406 U.S. 203 (1972).   [40] *Id.* at 216.

this has implications for the *forum internum*. This would be presented most starkly in a case in which a person was required to participate in the worship or rites of a religion with which he or she did not agree, or to recant his or her own religion. No such case has come before the Court. However, in an arguably similar situation the Court rejected two cases brought by Jehovah's Witness children who were punished for refusing to take part in what they perceived to be a military parade.[41] The applicants claimed that participation in such a parade violated their deeply held religious commitment to pacifism. In these cases the Court worked on the assumption that what was at stake was the right to manifest a religion, but, had the children been forced to participate in prayers (or penalized for not doing so), it is possible that the difficulty in maintaining the strict line between the internal and external aspects of religion or belief might have been more clearly perceived by the Court. To be forced to act in a way that the individual considers a serious violation of his or her religious beliefs is arguably equivalent to being forced to recant a religion or belief. The neat distinction between the internal and external realm is difficult to maintain in such a case.

Even the restrictive notion of the *forum internum* has not been applied consistently by the Court. This can be seen by comparing the school marching cases to *Darby v. Sweden* in which the Commission held that being forced to pay taxes to a Church to which one did not belong had serious implications for the *forum internum*.[42] While the Court decided the case on other grounds, the approach of the Commission is not easily reconciled with its decisions in cases such as those involving the Jehovah's Witnesses. Possibly the decision can be understood in the context that the applicant in *Darby* was being forced to participate in a religion in which he did not believe. The children were being forced to participate in a secular programme rather than directly in a religion. The way in which the applicants in each case perceived the issue at stake, however, may well have been very similar. In neither case did the action of the State go so far that it made it impossible (or even particularly difficult) for the individuals to maintain their internal beliefs, but in each case the State required the individuals to act in a way that they felt was in direct contradiction to

---

[41] *Valsamis v. Greece*, 2 Eur. Ct. H.R. (ser. A) 2312 (1996-VI); *Efstratiou v. Greece*, 27 Eur. Ct. H.R. (ser. A) 2347 (1996-VI).

[42] The law required taxes to be paid to the State Church of Sweden. Swedish residents who were not members of the Church of Sweden could apply for an exemption from paying at least part of this tax. Taxpayers such as Mr Darby, however, who earned money in Sweden but did not live there were not entitled to an exemption. *Darby v. Sweden*, 187 Eur. Ct. H.R. (ser. A) (1990) annex to the decision of the Court at para. 50–1, 60; T. Jeremy Gunn, *Adjudicating Rights of Conscience under the European Convention on Human Rights*, in RELIGIOUS HUMAN RIGHTS IN GLOBAL PERSPECTIVE: LEGAL PERSPECTIVES 305, 316–18 (Johan D. van der Vyver and John Witte Jr. eds., 1996).

the requirements of those beliefs. They were in effect being asked to recant, by their behaviour, their religion. This conflict between the behaviour required of them and their beliefs was such that it arguably interfered with the internal as well as the external realm.

Thus the crucial question is the point at which an action by the State is so intrusive that it is held to interfere, not merely with a person's right to manifest a religion, but also with his or her right to have a religion or belief. The answer so far seems to be that States have to act very repressively before the Court or Commission will hold that they have interfered with the *forum internum*. With the exception of the *Darby* case, there has been no other case in which the State ordering some action that was against the conscience of the individual or penalizing religious behaviour has been found to be an interference with the *forum internum*.[43] As Professor Evans puts it, people have to expect to 'pay a price' for their religion or belief[44] and the mere imposition of some burden on a person who is trying to practise their religion or belief is insufficient to be a breach of the first part of Article 9(1).

While some prices may be too high (e.g. torture or imprisonment), some reasonably serious burdens have not been held to be a breach of the first part of Article 9(1). A military judge who was dismissed from his job for being a member of a fundamentalist Islamic group was held by the Court (reversing the decision of the Commission) to have no case under the Convention, including Article 9.[45] The Court justified this decision in part on the grounds that in entering the army the applicant had voluntarily accepted certain limits on his rights and freedoms[46] but partly on the grounds that he was not dismissed on the basis of his opinions but on the basis of his conduct and attitude. Yet the conduct and attitude which formed the basis of the dismissal were the adoption of 'unlawful fundamentalist opinions'.[47] Vague allegations were made about the fact that his conduct was a breach of military discipline but no details were given and it is not clear what acts (if any) constituted this indiscipline.[48] This case seems to fall into the first class of interference with the *forum internum* described by Tahzib, that of discrimination on the basis of holding a particular religion and penalization for holding particular views. This is particularly so as there was no evidence that his religion was interfering with his performance of his role in the army, and the Commission had held that his dismissal

---

[43] Many of the issues that arise in relation to this problem are discussed in Chapter 8.

[44] EVANS, above, note 23, at 300–3.

[45] *Kalaç v. Turkey*, 41 Eur. Ct. H.R. (ser. A) 1199 (1997-IV). Ironically, EVANS, above, note 23, at 304 had written of the Commission case as demonstrating that there were some limits to how far the State could go in burdening the *forum internum*.

[46] This is discussed further at Chapter 6.7.2.

[47] *Kalaç v. Turkey*, 41 Eur. Ct. H.R. (ser. A) 1199 at 1203 (1997-IV).

[48] *Id.* at 1209.

amounted to a breach of Article 9.[49] In overruling that finding, the Court used such a narrow definition of freedom of religion or belief that it is difficult to see how any but the most totalitarian State could breach it. Thus, in most cases, the State can make it unpleasant or burdensome to hold a religion or belief without actually intruding on the *forum internum*.

It is possible, however, that there has been a shift at least by some members of the Court toward a broader view of the protection granted by the first limb of Article 9(1). In *Tsavachidis v. Greece*[50] a number of members of the Commission argued that the systematic surveillance by the secret police of a person on the basis of his religion or belief violated the very right to hold a belief. The majority only agreed that such surveillance amounted to a breach to the right of privacy (and thus could be overridden under Article 8(2) if necessary in a democratic society), but it is possible that some form of organized intimidation of a religious group by agents of the State might amount to an interference with the *forum internum*. The issue never reached the Court as the parties came to a friendly settlement.[51] However, in a recent case the Court was willing to find that the co-operation of State agents, particularly the police, with family members who detained their adult children against their will in order to 'de-programme' them from their religious beliefs, was a breach of the right not to be falsely imprisoned.[52] Unfortunately, although Article 9 was raised by the applicants, the Court decided that the claim was primarily based on Article 5(1) and thus Article 9 did not require separate investigation. This case, however, may also indicate some willingness on the part of the Court to protect the right to freedom of religious belief (even highly controversial religious belief) even if that protection was gained under another article of the Convention.

While the Court and Commission have been relatively limited in holding that a State has interfered in the *forum internum* by forcing participation in a non-religious programme, arguably different considerations should apply when the State is or appears to be involved in promoting a particular religious viewpoint. There are two primary contexts in which this could be said to occur. The first is in establishment of a State Church. The second is in education of children in State schools. Each of these areas has implications for the *forum internum*.

[49] *Id.* at 1211, opinion of the Commission, annex to the decision of the Court. The Commission, however, did not discuss the issue of the *forum internum* but based its decision on the grounds that Kalaç's dismissal was based on a manifestation of his beliefs but was not 'prescribed by law' with sufficient clarity.

[50] *Tsavachidis v. Greece*, App. No. 28802/95, Eur. Comm'n H.R., 4 Mar. 1997, unreported.

[51] *Tsavachidis v. Greece*, App. No. 28802/95, Eur. Ct. H.R., 21 Jan. 1999, unreported.

[52] *Riera Blume and others v. Spain*, App. No. 37680/97, Eur. Ct. H.R., 21 Sept. 1999, unreported.

5.4 THE STATE CHURCH

At the time when the Convention was drafted, many of the parties involved in the drafting process had some form of established or State Church.[53] Today numerous Contracting Parties make mention of a particular Church or religion in their constitutions.[54] None of these States has an official policy of persecution or intolerance of other religions, as historically was sometimes the case.[55] Most, however, give certain privileges or comparative benefits to a particular Church or Churches *vis-à-vis* other religions or Churches.

The first question that arises in the context of State Churches is whether their mere existence is a breach of freedom of religion or belief. The United Nations instruments dealing with religious freedom tend to avoid the issue, although the Draft Declaration on the Elimination of Intolerance or Discrimination on the Basis of Religion or Belief of 1967 stated at Article I(d) that neither the establishment of a religion nor recognition of a religion or belief by the State should in itself be considered a form of intolerance or discrimination.[56] This provision was not included in the final Declaration.

The Court and Commission have also decided that an establishment of a Church is not, in and of itself, a breach of the Convention.[57] The Commission, in the case of *Darby v. Sweden*,[58] held that

A State Church system cannot in itself be considered to violate Article 9 of the Convention. In fact, such a system exists in several Contracting States and existed there when the Convention was drafted and when they become parties to it. However, a State Church system must, in order to satisfy Article 9, include specific safeguards for the individual's freedom of religion.[59]

An established Church is not, therefore, given a *carte blanche*. In particular, the State cannot force people to join the Church or prohibit people from leaving it.[60] Were it to do so, this would be a clear case of interference in the *forum internum*. The fact that an established Church is allowed to

---

[53] *Darby v. Sweden*, 187 Eur. Ct. H.R. (ser. A) (1990), annex to the decision of the Court at para. 45.

[54] See the discussion at Chapter 2.2. For an overview of the various relationships between the State and Church worldwide see SUBRATA ROY CHOWDHURY, RULE OF LAW IN A STATE OF EMERGENCY: THE PARIS MINIMUM STANDARDS OF HUMAN RIGHTS NORMS IN A STATE OF EMERGENCY 223–9 (1989).

[55] Myres S. McDougal, Harold D. Lasswell, and Lung-chu Chen, *The Right to Religious Freedom and World Public Order*, 74 MICH. L. REV. 865, 868–9 (1976).

[56] McDougal, Lasswell, and Chen, *Id.* at 890, describe this as an 'unfortunate departure from the conventional wisdom that the establishment or recognition of an official religion may promote intolerance of other beliefs'.

[57] D. J. HARRIS, M. O'BOYLE, AND C. WARBRICK, THE LAW OF THE EUROPEAN CONVENTION ON HUMAN RIGHTS 361 (1995).

[58] *Darby v. Sweden*, 187 Eur. Ct. H.R. (ser. A) (1990), annex to the decision of the Court.

[59] *Id.* at para 45.　　[60] *Id.*

exist can, however, raise difficult questions about how much assistance the State can give to a Church before it is involved in actively promoting one religion in a way that puts inappropriate pressure on those outside the Church to become involved in the Church or improperly penalizes those who are not members. In his world-wide study of religious freedom, Arcot Krishnaswami noted that historically the 'mere existence in a country of an Established Church or of a State religion usually connoted severe discrimination—and sometimes even outright persecution—directed against dissenters', but warned that this is not always the case and that an Established Church in some countries today is more of a historic relic than a threat to religious freedom.[61] Thus in his analysis the mere existence of a State Church is not a breach of international treaties for the protection of religious freedom but it does give rise to the need for scrutiny as such Churches can involve the State in improper discrimination between members of different religions or beliefs.

This permissible level of State support for a Church has tended to arise most directly in cases of taxation and financial contributions to a Church or Churches, and in State control over those inside the Church, particularly religious personnel such as clergy and ministers. The influence of a State Church, however, can also be seen in cases concerning the requirement to take the oath before taking up a Parliamentary seat (which breached the Convention)[62] and laws forbidding blasphemy against only one religion (which did not breach the Convention).[63]

5.4.1 Financial Arrangements

The State may collect Church taxes directly for an established Church (or indeed for any other Church[64]) from people who are members of that Church. [65] For these purposes the State can require people to notify it of a change of religion—arguably an interference in the right not to be compelled to reveal one's religion. The State has been given 'a wide discretion' by the Commission in terms of what it may require by way of proper

[61] Krishnaswami study, at 46–7.

[62] *Buscarini and others v. San Marino*, App. No. 24645/94, Eur. Ct. H.R., 18 Feb. 1999, unreported.

[63] *Choudhury v. the United Kingdom*, App. No. 17439/90, 12 HUM. RTS L.J. 172 (1991); *Wingrove v. the United Kingdom*, 23 Eur. Ct. H.R. (ser. A) 1937 at 1955–6 (1996-V), although the Court in *Wingrove* described a law that only protected one religion as 'an anomaly'.

[64] In *Gottesmann v. Switzerland*, App. No. 10616/83, 40 Eur. Comm'n H.R. Dec. & Rep. 284 (1984), the applicants were made to pay a contribution to the Catholic Church (of which they were members) even though it was not the State Church of Sweden.

[65] *Darby v. Sweden*, 187 Eur. Ct. H.R. (ser. A) (1990), annex to the decision of the Court; *X v. Austria*, App. No. 9781/82, 37 Eur. Comm'n H.R. Dec. & Rep. 37, 42 (1984). See also Gunn, above, note 42, at 316–18.

notification.[66] It cannot, however, put undue burdens on people who are not members of a Church to escape the imposition of Church taxes. In the *Darby* case,[67] for example, the Commission held that expecting a man to change the State in which he resided in order to gain an exemption from paying taxation for the State Church was a breach of Article 9.[68] The State, however, is allowed to act as agent for the Church in collecting moneys from members for religious purposes, interfering in what would otherwise be a private arrangement. The State may also authorize Churches to require direct payment of Church taxes and permit the Church to use the judicial machinery of the State to enforce payment.[69] In assessing these cases, the Commission has sometimes equated membership of a Church with membership of a private organization that can claim dues from its members and use the State to help collect or enforce payment of these dues when the State is willing to do so.[70] It has not given consideration to the fact that such arrangements require individuals to reveal their religion and any decision that they make about changing their religion to the State—something that may inhibit some individuals from freely exercising this choice and thus act as a constraint on the *forum internum*.[71]

The Commission has also permitted a State to require a non-believer to pay the proportion of taxes to a State Church that is required for the Church to carry out its 'secular functions', such as keeping records of births and deaths, performing marriages, and arranging funerals. The individual may be forced to pay this tax even though he or she is strongly opposed to the relationship between the State and Church that these 'secular functions' imply.[72] Individual members of one Church were also held to have no case under Article 9 when they objected to the way in which their Church tax was distributed among a number of religions rather than being used only for their own Church—even though their objection was so strong that they felt that they had to leave the Church rather than tolerate such an arrangement.[73]

---

[66] *Gottesmann v. Switzerland*, App. No. 10616/83, 40 Eur. Comm'n H.R. Dec. & Rep. 284 (1984).

[67] *Darby v. Sweden*, 187 Eur. Ct. H.R. (ser. A) (1990), annex to the decision of the Court.

[68] *Id.* at para. 52.

[69] *E & G.R. v. Austria*, App. No. 9781/82, 37 Eur. Comm'n H.R. Dec. & Rep. 42 (1984).

[70] *Id.* at 45; *Schubert v. Germany*, App. No. 9183/80, Eur. Comm'n H.R., 5 Oct. 1981, unreported.

[71] P. VAN DIJK AND G. J. H. VAN HOOF, THEORY AND PRACTICE OF THE EUROPEAN CONVENTION ON HUMAN RIGHTS 542 (3rd edn. 1997) conclude that the first limb of Art. 9 prohibits the State from obliging one to reveal one's religion or belief even in a census or other form of registration.

[72] In *Kustannus Oy Vapaa Ajattelija AB and others v. Finland*, App. No. 20471/92, 85-A Eur. Comm'n H.R. Dec. & Rep. 29 (1996) the Commission held that a company set up with the specific purpose of promoting atheism and freethinking, and in opposition to State involvement with religion, was required to pay Church taxes.

[73] *Schubert v. Germany*, App. No. 9183/80, Eur. Comm'n H.R., 5 Oct. 1981, unreported.

The State may also enter into arrangements that provide benefits to one or a number of Churches over other Churches or religions. In *Iglesia Bautista 'El Salvador' and Ortega Moratilla v. Spain*[74] the Commission held that a taxation system which gave preferential treatment to the Catholic Church compared to Protestant Churches did not breach Article 9 or Article 14. In Spain, the Catholic Church enjoyed a tax exemption from property tax in relation to its places of worship. The applicants, a Protestant Church and a Protestant minister, requested a similar exemption and were refused it on the basis that the Catholic Church received such concessions under a Concordat between the Catholic Church and Spain. In the absence of such an agreement with the Protestant Church, there was no legal basis for extending the exemption to it.[75]

The Commission held that there had been no breach of Article 9, either alone or in conjunction with Article 14.[76] The right to freedom of religion does not require that a Church be exempted from ordinary taxation obligations. The State is under no obligation to allow places of worship tax-free status.[77] Similarly, the State may grant one Church or religious organization tax exemptions without a breach of Article 14 if there are 'objective and reasonable' justifications for the difference in treatment.[78] The Commission held that, in this case, there were such justifications because of the existence of the Concordat. The Concordat placed obligations on the Catholic Church (e.g. to place its historical, artistic, and documentary heritage at the service of the Spanish people) in return for benefits from the State (e.g. tax exemptions).[79] As there was no comparable arrangement with the Protestant Church, there was no discrimination in allowing tax exemptions to the Catholic Church and not to the Protestant one.[80] Finally, the Commission dismissed the argument that, by not requiring the Catholic Church to pay tax but requiring the applicant Church to do so, the State was forcing one Church to subsidize the other.[81] The Commission stated that taxation was a neutral act with no conscientious implications.[82] Further, the applicant could not prove that the taxation from its property was used in any particular way or for any purpose relating to the upholding of the Catholic Church. Thus the State may legitimately tax one Church and not another, and give financial assistance to one Church and not another, if there is some arrangement between the privileged Church and the State which imposes reciprocal obligations on the two parties. The Commission did not explore the issue of whether the

---

[74] *Iglesia Bautista "El Salvador" and Ortega Moratilla v. Spain*, App. No. 17522/90, 72 Eur. Comm'n H.R. Dec. & Rep. 256 (1992).
[75] *Id.* at 260.   [76] *Id.* at 262.   [77] *Id.* at 261.   [78] *Id.*   [79] *Id.*
[80] *Id.* at 262.   [81] *Id.*
[82] For a general overview of the issue of taxation and freedom of religion or belief, see Chapter 8.3.

applicant Church had the right to require the State to enter into an arrangement with the Church (the Commission indeed specifically noted that the first applicant had not tried to do so), but implicit in the judgment is the suggestion that it does not have this right. This decision was presumably influenced by the fact that, if all religions had to be given the same privileges as the State Church, the whole notion of a State Church would be undermined.

5.4.2 Control over Church Personnel

Another set of legal difficulties caused by the establishment of a particular Church or religion within a society is that the secular authorities are given a role in making decisions regarding that religion that would otherwise remain internal religious matters.[83] The State may, for example, set down the employment criteria required for ministers or set out the State duties that the ministers will be required to perform. The State may also be involved in decisions as to when a minister has failed to perform these State duties properly and dismiss the person involved.

The State, where there is an established Church, has the right to set out conditions for employment in the Church generally or for a specific post.[84] The right of the State to require an oath of office and loyalty was implicitly upheld by the Commission in *Knudsen v. Norway*.[85] The Commission also upheld the decision of an employment board not to give a position to a pastor who opposed the ordination of women, on the grounds that in the new position he might have to work with female assistant priests.[86] The issue of the employment criteria of ministers is not the usual domain of the State and, were there not a State–Church relationship, such interference might well be construed as a breach of Article 9.[87] The State–Church relationship, however, does not merely legitimize the interference but requires State action and State responsibility under the Convention for some of the actions of the Church.

---

[83] Krishnaswami study, at 50, argues that the State does have a role in regulating the internal practices of religions, particularly to prevent public disorder, but that the role should be very limited.

[84] This is implied in *X v. Denmark*, App. No. 7374/76, 5 Eur. Comm'n H.R. Dec. & Rep. 157 (1976).

[85] *Knudsen v. Norway*, App. No. 11045/84, 42 Eur. Comm'n H.R. Dec. & Rep. 247 (1985). The Commission did not deal with this point specifically but it upheld the right of the State to dismiss the pastor from his post in part on the grounds that he had revoked his oath of loyalty.

[86] *Karlsson v. Sweden*, App. No. 12356/86, 57 Eur. Comm'n H.R. Dec. & Rep. 172 (1988).

[87] In *Finska Fosamling I Stockholm and Hautaniemi v. Sweden*, App. No. 24019/94, 85-A Eur. Comm'n H.R. Dec. & Rep. 94, 97 (1996) the Commission dismissed a claim against Sweden as the decision that was the source of the complaint was made by the autonomous Church Assembly of the Church of Sweden and the State was therefore not responsible for the decision.

The rights of ministers or members of a religion are also limited. In a State–Church system, the State has the ability, at least in some circumstances, to require a minister either to behave in a certain way or to resign. This is so even when the issue involved is an essentially religious one. Action taken by the State Church of Denmark to discipline a clergyman who tried to impose a requirement that parents take five lessons of religious instruction before he would baptize their children was upheld by the Commission.[88] The reasoning of the Commission in making this decision is important both in the context of State–Church relations and also in regard to the religious freedom of members of a Church, whether the Church is established or not. The Commission held that

A church is an organised religious community based on identical or at least substantially similar views. Through the rights granted to its members under Art. 9, the church itself is protected in its rights to manifest its religion, to organise and carry out worship, teaching, practice and observance, and it is free to act out and enforce uniformity in these matters. Further, in a State church system its servants are employed for the purpose of applying and teaching a specific religion. Their individual right of thought, conscience or religion is exercised at the moment they accept or refuse employment as clergymen, and their right to leave the church guarantees their freedom of religion in case they oppose its teachings.

In other words, the church is not obliged to provide religious freedom to its servants and members, as is the State as such for everyone within its jurisdiction.[89]

Thus, the Church Minister had the ultimate say in what requirements would be set down for baptism. The pastor had the right to follow those directives or to resign. As long as the option of resigning is there, the Commission held that there is no breach of the right to freedom of religion.[90]

The Commission reiterated this finding when it approved the action of the secular Minister of Church and Education in Norway, who dismissed from his State post a clergyman who refused to carry out certain of his State functions in protest at a new, liberal abortion law.[91] His rejection of the law was consistent with the teaching of his Church. His removal from office was opposed, according to the applicant, by his parish and his bishop. His refusal related to only a small section of his duties (mainly relating to marriage).[92] Yet the Commission held that his actions in opposing the abortion law were not required by his religion. His refusal to carry out certain functions was merely motivated by his opposition to abortion, which was in turn motivated by his religion.[93] The freedom of ministers in

[88] *X v. Denmark*, App. No. 7374/76, 5 Eur. Comm'n H.R. Dec. & Rep. 157, 158 (1976).
[89] *Id.*   [90] *Id.*
[91] *Knudsen v. Norway*, App. No. 11045/84, 42 Eur. Comm'n H.R. Dec. & Rep. 247 (1985).
[92] *Id.* at 254.
[93] *Id.* at 258. Thus he was not entitled to protection as actions merely motivated by religion are not protected as manifestations of religion under Art. 9(1). See the discussion at Chapter 6.5.

established Churches is limited. The State could not force him to remain a member of the Church or the ministry but it could regulate his behaviour once he was a minister within the Church, as 'a clergyman within a State Church system, has not only religious duties, but has also accepted certain obligations toward the State'.[94]

Thus the State is given a considerable right to interfere with the organization and even religious requirements of a State religion. In particular, the State has a role in setting criteria for employment and dismissal of employees of the Church without much regard for religious freedom. There are, however, probably limits to the way in which the State can exercise this power. The Commission, in the *Knudsen* case, suggested that dismissal from a State office for disobedience may raise an issue under Article 9 'in some circumstances' but did not give any indication of what those circumstances may be.[95] The Commission, however, as part of its reasoning in holding that the government's actions were permissible, noted that the State only took away the State role of the minister, it did not interfere with his pastoral role.[96]

The role of the State in regulating the actions of leaders of non-State religious groups, however, is far more limited. In *Serif v. Greece*[97] the Greek government prosecuted Serif for claiming to be the Mufti of the local Muslim community in Rodopti and for wearing the robes of a Mufti. Serif had been elected by Muslims attending Friday prayers at the local Mosques and had a large following in the community, but another man had been appointed as Mufti by the Greek government. The Greek government claimed that it was necessary to regulate religious ministers as they were given certain rights under Greek law (such as the right to perform marriage ceremonies, limited rights of adjudication in family matters, and exemption from military service) and in order to protect the community from the tensions that might arise from the existence of two different religious leaders. The Court upheld the applicant's claim, holding that to punish a person 'for the mere fact that he acted as the religious leader of a group that willingly followed him can hardly be considered compatible with the demands of religious pluralism in a democratic society'.[98] While different considerations may have arisen if he claimed to carry out functions with legal effects, such as marriage ceremonies, the religious and moral leadership that he exercised was outside the control of the State. It was not for the State to take measures to unify the leadership of religious communities.[99]

---

[94] *Id.* at 257.   [95] *Id.*   [96] *Id.*
[97] *Serif v. Greece*, App. No. 38178/97, Eur. Ct. H.R., 14 Dec. 1999, unreported.
[98] *Id.* at para. 51.   [99] *Id.* at para. 52.

Thus while there are limits to the actions that a State can take against religious leaders (particularly those from non-established Churches) Article 9 allows considerable scope for the State to give privileges to established Churches and to exercise some degree of control over those Churches.[100] The issue of the extent to which the establishment of a Church may interfere in the *forum internum* of both members and non-members of the Church has rarely been considered and has only in the *Darby* case led the Commission to the conclusion that the State had gone too far in seeking to promote the interests of its Church. The historical importance of established religions in Europe seems to have made the Court reluctant to engage with the difficult philosophical questions that surround the extent to which such establishment might create an environment that interferes with the *forum internum* of both adherents and non-adherents of a particular religion.[101]

Yet the series of cases brought by religious minorities, especially the Jehovah's Witnesses, against Greece illustrate the potential problems when the State is too active in promoting the interests of one Church at the expense of others even when, as in the case of the Greek Orthodox Church, the Church maintains some degree of autonomy. The role of the State can be seen in the laws against proselytism, which were enforced strictly against the Jehovah's Witnesses but never used against the Orthodox Church.[102] Planning permission for mainstream Christian Churches was easily obtained but the Jehovah's Witnesses found that their applications could be delayed for years and had to pass through scrutiny by the local Orthodox bishop.[103] There was evidence of surveillance by the secret police against minority religious groups.[104] While these laws were held by the Court not to be a breach of the Convention in themselves (though they often applied impermissibly), the pattern of State distrust of certain religious minorities and efforts to make life difficult for them show the way in which the legislative and administrative arms of the State can put pressure on the *forum internum* of minority groups when the State perceives its interests to be allied to a particular religion or belief.

---

[100] Gunn, above, note 42, at 329, goes so far as to say that the Commission has 'an impermissible bias in favour of established religions'.

[101] For other problems that a State Church can cause to minority religions see PATRICK THORNBERRY, INTERNATIONAL LAW AND THE RIGHTS OF MINORITIES chapter 20 (1991).

[102] *Kokkinakis v. Greece*, 260-A Eur. Ct. H.R. (ser. A) (1993).

[103] *Manoussakis and others v. Greece*, 17 Eur. Ct. H.R. (ser. A) 1347 (1996-IV).

[104] *Tsavachidis v. Greece*, App. No. 28802/95, Eur. Comm'n H.R., 4 Mar. 1997, unreported.

5.5 FREEDOM OF RELIGION AND BELIEF AND THE *FORUM INTERNUM* IN EDUCATION

5.5.1 Background

Another area of great contention in relation to the *forum internum* is the education of children.[105] This is one area in which a modern, democratic State has the opportunity, even the obligation, to become involved in shaping the views and ideas of particularly vulnerable members of society. The line between indoctrination that is prohibited as an intrusion into the *forum internum* and an education that appropriately assists young people to deal with the (often religiously pluralistic) society in which they find themselves can be a difficult one to draw.

As discussed in Chapter 3, the drafters of the Convention were divided over how to protect the rights of parents over their children's religious and moral education.[106] It was generally agreed that using a school for religious or moral indoctrination was abhorrent and could become a tool of a totalitarian government. There were, however, concerns that any protection of the rights of parents to determine the religious and moral upbringing of their children should not involve expense to the State. Thus, while parents should be able to require the State *not* to teach their child in a particular way, they should not be able to demand that the State fund religious or moral education of a particular kind.

The Court and Commission have had to deal with a variety of cases claiming that the State was required to fund a particular type of education or educational philosophy. They have consistently rejected the notion that the State is obliged to fund private schools,[107] to provide grammar or selective schools,[108] to provide teaching or curricula in any particular manner (as long as such teaching does not amount to

---

[105] For a good overview of the US position regarding education and religion, see JOSEPH SCHUSTER, THE FIRST AMENDMENT IN THE BALANCE chapter 17 (1993). The usefulness of the US cases in relation to schooling is limited, however, because of the effect of the non-establishment clause.

[106] See discussion at Chapter 3.2.4.

[107] *X v. the United Kingdom*, App. No. 7782/77, 14 Eur. Comm'n H.R. Dec. & Rep. 179, 180 (1978), the government could provide less in the way of subsidies to a non-denominational private school than it did to State-run schools; *X and Y v. the United Kingdom*, App. No. 9461/81, Eur. Comm'n H.R. Dec. & Rep. 210 (1982), the United Kingdom need not subsidize places at the Rudolf Steiner school even if parents felt that they need to send their children there in order to ensure that they would be taught in a manner consistent with their anthroposophical views; *W and KL v. Sweden*, App. No. 10476/83, 45 Eur. Comm'n H.R. Dec. & Rep. 143, 148–9 (1985), students attending a private school could be means tested for certain grants that were given automatically to those in State schools.

[108] *X and Y v. the United Kingdom*, App. No. 7527/76, 11 Eur. Comm'n H.R. Dec. & Rep. 147, 150 (1977); *W and DM v. the United Kingdom*, App. No. 10229/82, 37 Eur. Comm'n H.R. Dec. & Rep. 96, 99 (1984).

indoctrination),[109] to fund tuition after elementary schooling,[110] to integrate disabled children into mainstream schools,[111] or to give approval to private schools which do not satisfy reasonable and objective criteria for establishment.[112] The financial burden on the State arising from Article 2 of the First Protocol is thus limited. In the often quoted words of the Court in the *Belgian Linguistics* case,[113] the right to education merely serves to guarantee

to persons subject to the jurisdiction of the Contracting Parties the right, in principle, to avail themselves of the means of instruction existing at a given time. The Convention lays down no specific obligations concerning the extent of these means and the manner of their organisation or subsidisation.[114]

Thus parents can organize private, religious schools but cannot expect government funding for them. The State can, however, choose to subsidize such institutions or pay for certain types of religious education (whether in State schools or not) if it so desires. The concern of the drafters of the Convention was not (compared with the framers of the United States Constitution[115]) to keep the State out of religion, including religious education, but rather to ensure that the State was not subject to financial demands that it did not wish to meet. The ability to operate independent schools has been perceived to be an important part of ensuring that there are educational facilities available for those who disagree with the moral or religious teaching that their children are

[109] *X, Y and Z v.Germany*, App. No. 9411/81, 29 Eur. Comm'n H.R. Dec. & Rep. 224 (1982), no right to have a child taught mathematics by the Sachrechnen method rather than by the modern mathematics methods used in German elementary schools.

[110] *15 Foreign Students v. the United Kingdom*, App. No. 7671/76 and 14 other applications, 9 Eur. Comm'n H.R. Dec. & Rep. 185, 187 (1977) held that 'the right to education envisaged in Art. 2 is concerned primarily with elementary education and not necessarily with advanced studies'. When the State provides education which is not compulsory, that education must still respect the parents' religious and philosophical beliefs: *40 Mothers v. Sweden*, App. No. 6853/74, 9 Eur. Comm'n H.R. Dec. & Rep. 27, 30 (1977).

[111] *PD and LD v. the United Kingdom*, App. No. 14135/88, 62 Eur. Comm'n H.R. Dec. & Rep. 292 (1989); *Simpson v. the United Kingdom*, App. No. 14688/89, 64 Eur. Comm'n H.R. Dec. & Rep. 188 (1989); *Graeme v. the United Kingdom*, App. No. 13887/88, 64 Eur. Comm'n H.R. Dec. & Rep. 158 (1990).

[112] *Family H v. the United Kingdom*, App. No. 10233/83, 37 Eur. Comm'n H.R. Dec. & Rep. 105 (1984), parents who did not meet the required educational standards or co-operate with the authorities regarding the home education of their dyslexic children did not gain the protection of the article. *Ingrid Jordebo Foundation of Christian Schools and Jordebo v. Sweden*, App. No. 11533/85, 51 Eur. Comm'n H.R. Dec. & Rep. 125, 128–9 (1987), a government decision to refuse to allow a private school to extend teaching to higher education was upheld on the basis that the reason for the decision was the failure of the school to provide proper educational standards.

[113] *Case Relating to Certain Aspects of the Law on the Use of Languages in Education in Belgium*, 6 Eur. Ct. H.R. (ser. A) (1968).

[114] *Id.* at 31.

[115] Schuster, above, note 105, at 289–90, notes a variety of views held on the rationale for the 'wall of separation' between religion and State in the US Constitution.

receiving in State institutions. Such schools are an important part of a religiously pluralist society.[116]

Not all children will attend independent religious schools, however, and the State thus also has an obligation to ensure respect for the beliefs of parents within the State school system. Were this not the case, the right to respect for religious beliefs in education would only be protected for those who could afford to pay the fees at private schools and whose religious group had sufficient membership and resources to make operating a school practical.[117] The extent of the State's obligation in relation to education in State schools has been the source of some controversy, as it is here that the issues of indoctrination and interference with conscience come into sharp focus. The way in which the Commission has dealt with these cases illustrates the limited nature of the protection granted by the first part of Article 9(1) in relation to the *forum internum*.

5.5.2 The Scope of the School's Authority

When faced with a school that wishes to teach a particular course and with parents who want the course either to be taught differently or not at all, or for their child to be excused from all or part of a course, the Court is faced with a difficult dilemma. There is a need to protect children from indoctrination and to protect the rights of parents to choose the religious and moral education of their children. The Court must also consider, however, the right of a child to a full education and the practical difficulties caused to schools if too many exemptions are given from attending certain subjects. There is also the issue of whether society has a legitimate interest in seeing that all children are given a good, general education that may include information about issues which are morally or religiously controversial.

The Court tried to deal with the tension between these various factors in *Kjeldsen, Busk Madsen and Pedersen v. Denmark*.[118] In that case the Danish education authorities had set out an 'integrated' curriculum for

---

[116] Natan Lerner, Group Rights and Discrimination in International Law chapter 10 (1991). This has long been important to religious minorities, as can be seen from the pressure (especially from Jewish lobby groups) to have the right to separate educational facilities included in the Minorities Treaties established under the League of Nations. See Evans, above, note 23, at chapter 4. See also *Minority Schools in Albania*, 64 P.C.I.J. 64 (ser. A/B) 4 (1935) (Advisory Opinion) which held that the prohibition of privately owned schools by the Albanian constitution was a breach of Albania's obligations towards religious and linguistic minorities.

[117] *Kjeldsen, Busk Madsen and Pedersen*, 23 Eur. Ct. H.R. (ser. A) at 25, 28 (1982) noted that 'undeniable sacrifices and inconveniences' have to be made by those who chose private or home education for religious reasons, but the fact that this option exists is relevant to the scope of the State's duties under the Convention. The mere presence of private, religious schools (even State-subsidized ones) does not, however, excuse the State from respecting the beliefs of parents in State school education.

[118] *Kjeldsen, Busk Madsen and Pedersen*, 23 Eur. Ct. H.R. (ser. A) (1982).

schools which included the teaching of sexual education as part of a number of subjects. The parents of several schoolchildren protested that the integration of sexual education into the course made such education, in effect, compulsory. This offended against some parents' religious beliefs. Such education, according to these parents, should be given in the home where they could be sure that due weight would be given to the religious and moral context of sexuality. The school argued that the information given to the children regarding sexual intercourse was factual and that the school took no particular moral standpoint in teaching sexual education. The school further argued that society had an interest in ensuring that all its young people had access to this information. In the case of sexual education, society has a legitimate interest in preventing the transmission of sexual disease, unwanted teenage pregnancies, and abortions, and this could be done in part by presenting factual information on these subjects to students.[119]

The Court emphasized that the right to education and the limitation on that education being used by the State as a tool of indoctrination was aimed at 'safeguarding the possibility of pluralism in education' and creating the conditions which are necessary for a democratic society to flourish.[120] It rejected the argument by the Danish government that the requirement to respect parents' beliefs set out in the second sentence of Article 2 of the First Protocol applied only to religious, denominational instruction. The Court noted that the duty on the State to respect the parents' religious and philosophical convictions is one that extends throughout the State educational system.[121] It further stated that the obligation on the school to respect the religious and philosophical beliefs of parents is one which is closely linked to the right to education set out in the first sentence of Article 2 of the First Protocol.[122] The Court did, however, accept that the setting and planning of the curriculum falls within the competence of the Contracting States and that there is scope for schools or education authorities to deal with issues of expediency about which the Court would not rule.[123] The Court was sympathetic to the practical problems which allowing too great a scope to parental rights may create. The Court agreed that a State must be given some leeway to make educational decisions and held that

[T]he second sentence of Article 2 of the Protocol does not prevent States from imparting through teaching or education information or knowledge of a directly or indirectly religious or philosophical kind. It does not even permit parents to object to the integration of such teaching or education into the school curriculum, for otherwise all institutional teaching would run the risk of proving impracticable. In fact, it seems very difficult for many subjects taught at school not to have, to a greater or lesser extent, some philosophical complexion or implications. The same

---

[119] *Id.* at 27.   [120] *Id.* at 25.   [121] *Id.*   [122] *Id* at 26.   [123] *Id.*

is true of religious affinities if one remembers the existence of religions forming a very broad dogmatic and moral entity which has or may have answers to every question of a philosophical, cosmological or moral nature.[124]

The Court's decision in this regard was bolstered by a brief reference to the other rights in the Convention, especially Articles 8, 9, and 10,[125] and by the fact that the Danish government had made generous financial provision for private, religious schools or home education which parents who were displeased with the integrated school curriculum could use. The mere existence of such alternative educational methods, however, did not relieve the State of its obligation to respect parents' religious or philosophical convictions in State education.[126]

5.5.3 The Limits on the School's Discretion

The Court, having set out the area of discretion to be left to the State in setting the curriculum, then considered the limits which Article 2 of the First Protocol places upon the school authorities. It observed that

The second sentence of Article 2 implies on the other hand that the State, in fulfilling the functions assumed by it in regard to education and teaching, must take care that information or knowledge included in this curriculum is conveyed in an objective, critical and pluralistic manner. The State is forbidden to pursue an aim of indoctrination that might be considered as not respecting parents' religious and philosophical convictions. That is the limit that must not be exceeded.[127]

Thus, in order not to breach Article 2 of the First Protocol, a State need not shy away from presenting religious or philosophical material but must make sure that the context in which it is presented is 'objective, critical and pluralistic'. This will, according to the Court, prevent the threat of indoctrination without undermining other rights in the Convention or creating immense practical difficulties for State educational authorities. The outcome in this case was for the Court to hold that the integration of sexual education into the Danish school curriculum was not in itself a breach of the Convention. The Danish authorities were legitimately concerned with social problems that arose from a lack of proper sexual education and had chosen a reasonable way of introducing important issues into the school curriculum.[128] The Court did acknowledge that there was potential for

---

[124] *Id.*

[125] *Id.*, although the Court never makes clear how they are relevant to the determination of the case. Art. 8 (respect for private and family life) and Art. 9 seem to suggest that greater deference should be given to the rights of the child not to be exposed to information and ideas that clash with his or her religious or philosophical beliefs. Art. 10 (paraphrased by the Court as 'freedom . . . to receive and impart information and ideas') would tend to support the view that the school and child should be able to engage in a free exchange of ideas.

[126] *Id.* at 25.   [127] *Id.* at 26 (emphasis added).   [128] *Id.* at 27.

abuse by individual teachers who might, through carelessness or misplaced proselytism, communicate issues regarding sexuality in a manner which was offensive to parents' beliefs.[129] Such abuses, however, needed to be guarded against by parents and school authorities and dealt with on an individual basis, rather than in a general action such as the one before the Court. Alternatively, parents could choose to send their children to private schools where they did not receive such education.[130]

5.5.4 Application in Later Cases

The Court has heard a number of subsequent cases dealing with issues raised under the second article of the First Protocol, including the celebrated case dealing with corporal punishment, *Campbell and Cosans v. the United Kingdom*.[131] While *Campbell and Cosans* demonstrated that the protection of Article 2 extended to the requirement that schools respect the wishes of parents who wanted to prevent their children being subjected to corporal punishment, it drew largely on the legal framework set down in the *Kjeldsen* case.[132] The United Nations Human Rights Committee has taken a similar line to the Court and held that a course in the history of religion and ethics did not breach Article 18(4) of the I.C.C.P.R. if it was 'given in a neutral and objective way and respects the beliefs of parents and guardians who do not believe in any religion'.[133] The European Court has not revisited the issue of the content of school curricula but the Commission has dealt with the issue a number of times and it is the way in which the Commission has undertaken its task which demonstrates some of the pitfalls of the seemingly balanced test of the Court in *Kjeldsen*.

---

[129] *Id.* at 28.   [130] *Id.*

[131] *Campbell and Cosans v. the United Kingdom*, 48 Eur. Ct. H.R. (ser. A) (1982).

[132] Other cases dealing with corporal punishment of children and its relationship to Art. 2 of the First Protocol include: *X, Y and Z v. the United Kingdom*, App. No. 8566/79, 31 Eur. Comm'n H.R. Dec. & Rep. 50 (1982) which held that parents who did not have a coherent world view which prohibited corporal punishment and who had not communicated their views to the school fell outside the protection of the article; *B and D v. the United Kingdom*, App. No. 9303/81, 49 Eur. Comm'n H.R. Dec. & Rep. 44, 50 (1986) upholding an application by a parent whose child had been caned by the school for misbehaving; *Seven Individuals v. Sweden*, App. No. 8811/79, 29 Eur. Comm'n H.R. Dec. & Rep. 104, 115–16 (1982), where a claim by parents that the new Swedish code on parenting which disapproves of, while not criminalizing, parental chastisement was deemed inadmissible by the Commission; *Durairaj, Baker and Durairaj v. the United Kingdom*, App. No. 9114/80, 52 Eur. Comm'n H.R. Dec. & Rep. 13 (1987) and *Jarman v. the United Kingdom*, App. No. 11648/85, 56 Eur. Comm'n H.R. Dec. & Rep. 181 (1988), where a friendly settlement was reached in each case regarding children who were corporally punished or excluded from school because of their parents' opposition to corporal punishment.

[133] *Hartikainen v. Finland*, Communication No. 40/1978, Human Rights Committee, Selected Decisions under the Optional Protocol (2nd to 16th sessions) CCPR/C/OP/1, 19 Apr. 1981, 12th session.

One case which illustrates this problem is that of *Angeleni v. Sweden*.[134] In this case, the applicants claimed a breach of Articles 9, 14 and Article 2 of the First Protocol because their daughter (the second applicant), a junior school student, was not given an exemption from religious instruction classes. The applicants were atheists and claimed that to force an atheist to participate in religious instruction which focused predominantly on Christianity was a breach of both the parents' right to have their philosophy respected and the student's freedom of religion. The application under Article 2 of the First Protocol was dismissed as the Swedish government had entered a reservation to that article stating that exemptions from teachings in Christianity could only be granted to 'children of another faith than the Swedish Church in respect of whom a satisfactory religious instruction has been arranged'. Exemptions would not be granted to children whose parents had a philosophical rather than a religious difference with the Swedish Church or whose parents could not arrange satisfactory alternative religious instruction for their children. The Commission held that the reservation applied in this case to the claims under Article 2 of Protocol 1.[135]

The claims under Articles 9 and 14 of the student herself were, however, not subject to the same reservation. The Commission noted that the Swedish government wished to provide information about religion rather than instruction in religion and that it was a legitimate aim of the government to ensure that all students had some education in religion.[136] Thus no issue of discrimination under Article 14 arose as the only students who were exempted were those who had alternative classes in religion arranged for them. As regards the Article 9 claim, the Commission noted that the applicant had in fact been exempted from most religious instruction (albeit somewhat outside the operation of the Swedish Act) because of her determined opposition to the subject. The Commission held that the applicant had not been exposed to any religious indoctrination. Without further comment, it held that 'the fact that instruction in religious knowledge focuses on Christianity at junior level at school does not mean that the second applicant has been under religious indoctrination in breach of Article 9 of the Convention'.[137] Yet it is difficult to see how a test that requires information to be conveyed in a 'general and neutral' manner is not undermined by allowing most of the information so conveyed to be about a single religion. In a system where the teachers of the subject must have expertise in Christianity and only a fairly shallow knowledge of other religions, the danger that lessons could turn into proselytism or marginalize people of other religious faiths is at least increased. The test seems to

---

[134] *Angeleni v. Sweden*, App. No. 10491/83, 51 Eur. Comm'n H.R. Dec. & Rep. 41 (1986).
[135] *Id*. at 47.   [136] *Id*. at 50–1.   [137] *Id*. at 49.

have shifted from its emphasis on 'general and neutral' conveyance of information as a means of protecting against potential indoctrination to
requiring the applicant to show actual indoctrination—a far higher test for
the applicant to meet.[138]

Moreover, it can be argued that the Commission has been less sympathetic to atheists/agnostics who claim the need to be exempted from
religious instruction than to members of other religious faiths.[139] The
Commission encouraged a friendly settlement and helped applicants to
obtain an exemption from the same religious instruction in Sweden that they
had deemed permissible in *Angeleni* in a case where the applicants were
members of a dissenting Evangelical Lutheran Church.[140] This approach was
reiterated in *Bernard v. Luxembourg*,[141] where the Commission held that a
law that only allowed exemptions from religious lessons to students whose
religious communities could arrange instruction in their own faiths during
school hours was discriminatory, but was not in breach of Article 14 as there
were 'objective and reasonable justifications' for treating these students
differently to other groups (such as atheists) that also wanted an exemption
but could not arrange for instruction.

The failure of the Commission to look behind claims of generality and
neutrality, the move toward the higher test of 'indoctrination', and a lack
of sympathy to the claims of non-theistic beliefs was also evident in a claim
from an agnostic child in relation to religious instruction in Poland. In State
schools the religious instruction was in Catholicism but exemptions were
granted to students and the two applicant students applied for and were
given exemptions. In the opinion of the Commission this rendered the
course 'voluntary'. The applicants, however, claimed that this system led
to pressure on students to take religious instruction, particularly in the
context of widespread social discrimination against non-Catholics in
Poland. One of the applicants was a 12-year-old girl who was required to
wait in the corridor of the school while religious instruction classes were
held. She gave evidence that this led to frequent questioning from teachers
and pressure from a teacher and other students to take the classes.[142]
Ultimately, against her father's wishes, she capitulated and joined the
classes. In the Court's opinion this meant that her instruction in Catholicism

---

[138] *Bernard and others v. Luxembourg*, App. No. 17187/90, 75 Eur. Comm'n H.R. Dec.
& Rep. 57 (1993); *CJ, JJ & EJ v. Poland*, App. No. 23380/94, 84-A Eur. Comm'n H.R.
Dec. & Rep. 46 (1996).

[139] Gunn, above, note 42, at 311–12; cf. HARRIS, O'BOYLE, AND WARBRICK, above, note
57, at 360–1.

[140] *Karnell and Hardt v. Sweden*, App. No. 4733/71, 14 YB Convention on HR (Cmn)
676 (1971); Gunn, above, note 42, at 311–12.

[141] *Bernard and others v. Luxembourg*, App. No. 17187/90, 75 Eur. Comm'n H.R. Dec.
& Rep. 57 (1993).

[142] *Id.* at 47–8.

was not a breach of Article 9 as it was 'voluntary'.[143] It did not explore how voluntary a decision by a child in such a situation of social pressure could really be. It also refused to deal in any detail with the claim by the other applicant student (whose school offered the option of instruction in ethics as an alternative to religious instruction) that widespread social discrimination against non-Catholics, for example in the labour market, meant that there was pressure to take religious instruction rather than ethics. The Commission noted that Poland had laws that prohibited religious discrimination so that any prejudice suffered could only be of 'minor importance' and that the particular applicant was not prejudiced anyway as the subject that they had chosen did not appear on their reports.[144]

Tazhib suggested that being forced to reveal one's religion (even when there were not serious concerns over discrimination) is an invasion into the *forum internum*, and other authors have reiterated the importance of being able to keep one's religion a secret from the State.[145] The Commissioners in the Polish case said that the student was not forced to reveal her religion, as there is always the potential for someone to take a course in a religion to which they are not committed. This is true at one level but, in the case discussed above, the practical outcome was that a student is either required to take a course in Catholic teachings or to refuse to take such a course and thereby *de facto* reveal at least a serious level of disagreement with such teaching. At the lowest level it requires the student to reveal his or her religion to the school authorities. While the Commission considered this in the Polish case, it only did so in the context of Article 8 and held that such revelations were a minor intrusion on privacy that could be justified in a democratic society. Yet this revelation, especially in the context of a relatively religiously intolerant society,[146] has serious implications for the *forum internum*, which is subject to no limitations under Article 9(2).

Thus the education cases try to strike a difficult balance between the legitimate educational aims of the society and the right to freedom of thought, conscience, and religion. While the tests, such as 'general and objective' teaching, seem appropriate in the abstract, in application the Commission and Court have been reluctant to explore the way in which such teaching may put pressure on students to take religiously specific instruction and to reveal their religion to the State and school authorities.

---

[143] *Id.* at 56. The Commission commented that, 'The second applicant moreover decided herself ... to attend religious education.'

[144] *Id.* at 54.

[145] HARRIS, O'BOYLE, AND WARBRICK, above, note 57, at 361, argue that 'if there were conceivably good reasons, possibly in the context of national security, for the State to know what a person believes, the resistance to giving it the power to do so reflects the shade of the Inquisition and the coercive investigations of modern totalitarian regimes'. See also VAN DIJK AND VAN HOOF, above, note 71, at 397–8.

[146] KEVIN BOYLE AND JULIET SHEEN, FREEDOM OF RELIGION OR BELIEF: A WORLD REPORT 358–65 (1997).

5.6 FREEDOM TO CHANGE RELIGION OR BELIEF

The above discussion relates primarily to the right to maintain one's religion or belief without improper interference by the State, yet another important aspect of religious freedom is the right to change religion or belief. If the integrity and autonomy of the person underlies the right to religious freedom, it is clear that this autonomy cannot simply be a one-off exercise of choice of religion or belief which will, for most people, be made in the first instance for them by their parents during their childhood before they can properly make an autonomous choice. The right to determine one's religion or belief is an ongoing matter, a continuing exercise of self-definition, and thus any interference with the right to change religion or belief is an interference with the *forum internum.*

Despite the fact that freedom to change religion has been the subject of serious controversy in the United Nations,[147] it has not been so controversial in the Convention context. The right to change one's religion or belief was included without discussion in the drafts of Article 9 and in the final document. The Court has expressly upheld the importance of the freedom to change religion in some cases dealing with proselytism, which are discussed below.[148]

The Court and Commission have also dismissed a number of cases dealing with complaints levelled by members of a religion against that religion on the grounds that the individuals involved all had the opportunity to leave the Church if they so desired.[149] While none of these cases have expressly dealt with the ability to leave a religion or to join a new religion, they suggest that the Court attaches importance to the freedom to change religion as in part justifying their decisions in those cases. The case involving 'de-programming', discussed above, while not dealing specifically with the issue of religious freedom, indicated a willingness by the Court to support the right of an individual to make the controversial choice of changing from a mainstream religion to a so-called 'cult'.[150]

While the Court and Commission have been reasonably supportive of the freedom to change religion or belief, they have interpreted this freedom reasonably narrowly. In the one case that directly raised the issue of the right to leave a religion, a couple complained that they should not have to pay tax to the Catholic Church, as they had already made clear their desire to leave the Church, even though they had not complied with the State requirements for notification on leaving a

---

[147] See Chapter 3.1; Krishnaswami study, at 24–8.

[148] *Kokkinakis v. Greece*, 260-A Eur. Ct. H.R. (ser. A) (1993); *Larissis and others v. Greece*, 65 Eur. Ct. H.R. (ser. A) 363 (1998-V).

[149] See, for example, the discussion at Chapter 6.7.

[150] *Riera Blume and others v. Spain*, App. No. 37680/97, Eur. Ct. H.R., 9 Mar. 1999, unreported.

religion.[151] The Commission held that these regulations did not interfere with their right to leave their religion but were for the administrative purpose of determining who had to pay taxes to which Church. In this case the obligation to pay Church taxes was not a breach of Article 9 as the couple could have escaped the obligation by complying with some reasonably simple administrative requirements. The State was held to have 'a wide discretion to decide on what conditions an individual may validly be regarded as having decided to leave a religious denomination'.[152] In another, rather peculiar case, the Commission rejected a claim that the State should formally annul the applicant's baptism and confirmation, presumably on the grounds that such an annulment was not necessary in order for him to be able to reject his religion in practice.[153] Despite this slightly cautious approach by the Commission it is most unlikely that the Court would uphold a law that placed substantial burdens on the right of a person to leave a religion or change his or her belief, particularly as the Court has tended to adopt an approach to religion that equates religious organizations with voluntary organizations—an approach that presupposes the importance of the ability to leave organizations.[154]

In areas in which the potential pressures on people to change or maintain their religion or belief are subtler, the Court and Commission have been reluctant to deal with the issues raised. The case of the Polish schoolchild who felt pressured to take Catholic instruction, for example, raises some issues of freedom to maintain or to change one's religion that the Commission simply avoided.[155] The obligation to reveal one's religion or belief to the State or other institutions may also, at least in some societies, cause problems of pressure to maintain or to change religion or belief.[156] These problems may not exist in a relatively pluralistic or tolerant society, but in a society that is more religiously homogenous or intolerant, the right to maintain or change one's religion or belief may be influenced by pressure from employers, landlords, or other private institutions. If the State makes information about people's beliefs easily available in such a society, even indirectly through school reports, then it may assist in creating an environment that is hostile to people from the religious majority changing their beliefs and puts pressure on people from religious minorities to change

---

[151] *Gottesmann v. Switzerland*, App. No. 10616/83, 40 Eur. Comm'n H.R. Dec. & Rep. 284 (1984).

[152] *Id.* at 289. Krishnaswami study, at 25–6, concludes that formal registration of religion or belief and any change in religion or belief is commonly used by States and is often merely a formality but he warns that such formalities may 'in fact be employed as a means of dissuading an individual from changing his religion or belief'.

[153] *X v. Iceland*, App. No. 2525/65, 18 Collection 33 (1967).

[154] See discussion at Chapter 6.7.

[155] *CJ, JJ & EJ v. Poland*, App. No. 23380/94, 84-A Eur. Comm'n H.R. Dec. & Rep. 46 (1996).

[156] FAWCETT, above, note 31, at 243; HARRIS, O'BOYLE, AND WARBRICK, above, note 57, at 361.

to mainstream beliefs through prejudice or other forms of social pressure. It is possible that such pressures are beyond the competence of the Court or Commission, as such cases require a broad understanding of the society and the way in which the State's actions influence the behaviour of private parties. If, however, the freedom to maintain or change a religion or belief is of fundamental significance, as the Court and Commission have often stated, they should look at these types of cases more carefully.

One of the issues that has made the freedom to change religion or belief so controversial is its relationship with proselytism. Article 18(2) of the I.C.C.P.R. protects people from 'coercion which would impair [their] freedom to have or adopt a religion of [their] choice'. Article 1(2) of the Declaration on Religious Intolerance and Discrimination also prohibits coercion. This addition to the later United Nations instruments was a response to the fears of those who saw proselytism as a potentially abusive and coercive activity, although others were concerned to ensure that mere intellectual argument, debate, or persuasion did not come to be seen as 'coercion'.[157] Professor Shaw has argued that Article 17 of the Convention could play a similar role in the Convention as the prohibition on the use of coercion plays in the United Nations instruments. Article 17 states that 'nothing in this Convention may be interpreted as implying for any State, group or person any right to engage in or perform any act aimed at the destruction of any of the rights and freedoms set forth herein'. Thus any coercion exercised by the State or a private person to induce someone to change religion should not be protected by Article 9.[158]

Proselytism is itself a manifestation of religion, at least under the dichotomy used by the Court, but it is closely related to the *forum internum* right to change belief. This is one area to which the Court has given some thought and developed a reasonably coherent, if somewhat conservative, approach to the scope of the right to change religion or belief. The issue arose in the first case in which the Court held that there had been a breach of the right to freedom of religion and belief, *Kokkinakis v. Greece*.[159] The applicant in that case, Mr Kokkinakis, was an elderly Jehovah's Witness who was convicted of breaching the prohibition against proselytism in Greek law.[160] Proselytism was defined in Greek law as

---

[157] A/2929, chapter VI, para. 110, summarizing E/CN.4/SR.319, at 6–7 (Australia). See generally EVANS, above, note 23, at 198–9.

[158] Malcolm Shaw, *Freedom of Thought, Conscience and Religion*, in THE EUROPEAN SYSTEM FOR THE PROTECTION OF HUMAN RIGHTS 445, 452–3 (R. StJ. Mcdonald, F. Matscher, and H. Petzold eds., 1993), although he regrets that the prohibition of coercion was not made clearer in the Convention. The Court itself has not resorted to Art. 17 but has used Art. 9(2) to deal with State claims that it is necessary to limit the rights of proselytizers in order to protect the rights of those whom they attempt to convert. See the discussion at Chapter 7.7.4.

[159] *Kokkinakis v. Greece*, 260-A Eur. Ct. H.R. (ser. A) (1993).

[160] The prohibition on proselytism was established under the Metaxas dictatorship and continued under Law 1363/1938.

in particular, any direct or indirect attempt to intrude on the religious beliefs of a person of different religious persuasion (*eterodoxos*), with the aim of undermining those beliefs, either by any kind of inducement or promise of inducement of moral support or material assistance, by fraudulent means or by taking advantage of his inexperience, trust, need, low intellect or naivety.[161]

Mr Kokkinakis was convicted of proselytism because he went to the house of Mrs Kyriakaki, the wife of the local Greek Orthodox cantor, and told her about the Jehovah's Witnesses. Mrs Kyriakaki could remember little about the conversation and said that it had not affected her religious views at all. No evidence was given during the trial or appeals that she was particularly naïve or vulnerable in any way. Her husband called the police, who arrested Mr Kokkinakis and his wife (who accompanied him but did not contribute to the discussion). Mr Kokkinakis was convicted of unlawful proselytism and had his conviction affirmed in a series of appeals through the Greek courts. He then made an application to the Commission, claiming a breach of his rights under Article 9.

This case raises important issues for both the right to manifest a religion and legitimate limitations on the exercise of that right and it is discussed in these contexts in later chapters. For present purposes, one of the reasons that the Court held that there was a right to try to convince others of the truth of one's religion or belief was that otherwise the freedom to change one's religion 'would be likely to remain a dead letter'.[162] This reasoning can be seen as analogous to the reasoning in the freedom of speech cases where the importance of free media is underlined by the Court pointing out that limitations on the media do not merely interfere with the rights of those seeking to communicate but also with the rights of those who should be able to have access to this information.[163]

The Court was prepared, however, to hold that the aim of the Greek legislation in seeking to prohibit 'improper proselytism' was a proper purpose as the legislation had as its aim the protection of the rights and freedoms of others (though it went on to find that the means used in this case were not necessary in a democratic society). Judge Martens, in a separate but concurring decision, suggested that this conclusion did not give enough importance to freedom of religion and the right to change one's religion or belief. He noted that freedom of religion is an 'absolute' value in the Convention and that, accordingly, the Convention 'leaves no room whatsoever for interference by the State' in freedom to have or change religions.[164] The freedoms in Article 9 include the right to change one's religion,

[161] Law 1672/1939.

[162] *Kokkinakis v. Greece*, 260-A Eur. Ct. H.R. (ser. A) at 13 (1993).

[163] *Sunday Times v. the United Kingdom*, 30 Eur. Ct. H.R. (ser. A) at 40 (1979), where the Court held that Art. 10 incorporates distinct and independent rights to both impart and receive information.

[164] *Kokkinakis v. Greece*, 260-A Eur. Ct. H.R. (ser. A) at 33 (1993).

and thus it is of no consequence to the State whether or not someone chooses to change their religion or attempts to induce someone else to change their religion. Teaching, which is explicitly protected in the Convention, is the religious duty of many people of many faiths and it is not for the State to interfere with it.[165] He acknowledged that sometimes this teaching may 'shade off into proselytising' and thus cause some conflict with the rights of others to maintain their beliefs.

In principle, however, it is not within the province of the State to interfere in this 'conflict' between the proselytiser and the proselytised. Firstly because—since respect for human dignity and human freedom implies that the State is bound to accept in principle everybody is capable of determining his fate in the way that he deems best—there is no justification for a State to use its power 'to protect' the proselytised (it may be otherwise in very special situations where the State has a particular duty of care but such situations fall outside the present issue). Secondly, because even the 'public order' cannot justify the use of State power in a field where tolerance demands that 'free argument and debate' should be decisive. And thirdly, because under the Convention all religions and beliefs should, as far as the State is concerned, be equal.[166]

While the judge does not make the point explicitly, this reasoning suggests that the government does not have a legitimate role in the area of regulating the freedom to change religion, even to 'protect' people from proselytism. Thus, any legislation which has as its aim the limiting of attempts at religious conversion is, except in very limited cases, wholly illegitimate.[167] Such laws cannot have a legitimate aim because they are seeking to protect people from an experience that the State cannot say is right or wrong.[168] The issue lies wholly in the realm of individual conscience, the *forum internum*. The other judges were not prepared to take such a broad view of the issue, however, and under their analysis the right to change religion does not prevent the State from taking steps to 'protect' people from those who seek to convert them.[169]

---

[165] *Id.* at 34. [166] *Id.* at 34–5.

[167] Peter W. Edge, *Holy War on the Doorstep*, 1996 New L.J. 146, argues that laws that specifically target proselytism are inappropriate and any problems that arise from excesses (such as the use of violence) should be dealt with by general criminal or civil laws.

[168] Paul Hayden, *Religiously Motivated 'Outrageous' Conduct: Intentional Infliction of Emotional Distress as a Weapon Against 'Other People's Faiths'*, 34 Wm & Mary L. Rev. 579 (1993), gives some examples of the improper way in which a number of religions may seek to gain converts but argues that laws that restrict such groups tend to lead to discrimination and hysteria against minority religions.

[169] For arguments in favour of limiting some missionary activity see Krishnaswami study, at 27, 40–1; Kurland, above, note 34, at 50 who in discussing proselytism refers specifically to the 'virulent attacks on the beliefs of others' by the Jehovah's Witnesses and suggests that it 'is not infrequent that those who are most intolerant of the rights of others are the most vigorous in seeking the protection of their own'.

5.7 CONCLUSION

The Court has accepted that freedom of thought, conscience, and religion is of great importance to individuals and a pluralistic, democratic society. Yet it has failed to define this concept in any meaningful way and has given little scope for claims by individuals seeking to protect their freedom of religion or belief. While it has begun to develop a concept of a positive right of freedom of religion or belief, the main role of this positive obligation so far has been to legitimize State interference with other rights (such as freedom of expression) to protect religious sensibilities, with little consideration as to whether this is necessary to freedom of religion.

In defining the scope of the negative obligation of the State, the Court and Commission have taken a very narrow view of what is required of a State. The central role given to the ill-defined notion of the *forum internum* has allowed States considerable scope to require individuals to act in a way that violates their religion or belief, to reveal their religion to State organs, and to 'pay a price' such as a loss of a job for adhering to their religious beliefs. In these cases the Court and Commission have tended to assume that the issue of interference in the *forum internum* is not in question, without proper consideration of the way in which being forced to act in a manner that is prohibited by a religion or belief may have implications for the fundamental internal freedom of religion or belief as well as for its manifestations. Even in the areas of the establishment of a State Church and the education of children in a State school, where the danger of the State promoting or denigrating a religion is clear, the Court and Commission have been highly deferential to the needs of the State and the historical role of established Churches in Europe. While the individual is given some protection in theory (through requirements such as religious education being given in a neutral and objective manner), the practical application of such protection can leave the individual with little recourse against a State that is intertwined with a particular religion or belief.

Freedom to change religion or belief has been given better protection than the more abstract notion of a general freedom of religion, but even here the Court has been unwilling to deal with some of the subtle ways in which a State can encourage a vulnerable person, especially a child, to change religion or can discourage people from changing religion or belief, especially through laws restricting proselytism.

The first limb of Article 9(1), the right to freedom of religion and belief, has not been clearly defined and has been narrowly applied. Thus, most cases that come under Article 9 raise (or are assumed by the Court to raise) issues relevant to the second limb of Article 9(1)—the right to manifest a religion or belief in worship, teaching, practice, and observance.

6

The Right to Manifest a Religion or Belief

6.1 INTRODUCTION

The second part of Article 9(1) says that everyone has the 'freedom, either alone or in community with others and in public or private, to manifest his religion or belief, in worship, teaching, practice and observance'. Unlike the freedom to have a religion, the right to manifest a religion or belief is subject to limitations under Article 9(2). Nevertheless, it constitutes an important part of freedom of religion and belief, especially as the first limb of Article 9(1) has been given such a limited meaning.

Four types of manifestation are listed in Article 9(1) and they are open to a variety of interpretations. The Court and Commission have adopted relatively narrow definitions of each of the terms, particularly the potentially open-ended term 'practice'. This has made it difficult for applicants in most cases to demonstrate that their right to manifest their religion has been restricted. Even in cases where there is some restriction, applicants have to show that they have not 'voluntarily' abandoned their right to manifest their religion by, for example, subjecting themselves to the rules of a particular organization or taking up employment that is inconsistent with the practice of their religion or belief.

6.2 ALONE OR IN A COMMUNITY WITH OTHERS, IN PUBLIC OR IN PRIVATE

Whether a belief is practised 'alone *or* in community with others' and in 'public *or* private' is a matter of choice for the believer. In a case dealing with a Muslim schoolteacher who wished to take time off on Friday afternoons to attend worship at a local mosque, the United Kingdom argued that it was sufficient protection of his right to worship that he was given a room within the school in which he could pray in private.[1] The Commission rejected this argument. It said that the right to manifest one's religion in community with others

has always been regarded as an essential part of freedom of religion and finds that the two alternatives 'either alone or in community with others' in Article 9(1) cannot

---

[1] *X v. the United Kingdom*, App. No. 8160/78, 22 Eur. Comm'n H.R. Dec. & Rep. 27, 33 (1981).

be considered as mutually exclusive, or as leaving a choice to the authorities, but only as recognising that religion may be practised in either form.[2]

When it comes to justifying government restrictions on free practice of religion or belief, however, these distinctions may be relevant. It would, for example, be far more difficult for the State to show that it was necessary to prevent someone from private, solitary worship than to demonstrate the need to limit the right of a large group to worship in public.[3] That, however, is a matter for Article 9(2). For the purposes of Article 9(1) the decision of the Commission that it is for the individuals involved to decide how their religion or belief is best expressed must be correct, especially given that the religions of some people may require a level of communal worship, while other individuals (especially those who are not members of an organized religious community) may prefer or even require private worship.[4] It is not for the State to intrude on these questions, except in response to a pressing social need.

While it is clear that individuals have a right to gather together for worship or religious ritual, the issue of whether the right to manifest a religion or belief in community with others also allows for the creation of organizations, institutions, or other permanent groups to promote the interests of the religion or belief is less clear.[5] The Commission has decided that Article 9 does not give rise to a right to be formally recognized or registered as a religion in States that still distinguish between recognized and non-recognized religions.[6] Yet it can often be necessary for believers to form permanent organizations to ensure the effective exercise of their individual right to manifest a religion or belief. Such groups may be essential if places of worship are to be constructed and maintained, religious schools or classes are to be operated, or expensive ritual objects purchased.[7] As Professor Dinstein has argued, 'freedom of religion, as an individual right, may be nullified unless complemented by a collective human right of the religious group to construct the infrastructure making possible the full enjoyment of that freedom by individuals'.[8] The Declaration on Religious

---

[2] *Id.* at 34. The Commission rejected the application on other grounds. See the discussion at Chapter 6.7.2.

[3] *ISKCON v. the United Kingdom*, App. No. 20490/92, 76-A Eur. Comm'n H.R. Dec. & Rep. 90 (1994). Restrictions placed on a Hindu temple by the planning laws were permissible, even though they interfered with freedom to worship collectively in public, as the huge numbers of people coming to the temple significantly interfered with those who lived in the nearby village. Private worship is rarely likely to interfere with the rights of others in the same way.

[4] Kevin Boyle, *Freedom of Conscience in International Law, in* FREEDOM OF CONSCIENCE 39 (Council of Europe ed.,1993).

[5] Krishnaswami study, at 21–2.

[6] *X v. Austria*, App. No. 8652/79, 26 Eur. Comm'n H.R. Dec. & Rep. 89 (1981), although the situation would be different if members from non-recognized religions were prohibited from exercising their religion or belief.

[7] PATRICK THORNBERRY, INTERNATIONAL LAW AND THE RIGHTS OF MINORITIES 195 (1991).

[8] Yoram Dinstein, *Freedom of Religion and Religious Minorities, in* THE PROTECTION OF MINORITIES AND HUMAN RIGHTS 152 (Yoram Dinstein ed.,1992).

Intolerance and Discrimination reiterates the importance of some of these rights by recognizing as manifestations of religions or beliefs the right to establish and maintain places of worship or assembly, to establish and maintain appropriate charitable or humanitarian institutions, to appoint religious leaders, and to communicate with fellow believers both nationally and internationally.[9] Even if these rights are not clearly covered by Article 9, applicants can also rely on the provisions of Article 11, which concerns freedom of assembly, to assist them in ensuring their rights to form associations on a permanent basis. Such groups can, however, pose more of a threat to States than mere informal gatherings of like-minded believers and tend therefore to be subject to greater restrictions.[10]

6.3 WORSHIP, TEACHING, PRACTICE, AND OBSERVANCE

6.3.1 The Exclusive or Inclusive Nature of the List

The next question is whether the words 'worship, teaching, practice and observance' are intended to be an inclusive or exclusive list of the manifestations protected under Article 9. The United Nations material, especially the Krishnaswami study, indicates that the words were used to try to cover a wide range of manifestations of religions and beliefs and were not intended to be read in a limited manner. In his commentary on the Universal Declaration of Human Rights, Krishnaswami concluded that, bearing in mind that on the one hand 'the Declaration was prepared with a view to bringing all religions or beliefs within its compass, and on the other hand that the forms of manifestation and the weight attached to them, vary from one religion or belief to another, it may be safely assumed that the intention was to embrace all possible manifestations of religion or belief with the terms "teaching, practice, worship and observance"'.[11] However, specific words are used in Article 9(1) without any qualification to suggest that the list was intended to be representative or inclusive.

In *Arrowsmith v. United Kingdom*,[12] the United Kingdom argued that the list was exclusive, that it should be read restrictively so that all manifestations of religion were analogous to worship, and that the test of

---

[9] Declaration on Religious Intolerance and Discrimination, Arts. 6 (a), (b), (g), and (i) respectively.
[10] THORNBERRY, above, note 7, at 191; P. VAN DIJK AND G. J. H. VAN HOOF, THEORY AND PRACTICE OF THE EUROPEAN CONVENTION ON HUMAN RIGHTS 553 (3rd edn. 1997).
[11] Krishnaswami study, at 17.
[12] *Arrowsmith v. the United Kingdom (admissibility)*, App. No. 7050/75, 8 Eur. Comm'n H.R. Dec. & Rep. 123, 127 (1977). Ben Vermeulen, *Comment, in* FREEDOM OF CONSCIENCE 140 (Council of Europe ed., 1993) argues on the basis of the case law that 'external manifestations are only protected by Art. 9 if they are, from an objective point of view, to be considered as acts of worship'. This does not, however, tend to be the view of most authors.

whether or not something was a manifestation of religion or belief should be determined objectively and not on the subjective claims of the applicant.[13] The applicant argued that the list was not exclusive or, if it was, that her actions were part of the 'practice' of her belief, as the term practice should not be read in the restricted manner suggested by the United Kingdom.[14]

The Commission did not discuss these opposing approaches in detail but focused instead on the issue of whether the applicant's actions could be said to fit within the definition of 'practice'. It determined that her actions did not fall within the definition of 'practice' but did not go on to consider the applicant's argument that the list in Article 9(1) was inclusive rather than exclusive. By failing to follow up her claims that the list in Article 9 was inclusive the Commission implicitly rejected this claim.[15] Similarly, in a number of cases that argued for the notion of manifestation to be extended to things such as the right to a divorce or a right to entry permits for religious believers into a State, the Commission has assumed that such extensions could not be manifestations.[16] Thus the list tends to be interpreted as exclusive and the Court and Commission have been reluctant to extend Article 9 to allow for the creation of 'new rights' that are not explicitly mentioned in the Convention.[17] Part of the reason for this is probably that the term 'practice' has such a potentially wide range of meanings that the arguments about the scope of manifestations under the Convention tend to focus on how broadly the term 'practice' should be interpreted rather than on trying to extend the types of manifestation beyond the four listed.[18]

The right to manifest a religion can be exercised in both an active and a passive manner.[19] For example, the right to worship includes the right not to be forced into worship against one's will. Only a limited number of cases have found a violation of the passive right to manifest a religion and

---

[13] *Arrowsmith v. the United Kingdom (admissibility)*, App. No. 7050/75, 8 Eur. Comm'n H.R. Dec. & Rep. 123, 127 (1977).

[14] *Arrowsmith v. the United Kingdom*, App. No. 7050/75, 19 Eur. Comm'n H.R. Dec. & Rep. 5, 31 (1978).

[15] Although this is not clear from the case itself, which does say that proclaiming general pacifist views might have fallen within Art. 9 manifestations. Later cases, however, have tended to focus on the term 'practice' rather than on extending the list of manifestations. See Malcolm Evans, Religious Liberty and International Law in Europe 305–6 (1997).

[16] *Church of X v. the United Kingdom*, App. No. 3798/68, 29 Collection 70, 77 (1968). (Criticized by Francis Jacobs and Robin White, The European Convention on Human Rights 213 (2nd edn. 1996); Evans, above, note 15, at 302.) *Khan v. the United Kingdom*, App. No. 11579/85, 48 Eur. Comm'n H.R. Dec. & Rep. 253, 255 (1986), held marriage is not a manifestation of religion or belief.

[17] Evans, above, note 15, at 298.

[18] See the discussion of practice at Chapter 6.3.4.

[19] Evans, above, note 15, at 284; J. E. S. Fawcett, The Application of the European Convention on Human Rights 244 (1987).

not all these cases have an exact correspondence to one of the forms of manifestation outlined in Article 9(1). In *Buscarini*, for example, the right not to be required to swear on the Gospels was upheld, although it is not clear that this right has a positive counterpart in the list of worship, teaching, observance, and practice. The difficulty in deciding whether being forced to take an oath is an intrusion into the *forum internum* or only an interference with the passive right to manifest a religion or belief, demonstrates the way in which the line between the two can become blurred, especially as the Commission and Court have not developed their reasoning in these cases.[20]

6.3.2 Worship and Observance

'Worship' has been given the highest status of the manifestations listed in Article 9(1). The Commission, when giving an overview of Article 9, has said that it primarily protects personal beliefs and religious creeds and 'acts which are intimately linked to these, such as acts of worship or devotion'.[21] The Court has not explicated the precise scope of the term but there does not appear to have been any serious contest about its scope in the cases so far. A few cases have raised some problematic issues. In one case the Commission was prepared to hold that the presence of a Protestant minister and services in a jail met the requirement of a right to worship by a Church of England prisoner without considering whether that right included worship in the specific denomination of the believer.[22] The Court has been prepared to hold that interference with the ability to set up a place of public worship raises issues of the right to worship and observance. [23] The *Holy Monasteries* case[24] also implies that interference (e.g. through confiscation) with objects required for worship constitutes an interference with the right,[25] although State control of the land on which the monasteries stood was not a restriction on the right to worship.[26] The

---

[20] EVANS, above, note 15, at 284.

[21] *C v. the United Kingdom*, App. No. 10358/83, 37 Eur. Comm'n H.R. Dec. & Rep. 142, 147 (1983).

[22] *X v. Federal Republic of Germany*, App. No. 2413/65, 23 Collection 1, 8 (1966). Indeed, the Commission dismissed the case as there was no evidence of the *absence* of a Protestant pastor and rites of worship.

[23] *Manoussakis and others v. Greece*, 17 Eur. Ct. H.R. (ser. A) 1347, at 1361 (1996-IV).

[24] *Holy Monasteries v. Greece*, 301 Eur. Ct. H.R. (ser. A) 1347 (1994).

[25] See also Krishnaswami study, at 31.

[26] *Holy Monasteries v. Greece*, 301 Eur. Ct. H.R. (ser. A) at 38 (1994). The complaint made by the applicants concerned a law that effectively transferred control over agricultural and forestry property from the monasteries to the government. The Court, in dismissing the claim, noted that the Greek laws in question 'in no way concerned the objects intended for the celebration of divine worship and *consequently* do not interfere with the exercise of the right to freedom of religion' (emphasis added). The Court did, however, find a breach of Art. 1 of Protocol 1 in relation to the property of a number of monasteries.

differences between State restrictions on land and interference with objects of ritual is not as self-evident as the Court assumes it to be, as each could potentially restrict the ability of the religious communities to perform their rites.

The term 'observance' seems to have been conflated into a slightly extended notion of worship and has not been given separate consideration by the Court or Commission. In *Manoussakis v. Greece*,[27] for example, the prosecution of several Jehovah's Witnesses for setting up a place of worship without having obtained a government permit was held by the Court to constitute an interference with worship and observance. No distinction between these terms was drawn.[28] The Court and Commission generally treat the concepts of worship and observance as self-evident and not in need of definition.

6.3.3 Teaching

The term 'teaching' has been discussed in some detail, although, like worship and observance, it has not been defined particularly clearly.[29] In *Kokkinakis v. Greece*[30] the majority of the Court held that interfering with proselytism was an interference with the right to manifest a religion or belief, but did not discuss why this was so. While the manifestation did not seem to be wholly an issue of teaching, the Court held that attempting to inform others of one's religion or belief falls within the meaning of teaching,[31] though not if it shaded off into 'improper proselytism'.[32] Somewhat strangely, the Court—which referred to the obligation on many people to bear *Christian witness*[33]—drew on a report by the World Council of Churches as evidence of the type of behaviour that would take proselytism outside the realm of teaching, such as offering social or material advantages to particular converts, manipulating people in distress, or the use of violence or brainwashing.[34] While the Court refused to define 'improper proselytism' in the abstract,[35] it is clear from *Kokkinakis* and the later proselytism case of *Larissis*[36] that the Court is prepared to protect

---

[27] *Manoussakis and others v. Greece*, 17 Eur. Ct. H.R. (ser. A) 1347 (1996-IV).

[28] *Id.* at para. 36.

[29] Dinstein, above, note 8, at 153–4.

[30] *Kokkinakis v. Greece*, 260-A Eur. Ct H.R. (ser. A) (1993).

[31] *Id.* at 13. The majority held that Art. 9 'includes in principle the right to try to convince one's neighbour, for example through "teaching"'. Evans sees the use of the words 'for example' as indicating that the primary issue with which the Court was concerned was that of practice or the general notion of 'manifestation'. It seems, however, reasonably clear from the wording that the Court is acknowledging that teaching is one way in which proselytism can be carried out, even if it is not the only way. See EVANS, above, note 15, at 306.

[32] *Kokkinakis v. Greece*, 260-A Eur. Ct. H.R. (ser. A) at 17 (1993).

[33] *Id.*   [34] *Id.*   [35] *Id.*

[36] *Larissis and others v. Greece*, 65 Eur. Ct. H.R. (ser. A) 363 (1998-V).

the right to proselytize as, at least in part, a manifestation of teaching one's religion and belief.

Some judges on the Court, however, took a far narrower approach to the term 'teaching'. Judge Valticos argued that the teaching referred 'undoubtedly to religious teaching in school curricula or in religious institutions'.[37] The majority, however, rejected this approach, in part on the grounds that if some inter-faith teaching were not possible then the right to change religion or belief would be rendered pointless.[38] Judge Valticos, while affirming that a person has a right to have a conversation about his or her religious beliefs with another person, characterized the facts in *Kokkinakis* as a 'rape of the beliefs of others'.[39] He bolstered his conclusion that this is the sort of behaviour in which Mr Kokkinakis was indulging by reference to the *Hoffmann v. Austria*[40] case, which another Chamber was hearing at the same time, in which there was evidence that the applicant Jehovah's Witness made visits *once a week* to spread the faith. He considered this to be evidence that all Jehovah's Witnesses are engaged in 'a systematic attempt at conversion' which constituted an attack on the beliefs of others.[41] His definition of proselytism was 'zeal in spreading the faith and by extension in making converts, winning adherents'[42] and he concluded that this behaviour is not a manifestation of religion or belief. Judge Valticos's summary of the facts of the case demonstrates the gap that he saw between teaching that is protected by the Convention and the type of behaviour in which Mr Kokkinakis engaged.

Let us now look at the facts of the case. On the one hand, we have a militant Jehovah's Witness, a hardbitten adept of proselytism, a specialist in conversion, a martyr of the criminal courts whose earlier convictions have served only to harden him in his militancy, and, on the other hand, an ideal victim, a naive woman, the wife of a cantor in the Orthodox Church (if he manages to convert her, what a triumph!). He swoops on her, trumpets that he has good news for her (the play on words is obvious but no doubt not to her), manages to get himself let in and, and, as an experienced commercial traveller and cunning purveyor of the faith that he wants to spread, he expounds to her his intellectual wares cunningly wrapped up in a mantle of universal peace and radiant happiness. Who, indeed, would not like peace and happiness? But is this the mere exposition of Mr Kokkinakis's beliefs or is it not rather an attempt to beguile the simple soul of the cantor's wife? Does the Convention afford its protection to such undertakings? Certainly not.[43]

---

[37] *Kokkinakis v. Greece*, 260-A Eur. Ct. H.R. (ser. A) at 27 (1993), dissenting opinion of Judge Valticos.
[38] *Id.* at 13.   [39] *Id.* at 28.
[40] *Hoffmann v. Austria*, 255-C Eur. Ct. H.R. (ser. A) (1993).
[41] *Kokkinakis v. Greece*, 260-A Eur. Ct H.R. (ser. A) at 27 (1993), dissenting judgment of Judge Valticos.
[42] *Id.* at 28. The definition is taken from the Petit Robert dictionary.
[43] *Id.*

Two other judges who dissented in *Kokkinakis* took a somewhat more moderate approach to proselytism, by focusing on the term 'teaching' as the basis for claiming a right to proselytize. They argued that 'teaching' required of the teacher 'openness and uprightness and the avoidance of the use of devious or improper means or false pretexts'.[44] Furthermore, specialists in religion should not take advantage of those without training and in their attempts to teach should 'respect the religion of others'.[45] Thus, in order to constitute teaching the teacher must use self-restraint and act in a completely trustworthy way. In this case, they felt that the applicant was not engaged in teaching as he gained access to the house of the woman whom he sought to convert by claiming that he had 'Good News' for her, rather than clearly explaining his purpose in calling on her. Thus these judges placed a very high burden on the person who sets out to win converts, requiring the person both to act with absolute integrity (far greater than the standard of not engaging in improper proselytism used by the majority) and to determine the religious literacy of those with whom they interact, to ensure that they are not taking advantage of a person's lack of knowledge. This is a restrictive notion of the right to teach and not one that has been accepted by the Court as a whole, which has given reasonable scope to the right to teach, even in the relatively controversial area of proselytism.

Outside the proselytism context, the issue of the right to manifest a religion through teaching generally arises in the context of school education. As discussed in the last chapter, although people have a right to teach religion and to set up religious schools as long as they meet the State-required minimum education standards, the obligation of the State to respect the right to teach is essentially a negative one. While the State may not interfere in private religious teaching, it is not required to provide it or to subsidize it.[46] The right to ensure proper training for religious leaders and clergy either domestically or abroad may also arise from the right to manifest a religion in teaching, although again the State is only obliged to refrain from interfering with or prohibiting the education of religious leaders.[47] Such education of leaders is a right in itself and also provides an indirect benefit to religious communities who may rely on their leaders for religious education of other members of the community.[48]

6.3.4 Practice

The term 'practice' has proved the most difficult of the four listed manifestations of religion or belief to define. It could potentially be very wide,

---

[44] *Id.* at 37, joint dissenting opinion of Judges Foighel and Loizou.
[45] *Id.*   [46] See above at Chapter 5.5.   [47] Krishnaswami study, at 41–2.
[48] Declaration on Religious Intolerance and Discrimination. Art. 6(g), the right to freedom of religion includes the right 'to train, appoint, elect or designate by succession appropriate leaders . . .'.

including putting into action all of the dictates and teachings of one's religion or belief. At the opposite end of the spectrum, it could be narrow, referring only to directly religious practices that are similar in nature to worship.[49] The latter interpretation is sometimes argued on the basis of the French version of the text which uses the plural *les pratiques*,[50] which suggests something more akin to the English idea of 'practices' than practice. The French plural term has a more religious flavour than does the singular but it is not much clearer than its English counterpart.

Neither the Commission nor the Court has directly addressed this issue or the possible inconsistency between the English and French versions of the text, both of which are equally authoritative.[51] They have, however, shown a keen awareness of the potentially wide scope of 'practice' and have been wary of giving it too expansive a definition. The *Arrowsmith* case[52] was concerned with the idea of 'practice' and how to develop a test to distinguish a 'practice' which was a manifestation of a religion or belief from the broad range of actions which were merely inspired or motivated by a religion or belief. In some later cases, the Commission has assumed that the test that was necessary to contain the broad notion of practice is also relevant to the other types of manifestation listed in Article 9(1).[53] This has made claims under Article 9 very difficult and has arguably excluded worthy cases from proper consideration by the Court and Commission. As it was the *Arrowsmith* case which established the test, and as it is a good example of the difficulties presented by the term 'practice' in Article 9(1), it is necessary to consider the case in some detail.

6.4 THE *ARROWSMITH* CASE: THE NECESSITY TEST OF MANIFESTATION

6.4.1 Factual Background

Pat Arrowsmith, a committed pacifist, was convicted for distributing leaflets to soldiers that urged them not to accept a tour of duty in Northern Ireland.[54] The pamphlet was directed to the particular situation in

---

[49] EVANS, above, note 15, at 305–6.

[50] Both the LAROUSSE GRAND DICTIONNAIRE (FRENCH–ENGLISH) and HARRAPS STANDARD FRENCH AND ENGLISH DICTIONARY outline a number of definitions for 'pratique', the first of which is 'application of theory', but for 'pratiques' both use the example *pratiques religieuses*.

[51] The signature clause of the Convention reads 'Done at Rome this 4th day of November 1950 in English and French, both texts being equally authoritative'.

[52] *Arrowsmith v. the United Kingdom*, App. No. 7050/75, 19 Eur. Comm'n H.R. Dec. & Rep. 5 (1978).

[53] EVANS, above, note 15, at 306, argues that 'the key to understanding what amounts to a manifestation for the purposes of Art. 9 lies in determining the scope of "practice"'.

[54] *Arrowsmith v. the United Kingdom*, App. No. 7050/75, 19 Eur. Comm'n H.R. Dec. & Rep. 5, 6 (1978).

Northern Ireland, rather than being a general pacifist tract, and it contained practical information about the options of deserting or publicly refusing to serve (while warning that this would lead to a court martial and prison) as well as legal options for leaving the army (such as buying out).[55] The applicant had distributed the same leaflets before and the Director of Public Prosecutions had decided not to prosecute her. She and her friends then went to another army base and distributed the leaflets there. The police asked them to cease doing so and her friends complied but she refused to do so, saying that the Director of Public Prosecutions had already approved the content of the leaflets. She was then arrested and charged.[56]

Miss Arrowsmith was prosecuted under the *Incitement to Disaffection Act* 1934 (UK), which prohibited any person from 'maliciously and advisedly ... [seducing] any member of Her Majesty's forces from his duty or allegiance to Her Majesty'[57] or possessing or distributing documents likely to have this effect.[58] She was convicted by a jury and sentenced to eighteen months' imprisonment. Her sentence was reduced on appeal to the Court of Appeal to the time already served (a little less than nine months) but the conviction was upheld.[59] She made an application to the Commission claiming that her conviction was in breach of Articles 5, 9, 10, and 14 of the Convention. Her application was held to be admissible as raising serious issues under the Convention.[60] In the decision on the merits, however, the Commission held that the applicant had failed to make out her case under each of the relevant Articles.[61]

6.4.2 The Decision of the Commission

The Commission accepted the applicant's claim that she was a committed pacifist and held that pacifism can be defined as the 'commitment in both theory and practice, to the philosophy of securing one's political or other objectives without resort to the threat or use of force against another human being under any circumstances, even in response to the threat or use of force'.[62] The Commission was prepared to accept that, in light of this definition, pacifism was a belief, deserving of protection under Article 9.[63]

---

[55] *Id.* at 9–12.   [56] *Id.* at 12.

[57] Incitement to Disaffection Act 1934 (UK), section 1(1).

[58] Incitement to Disaffection Act 1934 (UK), section 1(2).

[59] *Arrowsmith v. the United Kingdom*, App. No. 7050/75, 19 Eur. Comm'n H.R. Dec. & Rep. 5 (1978). See also *Arrowsmith v. Regina*, All ER 463 (1975).

[60] *Arrowsmith v. the United Kingdom (admissibility)*, App. No. 7050/75, 8 Eur. Comm'n H.R. Dec. & Rep. 123 (1977).

[61] *Id.* at 26.

[62] *Id.* at 19. The definition was provided by the applicant and accepted by the United Kingdom and the Commission.

[63] *Id.*

Thus, it was for the applicant to show that her distribution of the leaflets was a manifestation of that belief as a 'practice' of pacifism.

The Commission began its consideration of the definition of practice with a note of warning. 'The Commission considers that the term "practice" as employed in Article 9.1 does not cover each act which is motivated or influenced by a religion or belief.'[64] It did not, however, make clear which acts are covered by the term 'practice' if the term does not cover all acts that are motivated by religion or belief. Some idea of its position can be found in its conclusion that

It is true that public declarations proclaiming generally the idea of pacifism and urging the acceptance of a commitment to non-violence may be considered as a normal and recognised manifestation of pacifist belief. However, when the actions of individuals do not actually express the belief concerned they cannot be considered to be as such protected under Article 9.1, even when they are influenced by it.[65]

The Commission decided on this basis that the distribution of leaflets did not constitute practice of the belief of pacifism as the leaflets were not about pacifism itself (indeed a number of quotations from Absent Without Leave soldiers used in the leaflets suggested that fighting in some circumstances would be appropriate) but rather about political opposition to government policy on Northern Ireland.[66] The leaflets could have been distributed by many people who were opposed to the actions of the government in Northern Ireland but who were not pacifists. Thus her actions could not be said to be a manifestation of Miss Arrowsmith's pacifism.[67] Strangely, the Commission also noted that the leaflets were directed only at soldiers who might be posted to Northern Ireland and not to the public more generally.[68] This point somehow assisted it in concluding that the advice in the leaflets 'was not clearly given in order to further pacifist ideas'.[69] As Mr Opsahl pointed out in his separate and partly dissenting opinion, the aim of influencing people who are responsible for the action to which one is opposed 'is an essential and legitimate aspect of the exercise of freedom of expression and opinion'.[70] It seems very peculiar to suggest that a pacifist who spends her time appealing to soldiers to refuse to participate in the use of armed force could be seen to be practising her belief less than someone who outlined the pacifist ideals to the world at large. This can be compared to the approach taken to proselytism discussed above, where the majority of the Court held that the attempt to convert non-believers was an essential part of the religious obligations of many Christians.

[64] *Id.* at 19. [65] *Id.* at 20. [66] *Id.* [67] *Id.* [68] *Id.*
[69] *Id.* [70] *Id.* at 28.

6.4.3 Dissenting Opinions in *Arrowsmith*

The two dissenting opinions point out some of the dangers of the position taken by the majority. While Mr Opsahl ultimately voted with the majority on the question of whether there had been a breach of Article 9, he described the answer the Commission came to as 'very doubtful' and says that he might have dissented had it not been for the fact that he believed that Miss Arrowsmith's actions were more appropriately protected under Article 10.[71] He agreed with the majority that not all acts that are motivated by religion or belief can be protected by Article 9. Ordinary crimes of theft or violence, for example, cannot be sanctioned because they may be inspired by a religion or belief.[72]

On the other hand, one cannot in my opinion generally exclude from Article 9 all acts which are declared unlawful according to the law of the land if they do not *necessarily* manifest a belief, provided that they are clearly motivated by it. On the contrary, as Article 9.2 shows in setting out a series of further conditions for an interference to be justified, an act cannot be interfered with merely because it has been declared unlawful. I consider that Article 9 must, in principle, be applicable to a great many acts which are not, on their face, necessarily manifesting the under-lying or motivating belief, if that is what they *genuinely* do.[73]

He argued that this is particularly so when the action is not protected by other rights in the Convention.[74] The fact that the applicant's actions could have been undertaken by someone who did not share her belief was irrel-evant; everyone is entitled to have his or her case determined by the particular facts of the case and not by some arbitrary or narrow notion of what a particular belief requires.[75] Freedom of religion and belief means that certain actions will have a greater significance and importance to some people (who will thus be entitled to protection under Article 9(1)) than they will have for others (who will not be entitled to the protection as a consequence).[76] Mr Opsahl concluded his consideration of Article 9 by sounding a warning note that 'the line [between protected and non-protected actions] should not be drawn too narrowly so that only certain, perhaps more traditional, types of manifestation are protected, irrespective of the genuineness of the motivation'.[77]

Mr Klecker, in his dissenting opinion, went even further and held that the conviction of Pat Arrowsmith was a breach of the United Kingdom's obligations under Article 9. He held that her distribution of the leaflets was 'not merely an extension of her belief but an integral part of it'.[78] His opinion pointed to facts that were not mentioned by the majority, such as the fact that Miss Arrowsmith had been involved in trying to convince the

---

[71] *Id.* at 26.   [72] *Id.*   [73] *Id.*   [74] *Id.* at 26–7.   [75] *Id.* at 27.
[76] *Id.*   [77] *Id.*   [78] *Id.* at 30.

IRA to cease their actions in Northern Ireland as well as targeting the British military,[79] and he concluded that the distribution of leaflets to soldiers was a manifestation of her pacifist beliefs.[80] By looking at her actions in context, he concluded that her real motivation was not to undermine government policy, as suggested by the majority, but rather a practical attempt to convince both sides of a dispute to use peaceful means to resolve their differences.

Mr Klecker's analysis is interesting in that it looks to the larger context of the belief system and actions of the applicant rather than taking a narrow, isolated view of the particular action in question. Such a broad view can often lead to different conclusions or at least raise more complex questions than the more narrow approach does. This is important in an area such as determining whether a particular action is a manifestation of a wider religious or other belief. To refuse to look at a particular action as part of a larger context of religion or belief is to ignore the reality of the belief system for the individual involved. For the individual any particular action is integrated into their life philosophy as a whole and to ignore this context, as the Commission did in the *Arrowsmith* case, has the potential to undermine the right to religious freedom.

6.5 THE *ARROWSMITH* TEST

6.5.1 The Nature of the Test

The test that was applied by the Commission in *Arrowsmith* is not completely clear on the face of the judgment. The Commission certainly held that not all actions which are motivated by religion or belief are covered by the protection in Article 9 but it did not set out any real test to determine which actions are covered. By excluding actions that are merely motivated or influenced by belief, the Commission suggested that a very direct link is needed between the belief and the action if the action is to be considered a 'practice' under Article 9.[81] This has come to be interpreted in later judgments of the Commission as a type of 'necessity' test, which will be referred to hereafter as the *Arrowsmith* test.[82] Such an interpretation of *Arrowsmith* requires applicants to show that they were required to act in a certain way because of their religion or belief. An examination of cases that have applied the *Arrowsmith* test demonstrates the lack of clarity and the difficulties inherent in applying this test in a coherent manner.

---

[79] *Id.*   [80] *Id.* at 32.

[81] Evans, above, note 15, at 307–12.

[82] Although the case itself does not make clear whether the applicant needs to show necessity or merely a strong, direct link between the action and the belief.

6.5.2 Application of the *Arrowsmith* Test

One of the issues that a necessity approach raises is whether behaviour that is merely encouraged or permitted by a religion but not required by it is protected under Article 9(1). The answer to this question seems to be that such behaviour is not protected, falling foul of the concern in *Arrowsmith* not to allow behaviour merely motivated or inspired by religion or belief to be protected as a manifestation under Article 9. A decision that supports this conclusion is *Khan v. United Kingdom*,[83] in which the Commission upheld the criminal conviction of a 21-year-old man who underwent an Islamic marriage ceremony with a 14½-year-old girl, contrary to the wishes of her parents. In Islamic law, the age at which a girl can marry without her parents' consent is 12, whereas under British law it is 18. The man was convicted of abduction of a girl from the possession of her father and was sentenced to nine months in prison. His complaint that this breached his rights to freedom of religion and to marry and found a family was dismissed by the Commission, in part for the reason that Islam merely permitted marriage at an earlier age than British law, it did not require it.[84]

Other cases have adopted similar reasoning. In *X v. Austria*[85] the Court held that the decision of the German government to prohibit followers of the so-called 'Moonie sect' from setting up a legal association was not an interference in religious freedom or the right to worship in association with others because it was not necessary to the practice of their beliefs that they be allowed to form a legal association. A Buddhist prisoner who was not permitted by prison authorities to send articles to a Buddhist magazine was held not to have a cause of action because he could not show that sending the letters was necessary to his religion.[86] The award of damages against a Jew who refused to hand a guett (letter of repudiation) to his wife after a civil divorce (thus preventing her from remarrying under Jewish law) was also found to raise no issue of freedom of religion as Jewish leaders stated that the refusal was not mandated by Judaism.[87] There have been a large number of claims made in relation to general and neutral laws (such as laws on taxation, compulsory vaccination, pension schemes, and planning) on the basis that they interfere with religion or belief. In the vast majority of these cases, the Commission has utilized the *Arrowsmith* test to hold people claiming exemptions from such laws were merely influenced or motivated by religion or belief rather than practising their religion or belief.[88]

---

[83] *Khan v. the United Kingdom*, App. No. 11579/85, 48 Eur. Comm'n H.R. Dec. & Rep. 253 (1986).
[84] *Id.* at 255.
[85] *X. v. Austria*, App. No. 8652/79, 26 Eur. Comm'n H.R. Dec. & Rep. 89 (1981).
[86] *X. v. the United Kingdom*, App. No. 5442/72, 1 Eur. Comm'n H.R. Dec. & Rep. 41 (1974).
[87] *D v. France*, App. No. 10180/82, 35 Eur. Comm'n H.R. Dec. & Rep. 199 (1983).
[88] See below at Chapter 8.3.1.

6.5.3 The Applicability of the Test Outside 'Practice'

The *Arrowsmith* test was originally devised as a way of defining and limiting the potentially open-ended term 'practice'. At times, however, the Commission has applied it to one of the other forms of manifestation listed in Article 9(1). The high-water mark in this line of reasoning is the controversial decision of *X v. the United Kingdom.*[89] The case involved the refusal of a school to rearrange its timetable to give a Muslim teacher a 45-minute extension of the lunch hour on Friday afternoons to allow him to attend prayers at a Mosque. While the case was ultimately decided on other grounds, the Commission suggested that no Article 9 issue was raised because the applicant had not shown that it was a *requirement* of the religion that he attend Friday prayers.[90] If the Commission had been forced to rely on this aspect of its judgment in coming to its final decision, it would have dismissed a claim relating directly to the right to worship (a right explicitly included in Article 9) on the grounds that the right to worship did not raise any issues of freedom of religion when it cannot be proved that such worship is *required* by the religion.

Such an approach would have been inconsistent with other cases, in which the Court and Commission have assumed that interference with the right to worship or teach is a *prima facie* breach of Article 9(1) without any reference to *Arrowsmith.*[91] In *Kokkinakis*, for example, the Court held without discussion that restrictions on the right to proselytize were caught by Article 9(1),[92] although the Court may have been assisted in coming to that conclusion by the fact that Greece conceded that proselytism was a manifestation of religion.[93] It was not clear whether proselytism was a manifestation because it was required by the applicants' religion, or because it was teaching, or simply because it was a form of religious practice with which the Commission was familiar and comfortable. The distinction between *Kokkinakis* and *Arrowsmith* can be a difficult one to draw, as both applicants aimed at changing the views of members of a community that was deeply opposed to them. Both acted in accordance with the dictates of their religion or belief, and both provoked hostility in response.[94]

---

[89] *X. v. the United Kingdom*, App. No. 8160/78, 22 Eur. Comm'n H.R. Dec. & Rep. 27 (1981).

[90] *Id.* at 34–5.

[91] e.g. *Manoussakis and others v. Greece*, 17 Eur. Ct. H.R. (ser. A) 1347 (1996-IV); *Chappell v. the United Kingdom*, App. No. 12587/86, 53 Eur. Comm'n H.R. Dec. & Rep. 241, 246 (1987); *Childs v. the United Kingdom*, App. No. 9813/82, Eur. Comm'n H.R., 1 Mar. 1983, unreported.

[92] *Kokkinakis v. Greece*, 260-A Eur. Ct. H.R. (ser. A) at 14 (1993).

[93] *Id.* at 13.

[94] T. Jeremy Gunn, *Adjudicating Rights of Conscience under the European Convention on Human Rights, in* RELIGIOUS HUMAN RIGHTS IN GLOBAL PERSPECTIVE: LEGAL PERSPECTIVES 305, 322 (Johan D. van der Vyver and John Witte Jr. eds., 1996) observes that 'Although it

Further inconsistencies in application have arisen when in some cases the Commission appears to have subtly changed the nature of the test. In *Karaduman v. Turkey*,[95] for example, the applicant was a Muslim woman who was denied the right to graduate from her University course on the basis that she refused to have her identity photograph taken while she was not wearing a headscarf. The University rules (in compliance with the Constitution and the rulings of the Turkish Constitutional Court and Council of State[96]) prohibited the wearing of headscarves in State institutions, including schools and Universities, as a breach of the principle of secularity. While the decision was ultimately made on other grounds, the Commission indicated that the refusal of the University to allow Miss Karaduman to wear a headscarf in her photograph was probably not a restriction on her right to manifest her religion.

The Commission also takes the view that a university degree certificate is intended to certify a student's capacities for employment purposes; it is not a document intended for the general public. The purpose of the photograph affixed to a degree certificate is to identify the person concerned. It cannot be used by that person to manifest his [*sic*] religious belief.[97]

The normal, *Arrowsmith* approach to this question would have been to question whether the wearing of the headscarf and refusing to remove it for a photograph was required by Islam. The shift of emphasis away from the issue of religious apparel, which seemed to be at the heart of the application, and on to the taking of the photograph, suggests a level of conceptual confusion within the Commission as to the appropriate way to apply the *Arrowsmith* test.

Thus the scope of the *Arrowsmith* test is not entirely clear. It seems that it is generally restricted to questions of practice but that the Commission or Court have some discretion in whether to characterize an issue as one of practice or another form of manifestation such as teaching. It also appears that there are some cases that the Commission is prepared simply to assume must fall outside the protection of Article 9, even without applying the *Arrowsmith* or any other test to explain why this is so. For example, a ban on the Church of Scientology advertising an 'E-meter' on the basis that the 'scientific' claims in the advertisement were misleading was held not to raise any issue of freedom of religion because the State

seems correct as a matter of fact and of law that Mr Kokkinakis's freedom to manifest his religion had been impaired, it is not entirely obvious why the Court reached its decision in such a conclusory manner, particularly in light of the *Arrowsmith*, *Karlsson*, and *Knudsen* decisions.'

[95] *Karaduman v. Turkey*, App. No. 16278/90, 74 Eur. Comm'n H.R. Dec. & Rep. 93 (1993).
[96] *Id.* at 103–4, outlines the relevant decisions of the Turkish Constitutional Court.
[97] *Id.* at 109.

was only regulating the commercial and not the religious activities of the Church.[98] A soldier whose lack of discipline and insubordination was linked to his Islamic faith was likewise unable to claim the protection of Article 9 when he was court martialled for insubordination, as rebelling from military authority was not the type of behaviour that is protected under Article 9.[99] A man who was not able to obtain a divorce in the Republic of Ireland, despite divorce being permitted by his Church, had his claim dismissed on the basis that divorce was a matter to which Article 9 could not 'in its ordinary meaning, be taken to extend'.[100] Once again, the logic of these decisions is not entirely clear and it is quite possible that the Court would take a different approach to the commercial/religious division, for example, if the advertising in question was not for an E-meter from a minority religion but for the Bible or a pilgrimage to the 'healing' waters at Lourdes advertised by mainstream Christian Churches.[101]

It is thus difficult to fit such cases into the overall approach of the Commission to the protection of manifestations of religion or belief. These cases aside, it appears to be the general (though not consistently applied) principle that the *Arrowsmith* test requires an applicant to show that a *practice* is necessary to his or her religion in order for it to be protected, but that applicants who raise issues concerning worship, teaching, or observance need only show that there was an interference in fact to prove a breach of Article 9(1). While this means that the application of the *Arrowsmith* test is limited, most applicants who claim a breach of Article 9 claim that it is their right to practise their religion or belief that has been restricted. Thus the practical importance of the test is significant, and is increased by the fact that it is sometimes inappropriately applied outside the definition of practice to other manifestations listed in Article 9.

---

[98] *X and the Church of Scientology v. Sweden*, App. No. 7895/77, 16 Eur. Comm'n H.R. Dec. & Rep. 68, 72 (1979). The Commission held that, while religions may advertise their arguments with freedom, a distinction should be drawn 'between advertisements which are merely "informational" or "descriptive" in character and commercial advertisements offering objects for sale. Once an advertisement enters into the latter sphere, although it may concern religious objects central to a particular creed, statements of religious content represent, in the Commission's view, more the manifestation of a desire to market goods for profit than the manifestation of a belief in practice, within the proper sense of that term.' No reasoning is given to support such a general conclusion.

[99] *Yanasik v. Turkey*, App. No. 14524/89, 74 Eur. Comm'n H.R. Dec. & Rep. 14 (1993).

[100] *Johnston v. Ireland*, 112 Eur. Ct. H.R. (ser. A) at 27 (1986), despite the strong dissenting opinion of Judge de Meyer, at 36.

[101] Gunn, above, note 94, at 328, argues that the rationale for restricting advertisements for the commercial sale of the E-meter would 'apply equally to an injunction banning book-stores from praising the virtues of the Bible'. EVANS, above, note 15, at 313.

6.6 ANALYSIS OF THE *ARROWSMITH* TEST

6.6.1 Methodology of the Court and Commission in Determining Necessity

The *Arrowsmith* test requires a determination of whether a restricted action is required by the religion or belief of the applicant. The Commission or Court determines this issue 'objectively' and does not seem to be prepared to take the applicants' claims about their religion or belief as particularly relevant to this determination.[102] As one author has noted, in the area of the margin of appreciation the Court has deferred to the judgment of States, believing them to better understand the vital forces at work in their own societies. It has not been prepared to be similarly deferential in relation to claims made by individuals about the importance of their own beliefs or the significance of a particular practice to them.[103]

The Court and Commission can be criticized for taking upon themselves the task of determining the requirements of a religion or belief and for often ignoring the claims of the applicants about their own faith.[104] Clear illustrations of the problems associated with the approach of the Court and Commission can be seen in the *Valsamis* and *Efstratiou* cases[105] brought against the Greek government by parents and students who were Jehovah's Witnesses. The cases arose out of the suspension of a number of Jehovah's Witness children from their school for several days for refusing to take part in a parade on Greek National Day (the day on which war broke out between Greece and fascist Italy). The parents of the students did not want their children to participate in the parade because they saw it as a celebration of war and thus a violation of their pacifist beliefs. They brought an action under Article 2 of the First Protocol and the students, on a similar basis, brought an action under Article 9. The majority of the Court dismissed the claims, saying that they could see nothing in the parade that could offend the applicants' religious convictions. The judges indeed determined that the parades served in part a pacifist objective.[106] In doing so,

---

[102] VAN DIJK AND VAN HOOF, above, note 10, at 550, note that this objective approach 'may in general be unavoidable' but that it could pose a threat to minorities who cannot show sufficient similarities between their religion or beliefs and traditional/mainstream religion or beliefs.

[103] Peter W. Edge, *The European Court of Human Rights and Religious Rights*, 47 INT'L & COMP. L.Q. 680, 685 (1998) notes that, 'The margin of appreciation is based, in part, on a recognition that the State is closer to the situation in discussion, and probably better informed of the exact circumstances than an international court. In sharp contrast to this deference to State expertise, the Court and Commission are much less willing to accept the individual believer's view of his or her beliefs.'

[104] *Id.* at 685–7.

[105] *Valsamis v. Greece*, 2 Eur. Ct. H.R. (ser. A) 2312 (1996-VI); *Efstratiou v. Greece*, 27 Eur. Ct. H.R. (ser. A) 2347 (1996-VI).

[106] *Valsamis v. Greece*, 2 Eur. Ct. H.R. (ser. A) 2312 at para. 11 (1996-VI); *Efstratiou v. Greece*, 27 Eur. Ct. H.R. (ser. A) 2347 at para. 11 (1996-VI).

they simply discounted the evidence of the applicants that such a parade conflicted with their religion, despite the fact that no reference is made in the judgment to any evidence (other than the judges' own assessments) that would counter the claims that the applicants made about what their religion required of them.[107]

6.6.2 Evidence of Necessity

The Commission and Court often simply state that there is no conflict between the religion or belief of an applicant and the action that is required by the State. This approach obscures the methodology by which the Commission and Court make such determinations. In some cases, where the judges do not merely rely on their own assessment of the obligations on the applicant, expert evidence from religious leaders is used.[108] The Muslim schoolteacher, however, was not permitted to bring such evidence (in part because the case was ultimately decided on other grounds) and the Commission does not normally hear such evidence.[109] In the *Kokkinakis* case the Court referred to a report by the World Council of Churches to determine that proselytism was part of the 'essential mission' of all Christians, but that improper proselytism was a 'corruption' of that mission.[110] It did not refer to any other religious authority, such as the rules of the Jehovah's Witnesses themselves. Given that the Commission and Court have been unwilling to accept the subjective assessment of the applicants themselves as to whether something is required by their religion or belief, one objective form of evidence would seem to be expert evidence from such leaders or reference to the rules or dogma of religious or belief-based groups.[111] The Court does seem to be willing to refer to such material

[107] cf. *West Virginia State Board of Education v. Barnette*, 319 U.S. 624, 642 (1943) which upheld exemptions from flag saluting for Jehovah's Witness schoolchildren. '[N]o official, high or petty, can prescribe what shall be orthodox in politics, nationalism, religion, or other matters of opinion or force their citizens to confess by word or act their faith therein.' Thus the children were entitled to the exemption because the Jehovah's Witnesses considered the salute to have religious implications, even though the Court also held that saluting the flag was a secular activity and therefore not banned by the anti-establishment clause.

[108] e.g. *D v. France*, App. No. 10180/82, 35 Eur. Comm'n H.R. Dec. & Rep. 199, 202 (1983). The Commission held that the refusal of a Jew to hand over a letter of repudiation to his wife after the divorce was 'at variance' with the 'religious leaders under whose authority he claimed to be acting'. This conclusion was derived from the decision of the French Court rather than expert evidence given directly to the Commission.

[109] *X v. the United Kingdom*, App. No. 8160/78, 22 Eur. Comm'n H.R. Dec. & Rep. 27, 35 (1981).

[110] *Kokkinakis v. Greece*, 260-A Eur. Ct. H.R. (ser. A) at 17 (1993).

[111] It is for applicants to prove that their actions are mandated by their religion or belief, but the Commission has given little guidance as to how this can be achieved. In *X v. the United Kingdom*, App. No. 8231/78, 28 Eur. Comm'n H.R. Dec. & Rep. 5, 27 (1982), for example, the application was denied because the applicant did not substantiate his claim that Sikh leaders refuse to wear prison clothes for religious reasons. No indication is given of what evidence would have been acceptable.

occasionally, but its use is haphazard and there seems to be no principle governing the use of expert evidence on religious matters. Thus the 'objective' approach of the Court to manifestations does not seem to be based on objective criteria but instead involves a substitution of the Court or Commission's judgment for that of the applicants.

6.6.3 Types of Belief Advantaged by *Arrowsmith*

Furthermore, whatever evidence is given, the very nature of the *Arrowsmith* test can have the unfortunate result of privileging committed and obedient members of certain types of religious organization over people with other religions or beliefs. For individualistic beliefs, such as Pat Arrowsmith's pacifism, there may be no higher authority or set of rules that can be consulted to determine what behaviour is required by the belief.[112] In religions that are non-hierarchical, it may be difficult to decide who is qualified to give expert evidence,[113] and in religions or beliefs that emphasize the development of individual conscience rather than adherence to a set of rules the very nature of the *Arrowsmith* test will make it difficult for an adherent to show that behaving in a particular way was a requirement of his or her religion or belief.

The *Arrowsmith* test can also act to the disadvantage of someone who is a member of a religious group but (either as an individual or part of a subset within the religion) does not accept all the teachings of that religion or who believes that his or her religion places additional demands on him or her.[114] For example, it may be easy for a Jehovah's Witness or a Quaker to show that their pacifism is a well-established part of their religion, but it may be more difficult for a Christian from another Church to make the same claim (even if the claim is genuine and based on his or her reading

---

[112] EVANS, above, note 15, at 308.

[113] Stephanos Stavros, *Freedom of Religion Claims for Exemption from Generally Applicable, Neutral Laws: Lessons from Across the Pond?*, 6 EUR. HUM. RTS REV. 607, 612 (1997), asks 'how many experts could the Commission find to support or refute the contention that a Hindu belonging to the Radhaswami sect is, upon "reaching the third stage of the activities of the sect" precluded from being a member of a trade union?'; Antonio Perotti, *Freedom of Conscience and Religion and Immigrants*, in FREEDOM OF CONSCIENCE 185–6 (Council of Europe ed., 1993), argues that one of the problems faced by some immigrant religious groups is their lack of clear, hierarchical leadership that can represent the group to the organs of the State.

[114] Edge, above, note 103, at 687, criticizes the idea that it could be for the Court to determine the nature of the criteria that applicants are entitled to use to determine whether their religious interests were affected. 'Not only would it place the Court in the position of acting as an authority on issues it is profoundly ill-suited to consider, it also creates a mechanism by which orthodoxies can establish their religious interests with greater ease than heterodoxies. If the Court seeks to enter into determining what one must believe, and how one must act, in order to meet religious duties in a particular tradition, it is more likely to have recourse to dominant, well-documented traditions than to the individual beliefs of the applicant.'

of the Gospels and understanding of the faith) when the Church of which they are a member does not support a general principle of pacifism.

Similarly, when there is disagreement between various members of a religion or belief over issues of doctrine and practice, the desire of the Commission to find an objective and authoritative answer to whether the practice is required can lead it to decide between competing approaches, sometimes rejecting an applicant's claim because it is outside the mainstream of his or her religion.[115] This stands in contrast to the approach taken by the United States Supreme Court, which, when dealing with the problem of a man who claimed that his religion forbade him from working in the direct production of armaments even though other members of the same religion did such work, held

Intrafaith differences of that kind are not uncommon among followers of a particular creed, and the judicial process is singularly ill-equipped to resolve such differences in relation to the Religious Clauses ... [T]he guarantee of free exercise is not limited to beliefs which are shared by all the members of a religious sect.[116]

Such an approach, however, requires the Court to be prepared to take the claims of applicants seriously rather than attempting to find some objective grounds to assess necessity.

6.6.4 Alternative Approaches to Manifestations

Given some of the problems with the *Arrowsmith* test, some judges have suggested alternative approaches to determining whether a certain practice is a manifestation of religion or belief. Indeed, the Commission itself has at times used a different formulation by asking whether the actions of the applicant 'give expression' to his or her religion or belief.[117] This appears to be less a restrictive test than requiring applicants to prove the necessity of their actions to their religion or belief and one that would allow applicants to succeed in a wider range of cases. It is closer to the test suggested by Mr Opsahl in *Arrowsmith* than the test normally used. It has, however, only been used on a handful of occasions and never in a case where an applicant has been successful.[118] In the cases that have used the 'giving expression' test, the applicants were held not to reach even this easier

---

[115] X *v. the United Kingdom*, App. No. 5947/72, 5 Eur. Comm'n H.R. Dec. & Rep. 8 (1976), the Commission accepted the determination of a rabbi that the food served in a prison was kosher and could be eaten by the applicant, despite his claims to the contrary.

[116] *Thomas v. Review Board of the Indiana Employment Security Division*, 450 U.S. 707, 714 (1981).

[117] See generally EVANS, above, note 15, at 312–13.

[118] e.g. *Knudsen v. Norway*, App. No. 11045/84, 42 Eur. Comm'n H.R. Dec. & Rep. 93 (1985); *X and the Church of Scientology v. Sweden*, App. No. 7805/77, 16 Eur. Comm'n H.R. Dec. & Rep. 68 (1980).

threshold. Given the fact that the *Arrowsmith* test continues to be used routinely, it is unlikely that the necessity test will be replaced by a test that is more generous to applicants.[119]

Judges Thór Vilhjálmsson and Jambrek proposed a potential alternative test in their joint dissents in *Efstratiou* and *Valsamis*.[120] They suggested that the Court should not make its own assessment of the validity of the beliefs or the importance of an action to applicants. Instead, they proposed that the applicants' 'perception of the symbolism of the school parade and its religious and philosophical connotations has to be accepted by the Court unless it is obviously unfounded and unreasonable'.[121] In similar vein, in relation to an Article 2, Protocol 1 claim, Judge Verdross held that the Court had to verify the truth of the statements made by applicants about their religious beliefs (to ensure that they were not acting fraudulently) but to 'respect the ideology of the persons concerned once such ideology has been clearly made out'.[122]

This alternative, which respects the right of applicants to determine whether being forced into a particular activity or prohibited from some type of action affects their religious sensibilities, is a clearer test and does not require judges to make determinations about a person's religious beliefs or the requirements of a religion. If such an approach were to be taken, the potential for abuse by applicants could be limited by the use of Article 9(2) and by the fact that 'obviously unfounded and unreasonable' beliefs (particularly those that are clearly fraudulent) would be excluded. The practice of the Supreme Court of the United States of America demonstrates that such an approach is practical, even in a relatively pluralistic society. The Supreme Court has shown reluctance to become involved in determining what is or is not required by a particular religion or belief. As a general rule, it does not question the claims of petitioners that some behaviour is required by or is not consistent with their religion or belief except where the claim is 'so bizarre, so clearly non-religious in motivation, as not to be entitled to protection under the Free Exercise Clause'.[123] This is because courts 'are not the arbiters of scriptural interpretation'.[124]

The approach of the Supreme Court takes the claims of petitioners far more seriously than does the approach of the European Court and demonstrates an understanding of the problems that can arise when a court

---

[119] Despite the cautiously optimistic conclusion drawn by Gunn, above, note 94, at 318.

[120] *Valsamis v. Greece*, 2 Eur. Ct. H.R. (ser. A) 2312 (1996-VI), *Efstratiou v. Greece*, 27 Eur. Ct. H.R. (ser. A) 2347 (1996-VI) dissenting judgments of Judges Thór Vilhjálmsson and Jambrek.

[121] *Id.* at para. 18 in each judgment.

[122] *Kjeldsen, Busk Madsen and Pedersen*, 23 Eur. Ct. H.R. (ser. A) at 32 (1976), separate opinion of Judge Verdross.

[123] *Thomas v. Review Board of the Indiana Employment Security Division*, 450 U.S. 707, 714 (1981); *Employment Division of Oregon v. Smith*, 494 U.S. 872, 886 (1990).

[124] *U.S. v. Lee*, 31 L. Ed. 2d 127, 132 (1982).

substitutes its decisions about what is required for those of the people affected. While this more subjective approach itself has some dangers (particularly in the potential for fraud) it is preferable to a test that requires judges to make a determination, often with little evidence, as to the requirements of a religion or belief. This is particularly important given that the Commission and Court have, at times, been accused of being unsympathetic to the claims of those from non-Christian traditions or religions without a long history in Europe.[125] They have never held in favour of an applicant in cases dealing with the wearing of religious apparel or having a particular appearance,[126] for example, which can be important to people from some religious traditions despite having little relevance in Christianity. On the other hand, they have been quick to hold that there is a right to proselytize (or bear 'Christian witness') despite the fact that this was highly controversial in the United Nations debates and remains contentious.[127] The role of the Court in determining what is and is not necessary to the religion or belief of an applicant increases the potential that it will single out for protection religious rites and practices with which the members of the court are familiar and feel comfortable. This can have serious implications for minorities and it demonstrates the dangers of the *Arrowsmith* test pointed out by Mr Opsahl—that it favours traditional types of religious practice over the practices of adherents of newer (at least in the European context) beliefs.[128]

6.6.5 United Nations Material

If the Court wished to add additional and more objective elements to the subjective claims of applicants that an action is a manifestation of a religion or belief, one resource could be scholarly studies into religious freedom, such as those conducted by the United Nations. These studies could be taken in conjunction with the claims of applicants to demonstrate some of the types of behaviour that are internationally accepted as manifestations

---

[125] Gunn, above, note 94, at 310–12; Peter Cumper, *The Rights of Religious Minorities: The Legal Regulation of New Religious Movements, in* MINORITY RIGHTS IN THE 'NEW' EUROPE 166, 174–5 (Peter Cumper and Steven Wheatley eds., 1999).

[126] Such as the growing of a beard, *X v. the United Kingdom*, App. No. 1753/63, 16 Collection 20 (1965).

[127] See the discussion at Chapter 5.6.

[128] *Arrowsmith v. the United Kingdom*, App. No. 7050/75, 19 Eur. Comm'n H.R. Dec. & Rep. 5, 27 (1978), separate opinion of Mr Opsahl. Karel Rimanque, *Freedom of Conscience and Minority Groups, in* FREEDOM OF CONSCIENCE 155 (Council of Europe ed., 1993), argues that 'To enjoy the protection of Article 9, a conduct or the refusal to perform a legal duty must be the direct expression of the spiritual or religious belief. For spiritual minorities, especially those which society has not become conversant with, this holds the danger that a behaviour will only then be considered the expression of a spiritual belief, when a sufficient resemblance can be found with the known patterns of familiar spiritual movements.'

of religion or belief. Thus an applicant who could show that the State restricted one of the types of manifestation outlined in internationally recognized studies as a manifestation of belief, and who made a reasonable claim that such a manifestation was an important part of his or her religion, should be presumed to have a case under Article 9(1) unless his or her claim can be shown to be fraudulent.

In his respected study on religious freedom, for example, Krishnaswami set out some of the manifestations of religion and belief that he considered to be protected under the Universal Declaration. They included practices involving marriage and divorce, the wearing of religious apparel, observance of burial rites, communication with co-religionists, and individual and corporate worship.[129] Similarly, the Declaration on Religious Intolerance and Discrimination lists a series of manifestations of belief including acquiring and using articles needed for religious rites, publishing and disseminating material on religion or belief and teaching in suitable places, observing days of rest, and celebrating holidays and ceremonies in accordance with the precepts of one's religion or belief.[130]

These United Nations materials could be a valuable resource for the Court as they draw on studies and input from the wider international community. While the overwhelming majority of judges on the Court come from States that are predominantly Christian, the United Nations studies incorporate comments from States with a far wider range of religious demographics. Groups such as Muslims, Hindus, or Buddhists, which are minorities in most Council of Europe States, form majorities in other United Nations member States. Because of this, an issue such as the wearing of religious apparel, which a number of Western authors[131] and judges[132] consider marginal to religion, has been given greater prominence in international materials.[133] Reference to such materials could prove useful to members of the Court in helping to ensure that majoritarian concepts of

---

[129] Krishnaswami study, at 31–42, and draft principles, especially Part II, attached to the report at Annexe 1.

[130] Declaration on Religious Intolerance and Discrimination, Art. 6. This is a more limited list than those in the Krishnaswami study or earlier drafts of the Declaration, although it includes some manifestations not included in those lists, such as the right to communicate with communities on issues of religion at a national and international level.

[131] e.g. Jacques Robert, *Freedom of Conscience, Pluralism and Tolerance, in* FREEDOM OF CONSCIENCE 30–1 (Council of Europe ed., 1993), who says that the wearing of headscarves in French schools could constitute forms of 'pressure, provocation, proselytism or propaganda . . .'. For a more balanced approach see Sebastian Poulter, *Muslim Headscarves in Schools: Contrasting Legal Approaches in England and France*, 17 Ox. J OF LEGAL STUDIES 43 (1997).

[132] *Karaduman v. Turkey*, App. No. 16278/90, 74 Eur. Comm'n H.R. Dec. & Rep. 93 (1993); *Goldman v. Weinberger*, 475 U.S. 503 (1986).

[133] Krishnaswami study, at 33, notes that there may be reasons for preventing the wearing of religious clothing but it is 'generally desirable that persons whose faith prescribes such apparel should not be unreasonably prevented from wearing it'. See also Dinstein, above, note 8, at 150.

what it is to manifest a religion do not gain inappropriate significance in the Court's case law.

6.7 'CONTRACTING OUT' OF RIGHTS

The difficulty caused to applicants by the restrictive test of manifestations used by the Court and Commission is increased by the rulings that, in some cases, applicants have voluntarily agreed to forgo their right to religious freedom.[134] In such cases the Commission has found that there is no breach of Article 9, as long as it is possible to change the situation.[135] The Commission has acknowledged that there may be situations in which the ability of applicants to change their position would require more than could reasonably be expected of them in order to be able to freely practise their religion or belief. In *Darby*, for example, the Commission rejected the argument of Sweden that Mr Darby could avoid paying Church tax by moving permanently to Sweden.[136] In this extreme case, the Commission recognized that the decision of the applicant to live 'voluntarily' in another State was not sufficient grounds to say that he had waived his right to freedom of religion in relation to Church taxes.[137]

There is some justification for this approach. It suggests respect for the autonomy of individuals who are given the opportunity to make choices, as long as they are prepared to live with the consequences of their decisions.[138] The Commission should not put individuals in a position where they are forced to comply with the tenets of their religion, even if they prefer, for example, to take up a job that required them to work on their Sabbath day.[139] The reasoning of the Commission appears to leave it up to individuals to make the choice between the dictates of their religion or belief and the advantages that might be gained by taking a course of action that is inconsistent with manifesting it. This can be important to protect people from the oppression of their own religious group. As former United

---

[134] EVANS, above, note 15, at 301 argues that requiring a degree of personal sacrifice as the price of exercising religious freedom is not incompatible with Art. 9.

[135] VAN DIJK AND VAN HOOF, above, note 10, at 553.

[136] *Darby v. Sweden*, 187 Eur. Ct. H.R. (ser. A) (1990), annex to the decision of the Court at para. 52. People who lived in Sweden could be granted an exemption from Church taxes, whereas people who lived in other countries but worked in Sweden, like Mr Darby, were not eligible for exemptions.

[137] Gunn, above, note 94, at 318; Stavros, above, note 113, at 615.

[138] Conference on Security and Co-operation in Europe, Document of the Copenhagen Meeting of the Conference on the Human Dimension of the CSGE, 1990, para. 32, belonging to a national minority is a matter of personal choice and (32.6) no disadvantage may arise for a person on account of the 'exercise or *non-exercise*' of their minority rights (emphasis added).

[139] One argument that is sometimes made against 'group' minority rights is that they interfere with the ability of members of the group to make precisely this type of autonomous choice.

Nations Special Rapporteur Francesco Caportorti has warned, 'To consider the protection of collective values of the group as the only goal worthy of pursuit by international norms concerning minorities is dangerous in that dissenting individual members could get dragged under the cover of the unitary policy actually carried out by its dominant circles.'[140] While it is worth keeping this caveat in mind, most of the cases that have come before the Commission and Court do not involve individual choice that has been limited by religious groups but rather individual choice limited by the State.

6.7.1 The Voluntary Model and State Churches

Sometimes, however, the Court and Commission apply the notion of voluntarily choosing between a religion or belief and an alternative course of action too simplistically. For example, when the State has acted in a manner that forces the individual to choose between a deeply held belief and some social role, the idea of free choice is strained. One of the contexts in which the problem arises in an acute form is in relation to freedom within a church or religious organization, particularly a State Church. The Commission has held a number of times that a Church is not required to grant religious freedom to its members, as long as those members are free to leave the Church.[141] This includes Church employees, such as ministers, who are required to follow the directions of their employer. As discussed in the previous chapter,[142] the rights of ministers in a State Church or the rights of members of a religion *vis-à-vis* that religion are very limited.

Such decisions treat religion as a type of voluntary, private organization. As long as people have a choice as to whether to remain in or leave a religion, they are subject to the rules of that body in the same ways as golfers must obey the rules of the club to which they belong and pay their dues or leave. This analysis does not consider the ways in which a simple 'obey or leave' model fails to do justice to the complexities of the relationship between a believer and a Church. This is particularly the case where there is involvement in the running of the Church by secular authorities. In the baptism case, the incompatibility between the clergyman remaining a minister of the Church to which he was otherwise committed and his conscientiously held religious beliefs (in relation to the importance of religious instruction before baptism) arose from the order of the secular authorities.[143] Similarly, in a case where a minister was dismissed from his State

---

[140] Francesco Caportorti, *Are Minorities Entitled to Collective International Rights?*, in THE PROTECTION OF MINORITIES AND HUMAN RIGHTS 509 (Yoram Dinstein ed., 1992).

[141] *Knudsen v. Norway*, App. No. 11045/84, 42 Eur. Comm'n H.R. Dec. & Rep. 247, 257 (1985); *Karlsson v. Sweden*, App. No. 12356/86, 57 Eur. Comm'n H.R. Dec. & Rep. 172, 175 (1988).

[142] See the discussion at Chapter 5.4.2.

[143] *X v. Denmark*, App. No. 7374/76, 5 Eur. Comm'n H.R. Dec. & Rep. 157, 158 (1976).

functions for refusing to carry out some functions in protest at the liberalization of abortion laws, his protest and position were well received by his parish and the Church authorities but unacceptable to the State authorities.[144] In such cases to talk about being able to leave the Church as being a sufficient safeguard of conscience denies the role of the State in creating a crisis of conscience in the first place.

Even when the State is not involved, leaving a religion is a far more complex matter than leaving other types of private organizations.[145] For many people religion is not 'voluntary' in the way in which social or political groups may be. To some people in some religions, their religion is the source of truth and salvation. They may disagree with a particular aspect of its structure, such as the requirement, backed by legal sanction, to pay Church taxes,[146] but leaving it could be seen to be of serious detriment to spiritual well-being. On other levels, the decision to leave a tight-knit religious community can be made difficult by the fact that a person has little social, economic, or personal independence from the group, even though they theoretically have a right to leave.[147] In these circumstances, the voluntary organization model that the Commission has used to assume that there is no need for freedom of conscience within a religious organization is problematic.

6.7.2 The Voluntary Model in Other Contexts

The idea of 'voluntarily' contracting out of rights in the context of non-religious groups causes another set of problems. It may be appropriate for the Commission to hesitate to interfere in the internal organization of a religion, not because religions are voluntary organizations, but because such interference runs the risk of itself being an intrusion into the religious freedom of other members of the group in order to protect the freedom of one member.[148] Such considerations do not, however, apply in the context of restrictions placed on religious freedom by non-religious organizations or individuals. In such cases, the Commission has found against Article 9

[144] *Knudsen v. Norway*, App. No. 11045/84, 42 Eur. Comm'n H.R. Dec. & Rep. 247, 257 (1985).

[145] *Fabian v. Switzerland*, App. No. 7562/76, Eur. Comm'n H.R., 16 May 1977, unpublished. The Commission held that no Art. 9 issue was raised by the lack of remedies to be taken against the sexton of a Church who was abusive to the applicants, in part because the applicants were free to continue to attend the Church or were 'free to choose another church'.

[146] *E & GR v. Austria*, App. No. 9781/82, 37 Eur. Comm'n H.R. Dec. & Rep. 42 (1984).

[147] Paul Hayden, *Religiously Motivated 'Outrageous' Conduct: Intentional Infliction of Emotional Distress as a Weapon Against 'Other People's Faiths'*, 34 WM & MARY L. REV. 579, 642–53 (1993), outlines some of the methods used against people who try to leave some religious communities.

[148] This is less the case when the crisis of conscience is not due to a debate within the religion itself but one imposed by State organs.

applicants who have voluntarily accepted employment, taken a university place, or joined an organization that had objects in conflict with their religion or belief. As long as applicants chose to join the organization or accept employment and can choose to leave there is no breach of Article 9 if the rules of the employer or organization are enforced in a way that interferes with their manifestation of a religion or belief.[149]

One example of this type of case is that of the Muslim schoolteacher who was dismissed for taking 45 minutes away from his job on Fridays in order to attend a local mosque.[150] The Commission held that in accepting a job as a teacher without mentioning his religious requirements he had chosen to take employment on the conditions offered, which did not include time off for Friday prayer.[151] In another case, a woman who objected to having to work a Sunday shift for religious and family reasons was held to have no case as she was free to leave her employment if she felt that she could not work on Sundays for religious reasons.[152] No breach of the Convention was found in relation to a Muslim student who was required to have an identity photograph taken without her headscarf (which was against her religious beliefs). The Commission found that, in entering a secular University, she had agreed to abide by the rules, which included the requirement not to wear a headscarf in identity photographs.[153] A military judge who was dismissed because of his alleged connections with fundamentalists,[154] and a military recruit who was disciplined for similar offences,[155] were held to have agreed to submit themselves to army discipline and rules when they joined the army and these rules included some restrictions on their religious freedom.[156]

---

[149] Compare with Catharina Dales, Minister of Home Affairs, the Netherlands, *Opening Speech, in* FREEDOM OF CONSCIENCE 7 (Council of Europe ed., 1993) who explicitly rejects the notion that, as no one is forced to be a public servant, there should be no right of conscientious objection in the public service.

[150] *X v. the United Kingdom*, App. No. 8160/78, 22 Eur. Comm'n H.R. Dec. & Rep. 27 (1981).

[151] *Id.* at 36. The applicant 'remained free to resign if and when he found that his teaching obligations conflicted with his duties as a Muslim'. Stavros, above, note 113, at 616.

[152] *Stedman v. the United Kingdom*, App. No. 29107/95, 89-A Eur. Comm'n H.R. Dec. & Rep. 104, 107–8 (1997). It is possible that, in this case, the *bona fides* of the applicant were somewhat suspect as she had worked on Sundays previously and there was no indication of why her religious needs had changed. Her claim seemed to be more based on problems of family life.

[153] *Karaduman v. Turkey*, App. No. 16278/90, 74 Eur. Comm'n H.R. Dec. & Rep. 93, 108 (1993).

[154] *Kalaç v. Turkey*, 41 Eur. Ct. H.R. (ser. A) 1199, at 1203 (1997-IV).

[155] *Yanasik v. Turkey*, App. No. 14524/89, 74 Eur. Comm'n H.R. Dec. & Rep. 14, 22 (1993).

[156] Though not all types of restrictions were legitimate. The Commission said that in entering a military academy, the applicant accepted that there would be limitations as to the time and place in which religious freedom could be exercised without 'negating it entirely'. In particular, time was put aside for prayer and religious duties. *Id.* at 26.

In all of these cases the Commission determined that the applicants' freedom of conscience and ability to manifest their religion was not infringed because they had some role in choosing the situation that made the exercise of their religion more difficult and they were free to change this situation to one that made the full exercise of their religion or belief possible. Yet the Commission did not consider the difficult situation that this created for many minority groups.[157] In the case of the Muslim school-teacher, for example, his choice was to take less remunerative part-time employment or to give up his profession. This is a choice that was far less likely to face members of England's predominantly Christian schoolteachers for whom the working week (not only in teaching but in most workplaces) had been set up to keep Sundays free. For the Muslim woman who wished to have her photograph taken while wearing a headscarf, her choice was to take up free State education but to compromise her religious beliefs or to pay (if she was able to) for private education in an environment where she could exercise her religious beliefs.[158] In these types of situations, the Commission talks about people having a choice or making a 'voluntary' decision in a context where they may only have a range of unpalatable choices.[159] Professor Malcolm Evans, in his analysis of the decisions of the Court and Commission, notes that the exercise of religious freedom need not be without cost[160] but he does not acknowledge that the price tends to have to be paid more often and more heavily by minorities than it does by the majority for whose beliefs social structures tend to be better designed.[161] A labour relations lawyer has noted the problems that individuals face when the courts assume that workers have contracted out of their rights: 'This insistence on the centrality of contract places the individual in a dilemma. Either the individual in question accepts the terms of the contract in which case he/she will be permitted a scope for the expression of the right depending entirely on the terms of the contract, or he/she declines to accept the terms in which case he/she may be out of employment for some time.'[162]

---

[157] Their minority status being compounded in some cases by the general vulnerability of employees to employer pressure. Gerard Quinn, *Conscientious Objection in Labour Relations*, *in* FREEDOM OF CONSCIENCE 110 (Council of Europe ed., 1993).

[158] Of course, Islam is the majority religion in Turkey but the secular nature of the constitutional and political structure is such that those who wish to exercise certain Muslim religious traditions are effectively turned into a minority.

[159] For a critique of the notion that someone with only a range of unpalatable choices is genuinely autonomous in his or her decision making see JOSEPH RAZ, THE MORALITY OF FREEDOM chapters 14–15 (1986).

[160] EVANS, above, note 15, at 300.

[161] See further discussion of this issue below at Chapter 8.4.5.

[162] Quinn, above, note 157, at 117.

6.8 CONCLUSION

The right to manifest a religion or belief is at the heart of the protection of freedom of religion or belief under the Convention. This is particularly so given that the Court and Commission have given such a narrow reading to the first limb of Article 9. In these circumstances, for all practical purposes, it is only behaviour that is held to be a manifestation of religion or belief that is likely to be given protection under Article 9. While the Court, particularly over the last few years, has been more active than previously in holding that State actions have restricted the right to manifest a religion or belief, it has tended to focus its protection on the core areas of Christian belief, such as worship and proselytism. Cases that have raised less traditional manifestations have been dismissed in part through the development of a restrictive test of practice and in part through determinations that applicants have voluntarily agreed to restrictions on their religion or belief.

Thus the relatively liberal approach taken by the Court and Commission to the definition of religion or belief is subtly undermined at the manifestation stage. As the Commission and Court have taken upon themselves the task of deciding what is necessary to a religion or belief, and as they have performed this task with little reference to expert evidence, international standards, or the claims of the applicants themselves, they have developed a conception of religion or belief that belies their expansive definition of religion or belief. While minorities and individualistic believers are recognized as deserving of protection under the Convention, that protection has only extended to manifestations that are highly analogous to Christian beliefs. Even when an individual has been able to show that a State action interfered with his or her religion or belief, the conception of religion as a voluntary 'club' that the Court and Commission have used has made it difficult for many applicants to make out their case. Both tests disproportionately affect minorities whose practices may be less familiar to the Court and who are likely to be subject to great social pressure from private actors such as employers to forgo their religious practices in order to better assimilate into the dominant culture.

Thus, while manifestation of religion or belief has been given more teeth than the internal freedom of belief, it has very limited scope and provides little protection to non-traditional forms of practice. The Court and Commission in constructing their test for whether there has been a restriction on religion or belief have been strongly sympathetic to the problems caused to States if the right to practise a religion or belief is interpreted too broadly and to the problems that may be caused by fraudulent claims. They have shown little regard for the plight of sincere, committed believers whose claims that States' actions interfere with their religion or belief are routinely dismissed by institutions prepared to substitute their judgement for the judgement of the believers.

7

Limitations on Manifestations of Religion or Belief

7.1 INTRODUCTION

For some believers, the dictates of religion or conscience are absolute. Such people are determined to follow the rules of their religion regardless of the law or the consequences to themselves, including torture or death.[1] Yet it does not follow that the State has to respect all the decisions taken by such people.[2] If freedom of religion is valued by the State and the community as a whole because it promotes autonomy and pluralism, then the State may have a right or even a duty to intervene in religious practices to ensure that they do not destroy the autonomy of others or threaten other aspects of the social order. At one extreme, it is clear that a State is not required in the name of religious freedom to tolerate ritual human sacrifice, even if it genuinely is an essential component of a religious practice.[3] Yet it is also clear that a State cannot cut across important religious practices for little or no reason. Article 9(2) tries to balance out the competing interests between the individual's freedom to manifest a religion or belief and the State's legitimate interests in ensuring that such manifestations do not unduly interfere in public health and order, morality, and the rights and freedoms of others. A number of writers in the field have warned of the difficulties of determining legitimate limitations on religious freedom in the abstract,[4] but some general principles can be extracted from the case law of the Court and Commission.

It might be thought that, as the Court and Commission have given a strict interpretation to the right to manifest a religion or belief, the ability of States to justify their actions under Article 9(2) would consequently be

---

[1] Krishnaswami study, at 1.

[2] Myres S. McDougal, Harold D. Lasswell, and Lung-chu Chen, *The Right to Religious Freedom and World Public Order: The Emerging Norm of Non-Discrimination*, 74 MICH. L. REV. 865, 873 (1976), acknowledge that 'Even so fundamental a freedom as that of religious inquiry, belief and communication must, of course, be exercised and protected with due regard for the aggregate common interest in the preservation of all basic human rights.' A. H. ROBERTSON AND J. G. MERRILLS, HUMAN RIGHTS IN EUROPE 147 (1993); Ben Vermeulen, *Scope and Limits of Conscientious Objection, in* FREEDOM OF CONSCIENCE 81–2 (Council of Europe ed., 1993).

[3] Brice Dickson, *The United Nations and Freedom of Religion*, 44 INT'L & COMP. L.Q. 327 (1995); Krishnaswami study, at 29.

[4] Krishnaswami study, at 29; Donna Sullivan, *Advancing the Freedom of Religion or Belief Through the UN Declaration on the Elimination of Religious Intolerance and Discrimination*, 82 AM. J. INT'L L. 487, 511 (1988).

interpreted restrictively. In the majority of cases that pass the Article 9(1) threshold, the applicant has had to prove that the action that the State has restricted is necessary for the practice of his or her religion or belief under the *Arrowsmith* test.[5] This suggests that the State should take this narrowly defined right seriously and have to discharge a high burden to show that limiting the practice was justified. As this chapter illustrates, however, this has not occurred. While the Commission and Court are prepared to scrutinize State action with some care in cases where there has been overt and intentional discrimination against members of a religious group, they have generally given States a wide margin of appreciation in determining whether or not a restriction on the manifestation of religion or belief is necessary. In most cases it seems to be sufficient in practice for the State to show that it has acted in good faith in order for it to be able to justify limitations on religion or belief under Article 9(2).

Because of the limited scope given to Article 9(1), relatively few cases have been decided under Article 9(2), although it has come to greater prominence recently. In most of these cases, the Commission and Court have paid scant attention to Article 9(1) and either held with little explanation that there has been a breach of Article 9(1) or ignored the Article 9(1) issue altogether.

7.2 THE APPROACH TO ARTICLE 9(1) IN CASES THAT DEAL WITH ARTICLE 9(2)

7.2.1 Cases That Do Not Address Article 9(1) Issues

In some cases the Commission did not consider whether the actions taken by the government restricted the right of freedom of religion or belief because those actions were in any event clearly justified under Article 9(2). This approach allowed the Commission to avoid difficult issues and justified State action without giving any clear indication of what the legal position would be should there be a change in the circumstances.

One such case is *Chappell v. the United Kingdom,*[6] in which a representative of the British Druids challenged the right of the government to ban Druids from Stonehenge during the summer solstice. The Commission decided not to determine whether Druidism was a religion but noted that, if it was, preventing Druids from carrying out their summer solstice rites at Stonehenge would be a limitation on their right to freedom of religion.[7] The Commission ultimately held, however, that the issues arising under Article 9(1)—particularly whether Druidism is a religion—did not need to

---

[5] See above at Chapter 6.5.

[6] *Chappell v. the United Kingdom,* App. No. 12587/86, 53 Eur. Comm'n H.R. Dec. & Rep. 241 (1987).

[7] *Id.* at 246.

be determined as the government had sound justifications under Article 9(2) for banning people from Stonehenge during the summer solstice, i.e. to prevent a repetition of the disorder and lawlessness that had occurred in previous years.[8] Thus the Commission moved straight to a consideration of Article 9(2) without determining whether there was a breach of Article 9(1).

The Commission, in so doing, avoided the difficult but important issue of defining religion or belief. By explicitly refusing to decide whether or not Druidism was a religion or belief, the Commission cast some doubt over the issue, without giving any indication of how the doubt might be resolved. The Druids were left in the position of not having any idea of the scope of their rights or even whether they had any rights under Article 9(1). The United Kingdom was informed that its actions had been justified but given no indication of what its position was should the circumstances that justified the actions change.

The Commission has also assumed a breach of Article 9(1) in cases concerning the scope of the right to manifest a religion or belief. In a case involving a Sikh who was convicted twenty times for failing to wear a motorcycle helmet while driving a motorbike (which he refused to wear as this would have required him to remove his turban), the Commission held that the law requiring the wearing of motorcycle helmets was necessary for the protection of health in accordance with Article 9(2).[9] It did not engage in any discussion of whether a law such as this was a restriction (albeit a permissible one) on the rights of Sikh motorcyclists, merely saying that 'any interference that there *may* have been with the applicant's freedom of religion'[10] was justifiable. A more detailed consideration of the importance of the wearing of a turban to Sikhs and the extent to which the law interfered with that freedom would have better set out the context in which the Commission had to determine whether the law was proportionate and at least made clear whether a law that required a Sikh to remove his turban would be permissible even if there was no pressing social need—a question of considerable importance to many minority religious groups in Europe that require the wearing of some religious apparel.

7.2.2 Cases That Do Find a Breach of Article 9(1)

Even in cases that do find a breach of Article 9(1) the reasoning of the Court or Commission is often sketchy. In *Kokkinakis v. Greece*, for example, it was simply stated in a single sentence by the Court that interfering with proselytism was a restriction on the right to freedom of

---

[8] *Id.* at 246–7.

[9] *X v. the United Kingdom*, App. No. 7992/77, 14 Eur. Comm'n H.R. Dec. & Rep. 234 (1978).

[10] *Id.* at 235 (emphasis added).

religion.[11] Similarly, in a case where a man was convicted for standing outside a cinema loudly proclaiming the sinfulness of drinking and watching pornography, the Commission merely said that it was 'of the opinion' that his conviction for disturbing the peace amounted to a restriction on his freedom to manifest his religion or belief.[12]

It might be argued that the role of the Court and Commission is to make determinations on the facts of particular cases and not to engage in theoretical discussions that are not required in order to settle a particular claim. There are, however, several advantages to the Commission or Court at least briefly addressing the Article 9(1) issues. The first is that such cases at least give some ruling about whether an activity is a manifestation of a religion or belief for the purposes of the Convention.[13] Even if the reasoning that brings the Commission or Court to that conclusion is not detailed, by getting an overview of the facts of various cases where a breach has been found it is at least possible to develop a rough idea of the types of activities that are protected under Article 9(1). Secondly, it gives both applicants and States a better idea of whether the applicant has a right which he or she is entitled to exercise except where the State has good reason to restrict that right or whether this is an area that is unprotected by the right to religious freedom and thus open to government regulation. If the particular circumstances justifying the restriction change, the parties are put in a better position to be able to determine their respective rights and duties without further reference to the Court or Commission.

Perhaps the most important reason, however, as to why the Court and Commission should be cautious in skipping over the Article 9(1) stage is that it is the stage that focuses on the position of the applicant. Such an examination can act as a reminder of the importance of the restricted activity to the believer and may help to focus the minds of judges on the situation of the applicant. Moving to a consideration of Article 9(2) with little or no discussion of Article 9(1) can lead the Court to pay undue attention to the arguments of the government about its justifications for the law and its application, and to lose sight of the importance to the individual of the manifestation of religion in question.

7.3 THE GENERAL APPROACH TO LIMITATION CLAUSES

Once it has been determined or assumed that an applicant's right to manifest a religion or belief under Article 9(1) has been restricted, it is necessary

---

[11] *Kokkinakis v. Greece*, 260-A Eur. Ct. H.R. (ser. A) at 14 (1993).

[12] *Håkansson v. Sweden*, App. 9820/82, 5 Eur. H.R. Rep. 297 (1983).

[13] Malcolm Evans, Religious Liberty and International Law in Europe 330–2 (1997) argues that the Court and Commission have used Art. 9(2) to avoid the complex issue of what constitutes a religion or belief and what amounts to a manifestation of these.

to determine whether this interference can be justified under Article 9(2). Article 9(2) requires States to show that the limitations are 'prescribed by law and are necessary in a democratic society in the interests of public safety, for the protection of public order, health or morals, or for the protection of the rights and freedoms of others'. This structure is similar to that used to determine permissible limitations to a number of other rights in the Convention, in particular Article 8 (the right to privacy), Article 10 (freedom of expression), and Article 11 (freedom of peaceful assembly and association).[14] It is thus worthwhile considering how the Court and Commission generally deal with such clauses, as well as looking at the specific issues raised by freedom of religion or belief.

The Court has taken a similar approach to interpreting the limitation clauses in all the Articles outlined above despite the fact that although the Articles are similar, they are not identical. As outlined in Chapter 3, the drafting of the limitations clause for Article 9 was a controversial process and the drafters rejected the notion that all the rights in the Convention should be subject to the same limitations clause (as had been the case for the Universal Declaration).[15] The final draft of Article 9(2) was the narrowest of the proposed Articles, so the right to manifest a religion or belief is subject to fewer limitations than any of the other rights listed above. The freedom to have or change a religion or belief is subject to no limitations at all. The Court and Commission, however, have tended to deal with Article 9(2) in a roughly similar way to the other limitations clauses. They have interpreted its wording so broadly that there seems to be little difference in practice between the way in which Article 9(2) restricts State action and the way in which the less stringent Article 10(2) does. For example, in the case of a man convicted for Nazi activities, the Commission conflated the Article 9 and Article 10 issues and referred *inter alia* to the State's actions being justified for reasons of 'national security'—a justification that is not mentioned in Article 9.[16] The blurring of boundaries between the different types of justification for restricting manifestations of religion or belief undermines the principle set out by the Court that exemptions to a Convention right must be narrowly construed.[17]

---

[14] Loukis G. Loucaides, Essays on the Developing Law of Human Rights 183–5 (1995).

[15] See the discussion at Chapter 3.2.3.

[16] *X v. Austria*, App. No. 1747/62, 13 Collections 42, 54 (1963); cf. *X v. Italy*, App. No. 6741/74, 5 Eur. Comm'n H.R. Dec. & Rep. 83, 85 (1976), where a very similar conviction was justified only on the basis of the protection of public safety and the rights and freedoms of others.

[17] *Klass v. Germany*, 28 Eur. Ct. H.R. (ser. A) at 21 (1978); *Sunday Times v. the United Kingdom*, 30 Eur. Ct. H.R. (ser. A) (1979).

7.4.1 The General Approach

Articles 9, 10, and 11 all require that any limitations of the rights set out in these articles must be 'prescribed by law'.[18] Article 8 uses the words 'in accordance with law' but it is interpreted in the same manner as the other Articles.[19] The purpose of this requirement is to ensure that rights and freedoms are not restricted except by due process of law, in part because of the procedural safeguards that this implies and in part because of the rule-of-law requirement that a person should know in advance what conduct is prescribed and be able to adjust his or her behaviour accordingly.[20] In most of the cases in which the applicant claims that a restriction was not prescribed by law (and in all of the relevant Article 9 cases) there has been a law of some kind regulating the area. Applicants therefore tend not to complain of the absence of law but rather that the law is not sufficiently clear for the restriction in question to be said to be prescribed by law.

A law that is too vague and general in its terms may not be sufficiently clear for a restriction contained in it to be prescribed by law. In determining the degree of specificity required by the Convention, the Court has set out a test that is reasonably generous to States.

First the law must be adequately accessible: The citizen must be able to have an indication that is adequate in the circumstances of the legal rules applicable to a given case. Secondly, a norm cannot be regarded as a 'law' unless it is formulated with sufficient precision to enable the citizen to regulate his conduct: he must be able—if need be with appropriate advice—to foresee, to a degree that is reasonable in the circumstances, the consequences which a given action may entail. These consequences need not be foreseeable with absolute certainty: experience shows this to be unattainable. Again, whilst certainty is highly desirable, it may bring in its train excessive rigidity and the law must be able to keep pace with changing circumstances. Accordingly, many laws are inevitably couched in terms, which, to a greater or lesser extent, are vague, and whose interpretation and application are questions of practice.[21]

Thus, a law that is drafted in a somewhat vague or broad manner can be given sufficient precision by the interpretation of domestic courts or the agencies that apply the legislation.[22]

---

[18] On the requirement that a restriction be prescribed by law, see generally FRANCIS JACOBS AND ROBIN WHITE, THE EUROPEAN CONVENTION ON HUMAN RIGHTS 302–4 (2nd edn. 1996); LOUCAIDES, above, note 14, at 186–9.

[19] *Sunday Times v. the United Kingdom*, 30 Eur. Ct. H.R. (ser. A) at 30 (1979); EVANS, above, note 13, at 318. The French text uses the same term in all these articles.

[20] *Sunday Times v. the United Kingdom*, 30 Eur. Ct. H.R. (ser. A) at 30–1 (1979).

[21] *Id.* at 31.

[22] *Id.* at 30, held that the requirement of prescription by law can be met by the common law. *Kokkinakis v. Greece*, 260-A Eur. Ct. H.R. (ser. A) at 15 (1993), held that the rulings of courts can give sufficient precision to a vague law.

7.4.2 Prescribed by Law and Article 9

A number of applicants in Article 9 cases have attempted to use the requirement that a restriction on freedom of religion or belief be 'prescribed by law' to turn their particular case into a test case to challenge the validity of the law more generally. This has been the case in particular with broadly drafted laws that specifically target religious behaviour and under which numerous members of a particular religious minority have been targeted. The challenges to the laws prohibiting proselytism in *Kokkinakis*[23] and the regulation of places of worship in *Manoussakis*[24] are examples of this type of case. So far, however, no Article 9 case has succeeded because a restriction on freedom of religion or belief was not prescribed by law. Generally the Court has explicitly held that the legislation under which State action was taken was prescribed by law, despite strong criticism of this approach by some dissenting members of the Court. In the recent *Manoussakis* case, however, the Court appeared to take a more cautious approach to the issue and made no explicit finding in relation to whether the regulations were prescribed by law.

The typical approach of the Court to the issue of whether a restriction is prescribed by law can be seen in *Kokkinakis*, in which the applicant challenged the Greek anti-proselytism law on the ground that the definition of proselytism was so vague that its prohibition was not prescribed by law. The definition of the term proselytism in the Greek law began with the words 'in particular' and caught both direct and indirect attempts to 'intrude' on the beliefs of others.[25] For these reasons, Mr Kokkinakis claimed that the offence was too vaguely defined to be prescribed by law. The majority noted that the law was general but held that any ambiguities in the wording of the law were compensated for by case law, which defined the offence more precisely.[26] They did not consider why, if the Greek courts had really defined the offence suitably, a conviction such as Mr Kokkinakis's could have been upheld through all the appeal levels of the Greek domestic legal system. Judge Pettiti was far more critical of the law. He noted that it was dangerously broad and, especially in an authoritarian

---

[23] *Kokkinakis v. Greece*, 260-A Eur. Ct. H.R. (ser. A) (1993).

[24] *Manoussakis and others v. Greece*, 17 Eur. Ct. H.R. (ser. A) 1347 (1996-IV).

[25] *Kokkinakis v. Greece*, 260-A Eur. Ct. H.R. (ser. A) at 8 (1993). Greek laws nos. 1363/1938 and 1672/1939 defined proselytism as 'in particular, any direct or indirect attempt to intrude on the religious beliefs of a person of a different religious persuasion, with the aim of undermining those beliefs, either by any kind of inducement or promise of an inducement or moral support or material assistance, or by fraudulent means or by taking advantage of his inexperience, trust, need, low intellect or naivety'.

[26] *Id.* at 15. For a discussion of this aspect of the case see T. Jeremy Gunn, *Adjudicating Rights of Conscience under the European Convention on Human Rights, in* Religious Human Rights in Global Perspective: Legal Perspectives 305, 323–4 (Johan D. van der Vyver and John Witte Jr. eds., 1996).

State, it could prove a dangerous weapon. He considered this to be particularly so given the 'vagueness of the charge and the lack of any clear definition of proselytism' in the laws.[27]

Judge Martens went further and held that Mr Kokkinakis's conviction was not only a breach of Article 9 but also of Article 7 of the Convention (which says that no one shall be held guilty of a criminal offence that did not constitute a criminal offence at the time when it was committed).[28] He held that Article 7 was designed to protect individuals from arbitrary prosecution[29] and that the Greek proselytism laws were arbitrary because the definition of proselytism was 'dangerously ambiguous'.[30] Judge Martens was particularly concerned by the fact that the law had the potential to be used as an instrument of oppression.

These deficiencies are such that, in an atmosphere of religious intolerance, section 4 of Law no. 1363/1938 provides a perfect and dangerous instrument for repressing heterodox minorities. The file suggests that in the past it has been indeed used for this purpose, whilst at present such use, to put it mildly, does not seem to be wholly excluded.[31]

He considered there to be serious potential for abuse of such laws, especially given the rise of religious intolerance in Europe.[32] He conceded that the Greek courts had tended in recent times to read the provisions of the law down to mitigate the ambiguity of the text but argued that court rulings are not sufficient protection as, in times of religious intolerance, courts have changed their case law to the detriment of minorities.[33] His concerns in this regard were reiterated by Judge Repik in the later case of *Larissis and others v. Greece*,[34] who noted that since *Kokkinakis*, the Greek courts had adopted an even more subjective approach toward the definition of proselytism and that some of the protections contained in earlier decisions had been undermined by later court cases.[35] These minority judges were prepared to interpret the requirement that restrictions on religious freedom be prescribed by law fairly strictly compared to the majority. Generally this has not been the approach of the Court as a whole, which has focused on the specific facts of the case before it rather than addressing the broader problem that the 'prescribed by law' issue raises. There is some indication, however, in the *Manoussakis* case,[36]

---

[27] *Kokkinakis v. Greece*, 260-A Eur. Ct. H.R. (ser. A) at 21–2 (1993).

[28] *Id.* at 30–3.

[29] *Id.* at 31. Compare with the approach of the majority who, at 18, held that the main purposes of Art. 7 are to prohibit retrospective criminal law and to ensure that the individual who consults the law can foresee whether or not his actions will be punishable.

[30] *Kokkinakis v. Greece*, 260-A Eur. Ct. H.R. (ser. A) at 31 (1993).

[31] *Id.*   [32] *Id.*   [33] *Id.*

[34] *Larissis and others v. Greece*, 65 Eur. Ct. H.R. (ser. A) 363 (1998-V).

[35] *Id.* at 390, partly dissenting opinion of Judge Repik.

[36] *Manoussakis and others v. Greece*, 17 Eur. Ct. H.R. (ser. A) 1347 (1996-IV).

that the Court may be increasingly prepared to subject laws to slightly greater scrutiny. The law in question was set out in a Royal Decree under Law no. 1363/1983 of the Greek parliament, which outlined the criteria that had to be met by applicants in order to operate a place of worship. The wording of the decree 'conferred a number of discretionary powers, each of which was sufficient basis for a negative response to the application'.[37] It also involved the local Orthodox bishop in making decisions as to whether there was a need for additional places of non-Orthodox worship in a particular locality.[38] The Court in this case, as compared to others that have raised the issue, did not expressly hold that the restriction met the 'prescribed by law' test. Rather it noted that this ground of the application was 'directed less against the treatment of which they themselves had been the victims than against the general policy of obstruction pursued in relation to Jehovah's Witnesses. . . . They are therefore in substance challenging the provisions of the relevant domestic law.'[39] The Court refused to deal with the issue of prescription by law as the restriction on religious freedom in *Manoussakis* was incompatible with the Convention on other grounds.[40] However, the Court did not explicitly hold that the regulations were prescribed by law (as it had done in previous cases), and when it came to look at the issue of whether the regulations were necessary in a democratic society it scrutinized the manner in which the regulatory and administrative agencies routinely used the law in a manner that was 'rigid, or indeed prohibitive' to non-Orthodox religions, especially the Jehovah's Witnesses.[41] In relation to this law, as compared to the laws on proselytism, the fact that the Greek courts generally quashed improper convictions under the regulations was not sufficient protection of religious freedom.[42]

Nevertheless, in a case in which the Court clearly had concerns about the scope and potential for abuse of a law, it still refused to consider the issue of whether the restriction of religious freedom was prescribed by law. The reason for this seems to be that the applicant, by raising the issue, was trying to question the very law itself and the Court was reluctant to deal with this issue. Yet if the requirement that a regulation be sufficiently clear to guide the actions of those subjected to it is to be effective, the Court must sometimes be prepared to deal with challenges to the whole law. Given that the Court is supposed to be one of the primary organs for protecting human rights in Europe,[43] it should be prepared to take the wider view of cases such as *Kokkinakis* and *Manoussakis* where it is clear that an oppressive pattern of State behaviour has been conducted under the law in question. While the Court should not be too ready to

---

[37] *Id.* at 15.   [38] *Id.*   [39] *Id.*
[40] *Id.* Compare with the concurring judgment of Judge Martens, at paras. 2–3.
[41] *Id.* at 48.   [42] *Id.* at 48.   [43] See above at Chapter 1.3.2.

undermine State laws, at present the 'prescribed by law' requirement has little real efficacy in the Article 9 context.[44]

7.5 NECESSARY IN A DEMOCRATIC SOCIETY

7.5.1 The Role of the State in Determining Necessity and the Margin of Appreciation

If a restriction on religion or belief is prescribed by law, the Court or Commission then considers whether the law or the manner in which it was applied is 'necessary in a democratic society' for one of the reasons outlined in Article 9(2).[45] The test of what is necessary requires a balancing of a range of complex factors, and in *Handyside v. the United Kingdom*[46] the Court outlined the concept of necessity on which it has drawn in later cases.[47] In interpreting this requirement, the Court has recalled that Contracting States have the primary obligation for the protection of human rights. This is recognized by the Convention in a variety of ways, including the requirement that applicants exhaust domestic remedies before applying to the Court.[48] Thus the Court developed the notion that States have a 'margin of appreciation'[49] in determining whether a particular restriction on a right is required in the given circumstance. This is because

By reason of their direct and continuous contact with the vital forces of their countries, State authorities are in principle in a better position than the international judge to give an opinion on the exact content of these requirements as well as on the 'necessity' of a 'restriction' or 'penalty' intended to meet them. The Court notes at this juncture that, whilst the adjective 'necessary' ... is not synonymous with 'indispensable', neither has it the flexibility of such expressions as 'admissible', 'ordinary', 'useful', 'reasonable' or 'desirable'. Nevertheless, it is for the national

---

[44] Compare with Evans, above, note 13, at 320, who argues that the requirement of prescription by law provides a 'potent source of restraint upon abuse of power'. This is certainly true in theory but has not proved true in practice in the Art. 9 context.

[45] On the general issue of necessity in a democratic society, see Jacobs and White, above, note 18, at 306–9.

[46] *Handyside v. the United Kingdom*, 24 Eur. Ct. H.R. (ser. A) (1976).

[47] The *Handyside* case itself was primarily concerned with freedom of expression, as it was to do with the circulation of the 'Little Red Handbook', an educational textbook on sexual matters which was banned under the Obscene Publications Act 1959 (U.K.). The principles developed in this case, however, have formed the basis of the Court's general approach to the issue of 'necessity' in limitation clauses.

[48] *Handyside v. the United Kingdom*, 24 Eur. Ct. H.R. (ser. A) (1976).

[49] See generally Howard Charles Yourow, The Margin of Appreciation Doctrine in the Dynamic of European Human Rights Jurisprudence (1995); Thomas O'Donnell, *The Margin of Appreciation Doctrine: Standards in the Jurisprudence of the European Court of Human Rights*, 4 Hum. Rts Q. 474 (1982); Timothy H. Jones, *The Devaluation of Human Rights Under the European Convention* 1995 Pub. L. 430; J. G. Merrills, The Development of International Law by the European Court of Human Rights chapter 7 (1993).

authorities to make the initial assessment of the reality of the pressing social need implied by the notion of 'necessity' in this context.[50]

Therefore, while the State is given some discretion in making judgements about the claims of necessity, it does not have infinite room to move. 'The domestic margin of appreciation thus goes hand in hand with a European supervision.'[51] The Court maintains its role as supervisor, granting some but not indefinite leeway to States. This can make it difficult to determine in advance how wide the margin of appreciation may be in any particular case.[52] Some relevant factors to the width of the margin that have been identified by the Court or Commission are the level of consensus on the issue among Contracting States,[53] the extent to which the matter interferes with the core of an applicant's private life,[54] the importance of the right to a democratic and pluralistic society,[55] and the circumstances and background of the particular case.[56] It is not a simple matter of saying that there is a wider margin of appreciation under some Articles than under others.[57]

7.5.2 The Margin of Appreciation in Article 9 Cases

While in theory there is no difference between the margin of appreciation in relation to particular Articles, State respondents in Article 9 cases tend to be given a wide margin of appreciation. The relationship between States and religions in their territories is an inherently controversial one. While Europe may not have the deep religious divisions that exist in some parts of the world, there are a variety of religious demographics in each Contracting State.[58] Consequently, it is difficult for the Court to draw on universal or near-universal European conceptions when determining the width of the margin of appreciation in Article 9 cases. In the *Otto-Preminger* case,[59] for example, the Court held that 'it is not possible to discern throughout Europe

---

[50] *Handyside v. the United Kingdom*, 24 Eur. Ct. H.R. (ser. A) at 22 (1976). For criticism of this approach see Jones, above, note 49, at 436–8.

[51] *Handyside v. the United Kingdom*, 24 Eur. Ct. H.R. (ser. A) at 23 (1976).

[52] Jones, above, note 49, at 432 warns that even when the Court does distinguish principles relevant to the margin of appreciation 'there is little consistency in the use made of them'.

[53] *Sunday Times v. the United Kingdom*, 30 Eur. Ct. H.R. (ser. A) at 36 (1979), held that the 'authority of the judiciary' was a 'far more objective notion' on which there was greater European consensus (and therefore a narrower margin of appreciation) than the area of public morality.

[54] *Manoussakis and others v. Greece*, 17 Eur. Ct. H.R. (ser. A) 1347 at 1364 (1996-IV).

[55] *Sunday Times v. the United Kingdom*, 30 Eur. Ct. H.R. (ser. A) at 40 (1979); *Klass v. Germany*, 28 Eur. Ct. H.R. (ser. A) at 21 (1978).

[56] P. VAN DIJK AND G. J. H. VAN HOOF, THEORY AND PRACTICE OF THE EUROPEAN CONVENTION ON HUMAN RIGHTS 89–90 (3rd edn. 1997).

[57] Though see the argument by Yourow, above, note 49, at 189–93, that a *de facto* hierarchy of rights is being created by the use of the margin of appreciation.

[58] See above at Chapter 2.2.

[59] *Otto-Preminger-Institut v. Austria*, 295 Eur. Ct. H.R. (ser. A) (1994).

a uniform conception of the significance of religion in society . . . even within a single country such conceptions may vary.'[60] In *Wingrove* it reiterated this position, noting that what is likely to cause offence to religious people will differ from time to time and place to place, and that States are in the best position to determine the restrictions on free speech necessary to protect those whose religious feelings would be offended.[61] Thus, at least in relation to the protection of the religious sensibilities of others (which was the issue at stake in these cases), there is a reasonably wide margin of appreciation.[62]

There have been a small number of cases, however, where the Court seems to have considered the issue of religious freedom at stake to be so important as to require a narrower margin. In *Manoussakis*,[63] for example, where freedom of public worship was at issue, the Court said that in 'delimiting the extent of the margin of appreciation in the present case the Court must have regard to what is at stake, namely the need to secure true religious pluralism, an inherent feature of the notion of a democratic society'.[64] One author has suggested that the Court and Commission are more likely to engage in a strict review of laws that seek to regulate religious conduct directly than of general and neutral laws that have the incidental effect of restricting freedom of religion or belief, where the margin of appreciation is wider.[65]

Thus, while the margin of appreciation appears to be relatively wide in relation to most Article 9 cases, the State is not given complete flexibility to decide when an action to restrict religious freedom is necessary. The limits on States' rights can be seen in particular in cases dealing with religious minorities in Greece.[66] Greece has arguably pushed past the limited level of consensus that has been achieved among European States by more vigorously promoting its national Church than other States with a State Church and, perhaps more importantly, by using the law to make it

---

[60] *Id.* at 19. The case itself raised Art. 10 issues as Austria sought to justify its decision to prohibit the showing of a film on the basis that it offended the religious sensibilities of others.

[61] *Wingrove v. the United Kingdom*, 23 Eur. Ct. H.R. (ser. A) 1937 at 1957 (1996-V).

[62] Peter W. Edge, *The European Court of Human Rights and Religious Rights*, 47 INT'L & COMP. L.Q. 680, 684–5 (1998), argues that it is too wide and vaguely defined in the Art. 9 context.

[63] *Manoussakis and others v. Greece*, 17 Eur. Ct. H.R. (ser. A) 1347 (1996-IV)

[64] *Id.* at 1364.

[65] Stephanos Stavros, *Freedom of Religion and Claims for Exemption from Generally Applicable, Neutral Laws: Lessons from Across the Pond?*, 6 EUR. HUM. RTS REV. 607, 620–2 (1997). See further below at Chapter 8.3.

[66] *Kokkinakis v. Greece*, 260-A Eur. Ct. H.R. (ser. A) (1993); *Manoussakis and others v. Greece*, 17 Eur. Ct. H.R. (ser. A) 1347 (1996-IV); *Larissis and others v. Greece*, 65 Eur. Ct. H.R. (ser. A) 363 (1998-V); *Tsavachidis v. Greece*, App. No. 28802/95, Eur. Comm'n H.R., 4 Mar. 1997, unreported.

difficult for minority Churches to operate in Greece. While the Court has been reluctant to hold that any Greek laws are in breach of Article 9 as such, it has been prepared to find that the actions of Greece in prosecuting particular individuals under those laws were not necessary in a democratic society, probably in part because those actions were more extreme than those used in most member States in dealing with groups like the Jehovah's Witnesses.

7.5.3 Proportionality

In determining whether a restriction is 'necessary in a democratic society', the Court and Commission also look to whether a law or its application in a particular case was 'proportionate'. In determining whether the test of proportionality is met the Court and Commission look to whether 'the disadvantage suffered by the applicant is excessive in relation to the legitimate aim pursued by the Government'.[67] Clearly this will depend to a significant degree on the particular facts of the case and the perception of the Court as to the relative importance of the right and the severity of the restrictions. In *Larissis v. Greece*,[68] for example, the conviction of a group of military officers for attempting to proselytize some of the men under their command was held to be proportionate to the end of preventing abuses of the rights and freedoms of others even though the conviction of the same men for attempting to proselytize civilians was held to be disproportionate to the end sought.[69] In this case, the Court was willing to accept that any attempt at proselytism by senior officers was an abuse of power, despite the arguments in the dissenting judgment of Judge Van Dijk, who considered this absolute approach to be disproportionate. He felt that there should be a presumption of abuse in such cases but that it should be rebuttable.[70] He decided that the presumption should have been rebutted in regard to one junior officer who claimed that he first approached the senior officers, that they never pressured him, and that he converted to the Pentecostal Church of his own free will.[71]

Ultimately, the notion of proportionality will always contain some subjective element and depend significantly on the context. The Court has

---

[67] *National Union of Belgian Police v. Belgium*, 1 Eur. H.R. Rep. 578, 595 (1979–80).

[68] *Larissis and others v. Greece*, 65 Eur. Ct. H.R. (ser. A) 363 (1998-V).

[69] *Id.* at 381–2. This was so despite the fact the some of the civilians were in a state of some emotional vulnerability.

[70] *Id.* at 392.

[71] *Id.* at 393. Compare also to the approach of Prime Minister Nehru of India who, in speaking against a Bill to regulate conversion, argued that the Bill 'will not help very much in suppressing evil methods [of gaining converts], but it might very well be the cause of great harassment to a large number of people'. Cited in the Krishnaswami study, at 9.

always been rather vague about the idea of proportionality, and the role that it plays in Article 9 jurisprudence is somewhat obscure. It is useful to the Court in allowing it to hold that an application of a law in a particular case is not necessary in a democratic society, without undermining the integrity of the law as a whole. It was used in this way in *Kokkinakis* where the Court expressly approved the anti-proselytism laws but held that Mr Kokkinakis's conviction under them was not necessary to preserve the rights and freedoms of others.[72] Judge Martens took a more robust approach to the role of proportionality in the case, and criticized the Court's judgment as touching only 'incidentally' on the crucial question of whether the State is allowed under Article 9 to make proselytism a *criminal offence*.[73] Judge Pettiti also concluded that the use of a general criminal law for this purpose was inappropriate.[74] While he conceded that governments need to protect small groups of particularly vulnerable people (for example, minors and the intellectually handicapped) that could be done by very specific legislation. Otherwise, proselytizing should only be a criminal offence if it breached other, general laws such as 'misrepresentation, failure to assist persons in danger and intentional or negligent injury'.[75] A vaguely worded law criminalizing proselytism *per se* was not proportionate to the aim of protecting a small number of vulnerable people.

The majority took none of this reasoning into account. They moved from the position that proselytism can be improper because it may interfere with the rights and freedoms of others to the conclusion that the State must have the right to make proselytism a criminal offence. This does not necessarily follow. It may be quite possible for States to prevent the harm that may be done without targeting specifically religious behaviour such as proselytism.[76] Proportionality could be used in Article 9 cases to question whether the whole law, particularly when the law imposes criminal penalties, is necessary in a democratic society. Yet, at least in the Article 9 context, the Court has been reluctant to push the doctrine of proportionality further than the very factual/contextual approach that does not call the law itself into question. It has not, for example, used the notion of proportionality to question whether laws could have been drafted in a way that was less restrictive to the right to freedom of religion or belief without damaging the overall aim of the legislation[77] or whether civil remedies might be a more appropriate response to complex issues such as proselytism rather than the criminal law.

---

[72] *Kokkinakis v. Greece*, 260-A Eur. Ct. H.R. (ser. A) at 17 (1993).
[73] *Id.* at 33, partly dissenting judgment of Judge Martens.
[74] *Id.* at 22, partly concurring judgment of Judge Pettiti.
[75] *Id.* at 21–2.
[76] JACOBS AND WHITE, above, note 18, at 214–15.
[77] Discussed further below at Chapter 8.4.2.

7.6 LEGITIMATE AIM

Any restriction placed on freedom to manifest a religion or belief must be necessary in a democratic society 'in the interests of public safety, for the protection of public order, health or morals, or for the protection of the rights and freedoms of others'. Thus States cannot simply argue that their actions were necessary for the pursuit of any State interest, but have to show that the actions had a 'legitimate aim'. For example, a law that has the protection of public order as its aim has a legitimate aim for the purposes of justifying a restriction on a manifestation of religion or belief. On the other hand, a law that has the (otherwise entirely proper) aim of advancing scientific knowledge does not have a legitimate aim in so far as justifying breach of the Convention is concerned. At least in theory, limitations such as national security that are mentioned in other Articles but not in Article 9 should not be considered a legitimate aim to justify the restriction of religious freedom.[78] The Court has not been prepared to uphold the claims of States that have argued in favour of certain restrictions on the basis that they had a legitimate aim because they upheld tradition or historical links between a religion and the State.[79] While in these cases the Court has not addressed the issue explicitly, the failure of the Court to acknowledge the legitimacy of these aims suggests that it recognizes that the reasons that States may give for restricting freedom of religion or belief are limited to those in Article 9(2).

One of the key issues in determining whether a law has a legitimate aim is the extent to which the Court or Commission is prepared to accept a State's assertions as to the aim of the legislation in question. In *Kokkinakis v. Greece*, for example, the majority was prepared to accept that Greek laws on proselytism had the aim claimed by the Greek government, i.e. the protection of the rights and freedoms of those who may be subject to proselytism.[80] As discussed in Chapter 5,[81] Judge Martens questioned whether the State was justified in attempting to 'protect' others from proselytism,

---

[78] Yoram Dinstein, *Freedom of Religion and Religious Minorities, in* THE PROTECTION OF MINORITIES AND HUMAN RIGHTS 152 (Yoram Dinstein ed., 1992). The International Covenant on Civil and Political Rights does not permit limitations on the basis of national security either. See United Nations Human Rights Committee, General Comment on Article 18.

[79] *Manoussakis and others v. Greece*, 17 Eur. Ct. H.R. (ser. A) 1347 at 1362 (1996-IV). The Greek government argued that the laws restricting the building of non-Orthodox temples had a legitimate aim in part because of the role of the Orthodox Church in keeping 'alive the national conscience and Greek patriotism during periods of foreign occupation'. In *Buscarini and others v. San Marino*, App. No. 24645/94, Eur. Ct. H.R., 18 Feb. 1999, unreported, at para. 32, the government of San Marino argued that an oath of office was not religious but had 'historical and social' significance and was based in tradition. The Court did not address either argument explicitly but in neither case did it find that the claims constituted a legitimate aim.

[80] *Kokkinakis v. Greece*, 260-A Eur. Ct. H.R. (ser. A) at 16 (1993).

[81] See above at Chapter 5.6.

as the State should be entirely indifferent as to whether a person maintained or changed his or her religion. The majority did not explore this issue, nor Judge Pettiti's claim that the purpose of the law was to give the State 'the possibility of arrogating to itself the right to assess a person's weakness in order to punish a proselytiser, an interference that could become dangerous if resorted to by an authoritarian State'.[82] The majority did not consider the evidence provided by the applicant that the broadly drafted laws, which seemed on their face to be aimed at improper proselytism, were actually used as tools by the Orthodox majority to repress religious minorities. The evidence of the applicant in this regard seemed quite strong, as no member of the Orthodox Church had ever been charged under the laws, while between 1975 and 1992, 4,400 Jehovah's Witnesses were arrested, 1,233 were committed for trial, and 208 were convicted for breaches of the law.[83] In light of these criticisms, there seems to be reason for the Court to give critical consideration to whether Greece's claims about the aims of the legislation could be justified.[84]

The reasons for the Court's reluctance to test whether the justifications advanced by a State are a façade are fairly clear: the State is likely to have a better understanding of why a law was passed than the Court or Commission and, if the Court challenges the State's purported purpose, it is accusing the State of bad faith and mendacity. The Court will therefore prefer to find that a law has the legitimate aim that a State has claimed.[85] While this is understandable, it has, at times, tied the Court's hands in cases where the law seems to have an underlying improper purpose. The test of legitimacy of aim has become such a weak one that at present, at least in the Article 9 context, it places little constraint on States that can make a plausible case for saying that the aim of a law falls into one of the headings mentioned in Article 9(2).

The problem is exacerbated by the fact that the Court and Commission sometimes blur the boundaries between the types of justifiable limitation. In the early Commission cases, in particular, the Commission often merely

---

[82] *Kokkinakis v. Greece*, 260-A Eur. Ct. H.R. (ser. A) at 21 (1993), partly concurring decision of Judge Pettiti.

[83] *Id.* at 11. The figures were provided by the applicant but were not challenged by the Greek government, which merely noted that the number of prosecutions had decreased over the past two years.

[84] This conclusion by the Court leads Gunn, above, note 26, at 324 to conclude that the requirement that the law have a legitimate aim is 'in fact a meaningless requirement'.

[85] *Wingrove v. the United Kingdom*, 23 Eur. Ct. H.R. (ser. A) 1937 at 1955 and 1957 (1996-V). Even the British blasphemy laws that only protected the Christian religion had a legitimate aim of protecting religious sensibilities, even though it did not extend to all religions. Compare with the dissenting opinion of Judge Lohmus, at para. 4, 'The law of blasphemy only protects the Christian religions and, more specifically the established Church of England . . . The aim of the interference was therefore to protect the Christian faith alone and not other beliefs. This in itself raises the question whether the interference was "necessary in a democratic society".'

listed a number of limitations (for example, public order and the rights of others) and said that the actions taken by a State were necessary for those reasons, with little explanation given for why this was the case. In the *Chappell* case, for example, the Commission concluded that the decision of the government to close Stonehenge was necessary 'in the interests of public safety, for the protection of public order *or* for the protection of the rights and freedoms of others'.[86] The use of the word 'or' in particular creates the impression that the Commission was being vague about what it was that the government had proved.

Of course, there may be more than one ground for saying that a restriction is necessary under Article 9(2). A religious parade which is likely to lead to rioting and outbreaks of inter-faith hostility could be banned on the grounds that it is necessary to protect public order (to prevent rioting), to protect public health (of the people likely to be injured if public order breaks down), and to protect the rights and freedoms of others (for example, people who may be victimized because of their religion or belief, or property owners whose buildings may be damaged). Nevertheless, an approach that merely lists the possible grounds which a State could have for restricting the right to manifest a religion or belief without any explanation as to why they apply in this case or of the rights of applicants against which they have to be balanced [87] creates the impression that far more consideration is being given to the concerns of States than to the rights of individuals. Such an approach also tends to blur the distinction between a law having a legitimate aim in general terms and the question of whether the application of the law in the particular case was necessary and proportionate.

The way in which the Court and Commission look at the issue of whether a particular restriction has a legitimate aim and whether the particular restriction is necessary can be illustrated by looking at some cases that have arisen under each of the justifications set out in Article 9(2).

7.7 THE GROUNDS FOR RESTRICTING MANIFESTATIONS OF RELIGION OR BELIEF

7.7.1 Necessary in the Interests of Public Safety and for the Protection of Public Order

Manifestations of religious beliefs can give rise to real concerns over public safety and public order. These two heads of justification for restrictions on freedom of religion or belief tend to be taken together, with public safety

---

[86] *Chappell v. the United Kingdom*, App. No. 12587/86, 53 Eur. Comm'n H.R. Dec. & Rep. 241, 247 (1987) (emphasis added).

[87] Ironically, it was for precisely such lack of specificity that the Court condemned the Greek government in *Kokkinakis v. Greece*, 260-A Eur. Ct. H.R. (ser. A) at 17 (1993).

rarely being used as the sole ground for limiting manifestations of religion or belief. There is clearly a need to allow restrictions to protect public order and safety, as some religious groups may be involved in inciting or organizing acts of violence.[88] Such measures may also be necessary in societies where there is antagonism and intolerance between religious communities, where religious practices may become the focus for inter-religious hatred and public disorder.[89]

Yet the public order limitation also has the potential to be interpreted very widely to allow States to intervene in religious practices at any time that they become inconvenient or annoying to those in power.[90] This danger is increased by interpretations of these terms that broaden their scope. The Commission has, for example, held that a State was justified in using the public order justification to restrain someone whose actions caused 'public indignation'—a lower test than set out in the Convention.[91] Similarly some authors describe the public order and safety limitations as 'public interest limitations'.[92] This term is far more sweeping than the two more precise terms actually used in the Convention. The importance of not giving too wide an interpretation to the notion of public order is underlined by the French text. Rather than the relatively broad term *ordre public*, that could refer to a wide range of public interests and is used in a number of international instruments, the Convention uses the more restrictive term *la protection de l'ordre*.[93]

---

[88] A case that demonstrates the potential disruption to public order and safety that can be caused by a religious group is *Omkaranda and the Divine Light Zentrum v. Switzerland*, App. No. 8118/77, 25 Eur. Comm'n H.R. Dec. & Rep. 105 (1981) in which the leader of a religious group was imprisoned and faced expulsion because of his involvement with organizing the religious group which he led in acts of criminal violence. See also *X. v. the United Kingdom*, App. No. 6084/73, 3 Eur. Comm'n H.R. Dec. & Rep. 62 (1975), which held that free expression of belief does not include incitement to desert the army, murder officers, and supply weapons to the IRA.

[89] The Protestant marches that enter Catholic areas in Northern Ireland are an example of this problem. See generally Theo van Boven, *Advances and Obstacles in Building Understanding and Respect Between People of Diverse Religions and Beliefs*, 13 HUM. RTS. Q. 437, 441–2 (1991). Intolerance or antagonism may also arise between a religious group and non-religious groups, e.g. *Plattform Ärzte v. Austria*, App. No. 10126/82, 44 Eur. Comm'n H.R. Dec. & Rep. 65 (1985), involved clashes between a Catholic anti-abortion group and a socialist group supportive of the right to abortion.

[90] Luis Fernando Martinez-Ruiz, *Comment in* FREEDOM OF CONSCIENCE 66 (Council of Europe ed., 1993).

[91] In *Håkansson v. Sweden*, App. 9820/82, 5 Eur. H.R. Rep. 297 (1983), the conviction of a man for loudly proclaiming the evils of alcohol was found to be necessary for the protection of public order, even though the Swedish legislation only required, and the Commission merely held, that his actions had caused 'public indignation'.

[92] See e.g. EVANS, above, note 13, at 324.

[93] See SUBRATA ROY CHOWDHURY, RULE OF LAW IN A STATE OF EMERGENCY: THE PARIS MINIMUM STANDARDS OF HUMAN RIGHTS NORMS IN A STATE OF EMERGENCY 221 (1989); PATRICK THORNBERRY, INTERNATIONAL LAW AND THE RIGHTS OF MINORITIES 192 (1991). LOUCAIDES, above, note 14, at 189 notes that this is only one of a number of places in which the English and French texts of the limitations clauses are not precise equivalents.

One area in which public order has frequently been claimed as a justification is the prisoner cases.[94] In these cases it has simply been assumed that an enclosed and isolated prison community has a *'public* order'.[95] While it may be justifiable to assume that analogous reasoning applies to the order and safety of the enclosed prison community as to the broader public, the burden on the State to show why a restriction is required seems to be greatly reduced, in practice if not in theory, in prison cases.[96] This approach can be compared to the approach of the United Nations Human Rights Committee, which has noted that persons such as prisoners 'continue to enjoy their rights to manifest their religion or belief to the fullest extent compatible with the specific nature of the constraint'.[97]

An example of a case in which there was a reasonable argument for the need to restrict a prisoner's right to manifest his religion is *Childs v. the United Kingdom.*[98] The applicant in this case was a multiple murderer who had given evidence against a number of other inmates and was thus likely to cause disruption in the prison. He was held in solitary confinement and was generally not permitted to attend chapel services as the prison governor had determined that his presence would be likely to lead to a disturbance in the service. In this type of case, it is possible to see the relevance of public order limitations. A prisoner who is not only a dangerous criminal himself but who has incurred the enmity of other prisoners has the potential to create serious disruption to the prison community and to endanger his own safety and that of others (such as prison guards who would have to protect him against attacks from other inmates) if permitted to attend services. The Commission also noted that the applicant was visited by the prison chaplain on a regular basis and was allowed to attend some services.[99] The United Kingdom could therefore show that it was trying to protect the applicant's religious freedom as best it could in the circumstances.

---

[94] e.g. *X v. Austria*, App. No. 1753/63, 16 Collection 20 (1965); *Childs v. the United Kingdom*, App. 9813/82, Eur. Comm'n H.R., 1 Mar. 1983, unreported.

[95] EVANS, above, note 13, at 325. *Engles v. the Netherlands*, 22 Eur. Ct. H.R. (ser. A) at 41 (1977), held that public order 'also covers the order that must prevail within the confines of a special social group'. The case dealt with military discipline, but the principle extends to prison communities.

[96] At one time the Commission developed the notion that some rights contained an 'inherent limitation' which meant that they did not apply or applied in a more restricted way in the context of prisons. The Court, however, disapproved of the idea in *De Wilde, Ooms & Versyp v. Belgium*, 12 Eur. Ct. H.R. (ser. A) (1979–80). See JACOBS AND WHITE, above, note 18, at 297–301; COUNCIL OF EUROPE, HUMAN RIGHTS IN PRISONS 21–36 (1986).

[97] United Nations Human Rights Committee, General Comment on Article 18, para. 8; Resol. (73)5 of the Committee of Ministers of the Council of Europe, Standard Minimum Rules for the Treatment of Prisoners, Appendix of Standard Minimum Rules, Arts. 41 and 42.

[98] *Childs v. the United Kingdom*, App. No. 9813/82, Eur. Comm'n H.R., 1 Mar. 1983, unreported.

[99] The applicant claimed that this was not the case but the Commission referred to correspondence with the Bishop of Wakefield who stated that the prisoner was being seen regularly by the chaplain. *Id.* at 2.

Other cases that have relied on public order rationales in the prison context seem less justifiable.[100] In one such case the decision of the prison to deny a prisoner access to a journalist was justified, *inter alia*, on the grounds of public order, though it was not made clear whether it was disorder inside the prison that would occur if the prisoner was allowed to speak to a journalist or the likely disruption to order in the wider public if the journalists had been allowed access to the prisoner.[101] Neither outcome seems particularly likely and the Commission gave no explanation of its reasoning. In another case, a Buddhist prisoner claimed that he was not able to exercise his religion in a number of ways, including growing a beard and having a prayer chain.[102] In this case the Commission denied that either restriction was a breach of the Convention on the grounds that they were necessary in order to maintain public order. The refusal to let the prisoner grow a beard was based on a claim about the need to be able to identify the applicant (a claim that seems rather peculiar, particularly if he was the only prisoner whose religion required him to grow a beard).[103] The refusal to let him have a prayer chain was based in part on concerns for the prisoner's health and in part on prison discipline.[104] Similarly a prisoner who wished to communicate with co-religionists through the publication of articles in a Buddhist magazine was prohibited from doing so because of the extra administrative problems that this would cause the prison authorities.[105] In these cases fairly trivial justifications, which seem to be based largely on the need for rigorous prison discipline, were held by the Commission to justify a defence that the actions were needed in the interests of public order or safety.[106]

Outside the prison context, public order has been relevant to a number of cases although, as with the prison cases, it is often used as one of a number of justifications rather than the sole reason for a restriction. One area in which it has featured is that of public planning. In the case of *ISKCON v. the United Kingdom*,[107] local planning laws were enforced

---

[100] For an overview of the cases see COUNCIL OF EUROPE, HUMAN RIGHTS IN EUROPE 91–5 (1986).

[101] *X v. Belgium*, App. No. 3914/69, 34 Collection 20, 22 (1970).

[102] *X v. Austria*, App. No. 1753/63, 16 Collection 20 (1965).

[103] *Id.* at 26.   [104] *Id.* at 27.

[105] *X. v. the United Kingdom*, App. No. 5442/72, 1 Eur. Comm'n H.R. Dec. & Rep. 41, 42 (1974).

[106] Stavros, above, note 65, at 621, concludes that, 'It would not be unfair to say that the requirements of public order in prisons or on the streets were to a certain degree exaggerated in the Commission's reasoning' in a number of the cases discussed here. JACOBS AND WHITE, above, note 18, at 217 conclude that 'the Commission is somewhat unsympathetic to complaints of interference with religious freedom by prisoners'. Malcolm Shaw, *Freedom of Thought, Conscience and Religion, in* THE EUROPEAN SYSTEM FOR THE PROTECTION OF HUMAN RIGHTS 445, 459 (R. StJ. Mcdonald, F. Matscher, and H. Petzold eds., 1993), argues that 'the Commission has drawn too widely the principle with regard to prisoners'.

[107] *ISKCON and Others v. the United Kingdom*, App. No. 20490/92, 76-A Eur. Comm'n H.R. Dec. & Rep. 90, 91 (1994).

against a Hindu temple that had been built in a greenbelt area near a fairly small village. These planning laws restricted the uses to which the temple could be put and the number of people who could attend. The number of attendees had begun to exceed greatly the number for which the temple had originally been given permission to operate and the influx of people was beginning to cause problems in the village. The United Kingdom argued the case on the basis that it had acted to protect the 'rights and freedoms of others'—in this case the rights of people who lived in the village. The Commission agreed, but held that there was an additional justification, not suggested by the parties, for the restrictions. This justification was that the laws were for the 'protection of public order or health . . . in that planning legislation is generally accepted as necessary in modern society to prevent uncontrolled development'.[108] Similarly, in *Manoussakis*,[109] the Court held that laws requiring government permission for the establishment of a place of worship were justifiable in the name of public order as they allowed the State to ensure that a religious association was not carrying out harmful activities before giving the religion a permit to operate a place of worship. Thus, public order considerations can often be used to justify restrictions under planning laws, an area where the Court had already held that a State has a wide margin of appreciation.[110]

The *ISKCON* case, though subject to criticism,[111] shows up the areas in which public order justifications may be appropriate. Whether or not the Commission got the balance right in the particular case, there is a need for States to be able to protect a village flooded with thousands of visitors for whom there are inadequate facilities, just as it might be appropriate to subject religious processions to the same restrictions as other public processions or to require religious services to be conducted in a way that shows some respect for those who live in the vicinity of the place of worship. Here, the issue of proportionality again arises, and the need to weigh a range of complex and to a certain extent immeasurable factors causes

---

[108] *Id.* at 106.

[109] *Manoussakis and others v. Greece*, 17 Eur. Ct. H.R. (ser. A) 1347 at 1362 (1996-IV).

[110] *Sporrong and Lonnöth*, 52 Eur. Ct. H.R. (ser. A) at 26 (1982), cf. *Manoussakis and others v. Greece*, 17 Eur. Ct. H.R. (ser. A) 1347 at 1369 (1996-IV), concurring decision of Judge Martens, who noted that the requirement of prior authorization for building a place of worship may be appropriate in some circumstances but could also be used to disguise intolerance. When planning permission is required for places of worship, it should be absolutely clear that the permission in no way depends on the tenets of the religion and permission should be given unless 'very exceptional, objective and *insuperable* grounds of public order make that impossible'.

[111] Stavros, above, note 65, at 622 notes that in this case the Commission's usual test of whether there was a 'pressing social need' for the law was replaced by questioning whether the authorities had given 'adequate weight' to the religious needs of the Hindu community. See also Sebastian Poulter, *Rights of Ethnic, Religious and Linguistic Minorities*, 3 Eur. Hum. Rts. L. Rev. 254, 259 (1997); Shantilal Ruparell, *ISKCON: More than a Planning Dispute*, 6(43) Lawyer 10 (1992).

significant difficulties. It is difficult to argue, for example, that there is any 'objective' way in which to balance the inconvenience caused to people wakened by an amplified Muslim call to prayer in the early hours against the damage done to religious freedom by prohibiting such calls. The difficulty in balancing these factors tends to lead to the argument that such decisions are best left in the hands of the domestic governments. The rationales given by States in this type of case therefore do not seem to be subject to a significant degree of scrutiny by the Commission. While public planning concerns are legitimate and can probably appropriately be dealt with under the heading of public order and safety, there seems to be little explicit recognition by the Commission that these concerns are not, in all cases, overwhelming.

Proportionality requires a balancing of general public concerns with the rights that are at stake and, in a number of cases dealing with public order and safety limitations, the Commission seemed more concerned to determine whether there was any justification for a State's claim of public policy than to weigh this against the restrictions on religious freedom. Public safety and order can, in some contexts, be vital justifications for restricting manifestations of religion or belief in order to protect lives and prevent widespread social disorder. Yet in other contexts, such as the details of prison or planning laws, the social need is less pressing and more attention needs to be paid to the burden that such restrictions place on applicants. There is a danger that, in the Article 9 context, public safety and order may become equated with mere administrative convenience.[112]

Recently, however, the Court seems to have recognized the potential dangers in allowing the public order arguments to extend too far. In the *Buscarini* case,[113] for example, the argument of the government that a religious oath was necessary to maintain public trust in the legislature and therefore to protect public order was dismissed by the Court, which simply held that such an oath was not necessary in a democratic society.[114] The argument of San Marino in this case was so weak that it may not signal a real change of approach to the interpretation of public order, but the decision of the Court in *Serif v. Greece*[115] does indicate that States may now have their claims under Article 9(2) subject to greater scrutiny. In that case the Greek government argued that it needed to prosecute a man claiming to be the Mufti of a local Muslim community because of the

---

[112] Krishnaswami study, at 23, warns that 'while the maintenance of social cohesion may be a legitimate aspiration, it has only too often been invoked by States and by predominant groups within States to justify tyranny and persecution'.

[113] *Buscarini and others v. San Marino*, App. No. 24645/94, Eur. Ct. H.R., 18 Feb. 1999, unreported.

[114] *Id.* at para. 39.

[115] *Serif v. Greece*, App. No. 38178/97, Eur. Ct. H.R., 14 Dec. 1999, unreported.

potential for public unrest and tension that could arise if two people claimed to be the legitimate leaders of the same religious community. This type of claim may well have succeeded in the past, but in *Serif* the Court rejected the arguments of Greece. It held that

Although the Court recognises that it is possible that tension is created in situations where a religious or any other community becomes divided, it considers that this is one of the unavoidable consequences of pluralism. The role of the authorities in such circumstances is not to remove the cause of tension by eliminating the pluralism, but to ensure that the competing groups tolerate each other.[116]

This strong affirmation of the importance of religious pluralism is a welcome development and one that has the potential to change the approach of the Court to the whole interpretation of Article 9(2), if it is followed in other cases. It may be that States that wish to argue that public order considerations make it necessary to limit religious freedom will now be expected to produce much more evidence of the threat to public order and also to show that they could not contain the tension by taking measures to improve inter-religious relationships.

7.7.2 Necessary for the Protection of Health

It is in the nature of some religious traditions that certain practices have the potential to cause physical or mental harm to participants or to outsiders. When it comes to the protection of the health of those who are not members of a religion, the issue is relatively simple and the need for the State to be able to intervene to protect third parties is clear. In some of the prison cases referred to above there was a threat to the health of others if the applicants had been allowed to fully manifest their religion. In *Childs*,[117] for example, there was a threat to the health and safety of others if the applicant's presence provoked violence at a religious service. Likewise, a case in which a prisoner was not permitted to have a religious book that included a section on martial arts was justified on the basis that the prisoner could use the knowledge gained from the book in a manner that threatened the health and safety of others.[118]

While laws to protect third parties from the detrimental physical effects of the exercise of religious freedom of others are relatively unproblematic, laws that seek to protect adult religious believers from risks that they have

---

[116] *Id.* at para. 53.

[117] *Childs v. the United Kingdom*, App. 9813/82, Eur. Comm'n H.R., 1 Mar. 1983, unreported.

[118] *X v. the United Kingdom*, App. No. 6886/75, 5 Eur. Comm'n H.R. Dec & Rep. 100 (1976). Although the Commission in this case used the justification that prohibiting the book was necessary to protect the rights and freedoms of others, presumably these rights and freedoms were largely related to freedom from physical harm.

chosen themselves raise more complex issues.[119] One of the key areas where problems have arisen in domestic jurisdictions has been that of the refusal of medical treatment, such as blood transfusions, on religious grounds.[120] This type of case has not yet arisen under the Convention and, if it did so, it would squarely raise the issue of whether the State is permitted under the Convention to force protection of health on to a person who, for religious reasons, rejects that protection.

There have been a number of cases that have come before the Commission that suggest that the State does have a right to force protection of health even on those who have a serious religious reason for rejecting the protection. One such case was that of the Sikh motorcyclist who was convicted twenty times for refusing to wear his motorcycle helmet, as this would have required him to remove his turban.[121] The Commission conflated the idea of a law having a legitimate aim (the protection of the safety of motorcycle riders) with the idea of necessity in application to hold that the claim was manifestly ill-founded. It was quite open to the Commission to hold that the law itself was valid, while its application to Sikhs was disproportionate to the end sought. While it might generally be appropriate to protect people from carelessness or recklessness for their health, it is not clear that it is necessary to protect people when they object on deeply held religious grounds to such protection. As Professor Raz concludes, using the Sikh motorcyclists as a case in point, if 'the ideals of autonomy and pluralism are not enough to enable a person to pursue his moral convictions at his own expense, then they count for very little indeed'.[122] One explanation for the outcome in the Sikh motorcyclist case is that the Commission and Court have been reluctant to hold that the application of a general and neutral law to a person can breach freedom of religion. This reluctance makes it difficult for adults to argue on religious grounds against the application to them of generally applicable safety laws.[123]

Other cases seem to bear out this conclusion. Both *Childs*[124] and the case in which the Buddhist prisoner was denied a prayer chain[125] used the harm

---

[119] J. E. S. Fawcett, The Application of the European Convention on Human Rights 249 (1987) argues that the protection under the Convention is of public health and it is thus difficult to see how injury caused by the individual to him- or herself can be covered by the provision.

[120] For an overview of American cases on this issue see Note, *Jehovah's Witnesses and the Refusal of Blood Transfusions, A Balance of Interests*, 33 Cath. Law. 361 (1991).

[121] *X. v. the United Kingdom*, App. No. 7992/77, 14 Eur. Comm'n H.R. Dec. & Rep. 234 (1978); Melanie DiPietro, *Fact Finding Faith*, 3 J. of Contemp. Health L. & Pol. 185 (1987).

[122] Joseph Raz, The Authority of Law 283 (1979). However, cases in the USA dealing with the refusal of medical treatment by adults have taken into account other factors, such as whether a person who refuses the treatment is pregnant or has responsibility for children, which can complicate the issue. See Note, above, note 120, at 372–9.

[123] See discussion at Chapter 8.3.

[124] *Childs v. the United Kingdom*, App. 9813/82, Eur. Comm'n H.R., 1 Mar. 1983, unreported.

[125] *X v. Austria*, App. No. 1753/63, 16 Collection 20 (1965).

that could come to the prisoner as a reason for refusing to allow the prisoner to manifest his religion or belief. While there may be a greater justification for such an approach in prison cases as compared to cases dealing with free adults, as the State has a higher duty of protective care to those in its custody than it has for other people, this aspect of the prison cases has never been explicitly examined by the Commission or Court. Outside the Article 9 context, however, the Court has held that the State had not breached various rights of the applicants who had been jailed for performing consensual sadomasochistic homosexual acts in their home.[126] The Court held that this was an area in which the United Kingdom could intervene to protect the health of those participating, even though such intervention was not welcome.[127] This suggests that applicants might have difficulty convincing the Court that the State had no right to protect them from damage caused to their health by reason of their religious beliefs. It is possible, however, that the Court would consider those who wished to injure themselves or allow harm to come to themselves because of deeply held religious beliefs as worthier of protection than a sado-masochistic group.[128]

The other area that tends to be controversial in the health context is that of children who are endangered by their parents' religious beliefs. This endangerment may take the form of their parents refusing medical treatment, such as a blood transfusion, on behalf of the child[129] or using religious practices (such as prayer treatment) instead of standard medical treatment,[130] or requiring the child to undergo a ritual that is physically harmful, such as female genital mutilation.[131] Such situations raise difficult issues for States and human rights bodies. Given the lack of consensus on how to deal with such cases, and the fact that States that used their powers to overrule parents and permit hospitals to treat minors would be acting to

---

[126] *Laskey v. the United Kingdom*, 29 Eur. Ct. H.R. (ser. A) 120 (1997-I).

[127] *Id.* at 132.

[128] Compare with JACOBS AND WHITE, above, note 18, at 221; Krishnaswami study, at 45, argues that the State may intervene to protect an individual who refuses 'scientific medical treatment' and thus endangers his life as it would to prevent someone from committing suicide.

[129] The consequences of such denial may include the death of the child. Jennifer Trahan, *Parental Denial of a Child's Medical Needs for Religious Reasons*, ANN. SURV. AM. L. 307 (1989); Judith Inglis Scheiderer, *When Children Die as a Result of Religious Practices*, 51 OHIO ST. L.J. 1429 (1990).

[130] Again, this may result in the death of the child. See Eric Treen, *Prayer-treatment Exemptions to Child-Abuse and Neglect Statutes*, 30 HARV. J. ON LEGIS. 135 (1993); Wayne F. Malecha, *Faith Healing Exemptions to Child Protection Laws, Keeping the Faith v. Medical Care for Children*, 12 J. ON LEGIS. 243 (1985) who argue that parents' religious freedom should not include the right to endanger the life of their children.

[131] HENRY J. STEINER AND PHILIP ALSTON, INTERNATIONAL HUMAN RIGHTS IN CONTEXT 240–354 (1996); Kay Boulware-Miller, *Female Circumcision: Challenges to the Practice as a Human Rights Violation*, 8 HARV. WOMEN'S L.J. 155 (1985); Alison T. Slack, *Female Circumcision: A Critical Appraisal*, 10 HUM. RTS. Q. 437 (1988).

protect the health of the child, it is likely that the actions of the State would fall within the margin of appreciation.[132] While the issue was not directly raised in the case, such a conclusion is broadly consistent with the approach of the Court in *Hoffman v. Austria*.[133] In that case the Court ruled that an Austrian court breached the right to family life when it held against a mother who would otherwise have been granted custody on the basis that she was a Jehovah's Witness. The issue of the mother's opposition to blood transfusions was considered in some detail by the domestic courts but it was not decisive in the Court's judgment. The Court referred to the provisions of Austrian law that allowed the Austrian courts to order blood transfusions for children whose lives were endangered, but it did not comment expressly on the propriety of such laws.[134] This implies that a decision by a domestic court to require a child to have a transfusion would be appropriate.

One case in which the Commission has held that the State can interfere in religious practices of parents in order to protect the health of their children involved a number of parents who challenged a law that prohibited parents from 'ordinary chastisement' of their children (though it did not set out any penalty for refusing to comply).[135] This was against the religious beliefs of the parents, who were members of a Protestant Free Church, which taught that the corporal punishment of children was biblically mandated. The Commission showed some concern with the way in which the law interfered with family life but ultimately held that there was no breach of Article 8 or 9. It concluded that the extension of the Swedish law on assault to apply to parental corporal punishment was 'intended to protect potentially weak and vulnerable member [*sic*] of society'.[136] This case establishes some right of the State to act paternalistically to protect young children from the actions of their parents, but it does not make clear where the boundaries between that right and the right of parents to have their children brought up in a manner that is consistent with their religious beliefs lie, especially as the Commission spent some time noting the non-penal nature of the provision and its limited scope.[137] Nor does it indicate the approach that should be taken to the case of a child who claims a

---

[132] *Prince v. Massachusetts*, 321 U.S. 158, 170 (1944) argued in favour of restricting religious freedom to protect children by saying, 'Parents may be free to become martyrs themselves. But it does not follow that they are free, in identical circumstances, to make martyrs of their children.'

[133] *Hoffmann v. Austria*, 255-C Eur. Ct. H.R. (ser. A) (1993).

[134] *Id.* at 11–12.

[135] *Seven Individuals v. Sweden*, App. No. 8811/79, 29 Eur. Comm'n H.R. Dec. & Rep. 104 (1982); GERALDINE VAN BUEREN, THE INTERNATIONAL LAW ON THE RIGHTS OF THE CHILD 88–9 (1998).

[136] *Id.* at 114. This was in relation to the Art. 8 claim but the Commission held that the same reasoning applied *mutatis mutandis* to the Art. 9 claim.

[137] *Id.* at 111, 113.

breach of Article 9 in his or her own name in relation to a protective action taken in relation to that child by the State.[138] It does, however, suggest that the Court will be reluctant to condemn State actions that are aimed at the protection of children from the harmful physical consequences of their parents' beliefs.[139] This conclusion is bolstered by reference to Article 5(5) of the Declaration on Religious Intolerance and Discrimination, which states that '[p]ractices of a religion or belief in which a child is brought up must not be injurious to his physical or mental health or to his full development . . .',[140] and by the provisions of the Convention on the Rights of the Child relating to the rights of the child to healthy development.[141]

7.7.3 Necessary for the Protection of Morals

Allowing a State to justify restrictions on the right to manifest a religion or belief by reference to morality potentially poses serious problems. Religion remains a significant factor in the development of individual and social morality, and not all religions share a common morality. One complex question that arises in this area is whether a general law based on moral conceptions that are part of the morality of the dominant religion, but not of some minority religions, is a justifiable infringement on freedom of religion or belief. This question was raised in a case that was decided under Article 12 (freedom to marry and have a family) but has implications for Article 9.[142] A Protestant married man from the Republic of Ireland complained to the Commission that Irish laws prohibiting divorce were, *inter alia*, an improper imposition on his freedom of religion. While the Catholic Church prohibits divorce in all but a limited number of circumstances, the Protestant Church, of which he was a member, permitted it. He wished to divorce and remarry in Ireland but the Commission held that the issue did not raise an Article 9 issue as Article 12 was the *lex specialis*

---

[138] Children have an independent right to freedom of thought, conscience, and religion. Art. 14, Convention on the Rights of the Child, 20 Nov. 1989, U.N.G.A. Res. 25(XLIV), U.N. Doc. A/Res/44/25 (1989). However, the child also has a right to care and protection by the State, especially in the areas of safety and health (Art. 3) and a right to life, survival, and development (Art. 7). SAVITRI GOONESEKERE, CHILDREN, THE LAW AND JUSTICE 89–94 (1998).

[139] R. BEDDARD, HUMAN RIGHTS AND EUROPE 78–87 (3rd edn. 1993).

[140] Though see the criticisms of Sullivan, above, note 4, at 512–14 regarding ambiguities in the Declaration on Religious Intolerance and Discrimination over the relationship between the rights of the child and the rights of the parent.

[141] Art. 6(2) requires State parties to protect the survival and development of the child. Art. 24(4) says that States must take 'all effective and appropriate measures with a view to abolishing traditional practices prejudicial to the health of children'. See also GOONESEKERE, above, note 138, at 90; Cynthia Price Cohen, *The Relevance of Theories of Natural Law and Legal Positivism, in* THE IDEOLOGIES OF CHILDREN'S RIGHTS 63 (Michael Freeman and Philip Veerman eds., 1992); VAN BUEREN, above, note 135, at 162–3.

[142] *Johnston v. Ireland*, 112 Eur. Ct. H.R. (ser. A) (1986).

of the Convention in relation to marriage. The Commission dismissed the claim under Article 12 stating that the Irish laws were not such as to subvert the right to marriage but merely regulated that right in a manner consistent with its obligations under the Convention. The case has been criticized for its focus on the right of the State to set out marriage and divorce regulations, without looking at whether such regulation, while not a limit on the right to marry, was an improper restriction on freedom of religion.[143]

Even if the issue was looked at specifically, however, it is unlikely that the Commission would have decided in favour of the applicant. Such a decision would have potentially serious consequences, as much of the law in Member States has been influenced by religious beliefs or takes its moral basis from the dominant religions or beliefs present in the State. This applies most obviously in areas of conflict between various religions and beliefs such as marriage, divorce, abortion, and homosexuality. A simple application of religious freedom notions is not a useful way of dealing with these social and moral controversies, and members of the Court and Commission are perhaps rightly concerned not to become involved in judicial legislation in this fraught area. The United Nations Human Rights Committee has warned States, however, that 'limitations on the right to manifest a religion or belief for the purposes of protecting morals must be based on principles not deriving exclusively from a single tradition'.[144]

Possibly for these reasons States rarely rely on the morals limitation on its own although, where it has been relevant, the Court and Commission have tended to grant States a wide margin of appreciation.[145] Often cases that raise 'moral' issues are intertwined with the protection of the rights and freedoms of others, as has occurred with the censorship of religiously provocative films discussed below. The Court and Commission emphasize the rights and freedoms of others in these cases, but it is possible that such cases could be more honestly dealt with in terms of competing moralities.

7.7.4 Necessary for the Protection of the Rights and Freedoms of Others

The exercise of religious freedom gives rise to a range of potential conflicts with the rights and freedoms of others.[146] Some of these conflicts overlap with other heads of permissible limitation discussed above. The right to

---

[143] Compare with EVANS, above, note 13, at 299; Krishnaswami study, at 38–9.

[144] United Nations Human Rights Committee, General Comment No. 22 on Article 18, para. 8.

[145] VAN DIJK AND VAN HOOF, above, note 56, at 323.

[146] Sullivan, above, note 4, at 490 states that, 'The norms stated in the Declaration hold a striking potential for conflict with other rights, consequently, the task of applying the Declaration to concrete situations will challenge human rights advocates to devise interpretative approaches that will maximise the protection to all the rights implicated.'

manifest one's religion through the torture of heretics, for example, interferes with public health and safety, as well as with the right of others to be free from torture. Other cases raise more complicated issues.[147] As the Court has noted, 'in democratic societies, in which several religions coexist within one and the same population, it may be necessary to place restrictions on [the freedom to manifest a religion or belief] in order to reconcile the interests of the various groups and ensure that everyone's beliefs are respected'.[148] There is thus little or no controversy over the fact that manifestations of religion or belief must sometimes be limited to protect the rights and freedoms of others. The controversies tend to arise in interpreting the scope of the rights and freedoms and in balancing the competing claims.[149]

One question that arises in interpreting the phrase 'the rights and freedoms of others' is whether these freedoms are limited to those that are set out in the Convention. So far, the Commission and Court have generally limited the meaning of the phrase in this way, but sometimes the vague way in which 'the rights and freedoms of others' is used suggests that the limitations clause may have a wider scope than the rights under the Convention.[150] In the *ISKCON* case, for example, the application of restrictive planning laws to a Hindu place of worship was justified in part by reference to the rights and freedoms of those who lived in the nearby village.[151] While clearly the village being flooded with thousands of people and cars inconveniences such people, it is difficult to pinpoint a Convention right that is interfered with in such a case. At the very least, however, it is clear that all of the rights in the Convention will constitute rights and

[147] Although it has not been a particular issue in the Convention case law, there is significant potential for conflict between the rights of women and the right to freely practise a religion that may include practices that emphasize the subordinate status of women. Sullivan, above, note 4, at 514–18; Donna Sullivan, *Gender Equality and Religious Freedom: Towards a Framework for Conflict Resolution*, 24 N.Y.U.J. LAW & POL. 795 (1992); Donna E. Arzt, *The Application of International Human Rights Law in Islamic States*, 12 HUM. RTS. Q. 202, 208, 218–21, 222–3 (1990); Panel, *Resolving Conflicting Human Rights Standards in International Law*, 85th A.S.I.L. Proc. 336 (1991); Rebecca J. Cook, *Reservations to the Convention on the Elimination of All Forms of Discrimination Against Women*, 30 VA. J. INT'L L. 643 (1990).

[148] *Kokkinakis v. Greece*, 260-A Eur. Ct. H.R. (ser. A) at 14 (1993). Krishnaswami study, at 18, concurs but warns that 'such limitations should not be of such a nature as to sacrifice minorities on the altar of the majority, but to ensure a greater measure of freedom for society as a whole'.

[149] One interesting feature of *Kokkinakis v. Greece*, 260-A Eur. Ct. H.R. (ser. A) at 17 (1993) is that the Court referred to balancing the 'rights and liberties of others against *the conduct of which the applicant stood accused*' rather than against the rights of the applicant (emphasis added).

[150] EVANS, above, note 13, at 328, argues that the rights and freedoms of others has become 'something of a catchall'.

[151] *ISKCON and others v. the United Kingdom*, App. No. 20490/92, 76-A Eur. Comm'n H.R. Dec. & Rep. 90, 106 (1994).

freedoms of others for the purposes of Article 9(2). Thus freedom of religion or belief is both a positive ground on which someone can claim a right, and also a ground on which the State can justify restricting the rights of others.[152] This raises the question of whether the scope of religious freedom as a positive right is the same as the scope of freedom of religion or belief as a justification for restricting rights.

As discussed in Chapter 5,[153] the cases that deal with the developing notion of a right not to be offended in one's religious sensibilities suggest that the extent to which rights and freedoms can be limited in the name of religious freedom may be more extensive than the right under Article 9 itself.[154] This is part of a trend in Article 9(2) case law, in which the rights and freedoms of others are often not clearly explained or linked to one of the other rights in the Convention. While the *Otto-Preminger* case[155] seemed to base the rights and freedoms argument on Article 9 notions of religious freedom, the *Wingrove* case[156] (at least according to one of the dissenting judges[157]) based the restriction entirely on Article 10(2)—suggesting that no link between the rights and freedoms of others in Article 10(2) and the rights set out elsewhere in the Convention need be shown.[158] Whether the rights and freedoms of others in these cases is derived solely from Article 10(2) or whether they are also assessed by looking at Article 9(1), some authors have expressed serious concerns that offence to religious sensibilities could be a basis for restricting Convention rights.[159]

In other cases the Court has been similarly vague about precisely what rights of others are being protected. In *Kokkinakis*, for example, the Court readily accepted that the Greek anti-proselytism laws had the legitimate

---

[152] D. J. HARRIS, M. O'BOYLE, AND C. WARBRICK, THE LAW OF THE EUROPEAN CONVENTION ON HUMAN RIGHTS 359 (1995) note that, 'Where there is a conflict between protected rights, the judgment of the Court in *Otto-Preminger-Institut v. Austria* speaks in favour of the strong regard to be had for religious beliefs (and therefore, Article 9 rights) in deciding priority between the competing rights.'

[153] See above at Chapter 5.2.

[154] Edge, above, note 62, at 682, concludes that 'the Court may be willing to frame Article 9 rights in broader terms when used to restrict the individual than when used as a protection against State power'.

[155] *Otto-Preminger-Institut v. Austria*, 295 Eur. Ct. H.R. (ser. A) at 20–1 (1994).

[156] *Wingrove v. the United Kingdom*, 23 Eur. Ct. H.R. (ser. A) 1937 (1996-V).

[157] *Id.* at 1962, concurring opinion of Judge Pettiti, who stated that, 'Article 9 is not at issue in this case and cannot be invoked. Certainly the Court rightly based its analysis on the rights of others and did not, as it had done in the *Otto-Preminger-Institut* judgment combine Articles 9 and 10, morals and the rights of others, for which it had been criticised by legal writers.' It is questionable whether this is a wholly accurate reflection of the majority position, as at 1955 the majority note that the aim of preventing insult to a religion is a legitimate aim under Art. 10(2) but is 'also fully consonant with the aim of the protections afforded by Article 9 to religious freedom'. The majority again use the phrase the 'right of citizens not to be insulted in their religious feelings'.

[158] Edge, above, note 62, at 683, argues that this is the preferable interpretation of the cases, as it does the least damage to Art. 9 jurisprudence.

[159] VAN DIJK AND VAN HOOF, above, note 56, at 551.

aim of protecting the rights and freedoms of others,[160] but it is not entirely clear from where the right to be free from proselytism is derived. Many authors and States tend to assume that one has a right to be free from proselytism as part of the right to freedom of religion or belief.[161] Yet this is not self-evident.[162] Judge Pettiti noted that proselytism is 'the main expression of freedom of religion' and that attempting to 'make converts is not in itself an attack on the freedom and beliefs of others or an infringement of their rights'.[163] Do politicians who show up on the doorstep of someone who intends to vote for another party and try to convince that person to change his or her mind about the way in which to vote present a threat to freedom of speech or thought? It is likely that the Court would consider laws that prevented such activity to be a serious breach of Article 10 and, as long as the person had the right to shut the door or refuse to listen, arguments that such lobbying breached the rights or freedoms of the householder would be given little consideration.

Yet the Court accepted Greece's distinction between 'bearing Christian witness and improper proselytism'[164] (which the Court refused to define in the abstract). The Court largely justified its decision by reference to a report of the World Council of Churches, which said that improper proselytism was a corruption of the mission of Christians.[165] This report condemned pressure being put on people in distress to change their religion or the use of violence or brainwashing techniques as a violation of the rights of others (although it does not conclude that all such proselytism should be made a criminal offence). Yet the law in question went far beyond this and allowed for the conviction of people such as Mr Kokkinakis who merely presented his views in a persuasive manner to another adult.[166] Given that Judge Martens presented a powerful case in favour of the notion that there was no justification for interfering in the right to proselytize, the majority should have been more precise about the way in which proselytism—especially when it amounts to no more than speaking—can interfere with the freedom of others.

---

[160] *Kokkinakis v. Greece*, 260-A Eur. Ct. H.R. (ser. A) (1993).

[161] Krishnaswami study, at 39–41, although he is more specific about the nature of improper conversion than many authors and also aware of the dangers of broad laws prohibiting proselytism; EVANS, above, note 13, at 332.

[162] Sullivan, above, note 4, at 494.

[163] *Kokkinakis v. Greece*, 260-A Eur. Ct. H.R. (ser. A) at 23 (1993), partly concurring judgment of Judge Pettiti; cf. EVANS, above, note 13, at 284 who argues that part of the conceptual confusion in this area may arise because Art. 9 assumes that the State rather than other individuals will be responsible for encroachments on the freedom to maintain a religion.

[164] *Kokkinakis v. Greece*, 260-A Eur. Ct. H.R. (ser. A) at 17 (1993).

[165] *Id.*

[166] Peter Cumper, *The Rights of Religious Minorities: The Legal Regulation of New Religious Movements, in* MINORITY RIGHTS IN THE 'NEW' EUROPE 166, 167–8 (Peter Cumper and Steven Wheatley eds., 1999), argues that legal institutions can exaggerate the problem of 'brainwashing' when there is little objective evidence that this is taking place in order to justify the repression of new religions or 'cults'.

The way in which proselytism might constitute an imposition on the freedom of others became a little clearer in the subsequent case of *Larissis*,[167] in which the Court held that the attempts of superior officers to proselytize to those under their command could be punished by criminal law. The reason for this was that the hierarchical structures of the military put pressure on subordinates that would not be felt by civilians who would feel free to accept or reject approaches in relation to religious issues. 'What would in the civilian world be seen as an innocuous exchange of ideas which the recipient is free to accept or reject, may, within the confines of military life, be viewed as a form of harassment or the application of undue pressure in abuse of power.'[168] As noted above, the Court was even prepared to hold that the State had a legitimate aim in protecting the rights and freedoms of one of the airmen, even though that man in no way complained of a breach of his rights and claimed that he had converted of his own free will. The Court was prepared to substitute its own judgment (based on the evidence of the man's father and the domestic courts) to hold that he must have felt constrained to enter into conversations and possibly even to convert.[169]

Such cases raise complex issues of competing rights, where it is not clear why one set of rights should take precedence over another. In some cases, the precedence of one person's rights is a little clearer. A man, for example, claimed that the decision of the mother of their child to have an abortion and the refusal of the State to allow him any say in this decision was in breach of his right to religious freedom.[170] The Commission held that any interpretation of the father's right must 'first of all take into account her [the mother's] rights, she being the person primarily concerned by the pregnancy and its continuation or termination'. For this reason the Commission concluded that any interference that there might have been with the applicant's rights was justified as being necessary for the protection of the mother's rights.[171]

Yet few cases yield such a simple solution. Given the way in which religion or belief affects many aspects of the life of the believer, the right to manifest a religion or belief will often have the potential to conflict with other rights and such conflicts often generate great anger and contention between the parties involved. As a consequence, the Court and Commission in these cases have often given a wide and vague mandate to States to interfere with manifestations of religion or belief in order to protect the rights and freedoms of others.

---

[167] *Larissis and others v. Greece*, 65 Eur. Ct. H.R. (ser. A) 363 (1998-V).
[168] *Id.* at 380.
[169] *Id.* at 381; cf. the partly dissenting judgment of Judge Van Dijk at 392–3.
[170] *H v. Norway*, App. No. 17004/90, 73 Eur. Comm'n H.R. Dec. & Rep. 155 (1992).
[171] *Id.* at 170.

7.8 ARTICLE 15

The limitation clause in Article 9(2) has been the justification that States have used to date to explain their need to interfere in manifestations of religion or belief. The other article in the Convention that could potentially be used as a justification for limiting rights under Article 9 is Article 15(1), which reads

In time of war or other public emergency threatening the life of the nation any High Contracting Party may take measures derogating from its obligations under this Convention to the extent strictly required by the exigencies of the situation, provided that such measures are not inconsistent with its other obligations under international law.

While some articles in the Convention are non-derogable under Article 15,[172] Article 9 is subject to it.[173] The whole of Article 9, and not just the right to manifest a religion or belief, is covered by the state of emergency derogation, although it is difficult to think of a situation that would 'strictly require' a State to interfere in the *forum internum* of believers. Some authors have argued that at least the right to freedom of religion and belief is non-derogable under Article 15, even though it is not specifically mentioned as such.[174] Article 18 of the I.C.C.P.R. is non-derogable in states of emergency in its totality;[175] even manifestations of belief cannot be derogated from, although this was a cause of considerable controversy during its drafting.[176] Council of Europe members who are also parties to the I.C.C.P.R. cannot therefore derogate from freedom of religion or belief in states of emergency, as the Convention cannot be used to limit obligations taken on in other treaties.[177] For other members, however, Article 15 may be used to limit Article 9.

The Court has looked at states of emergency only a small number of times and has given somewhat contradictory signals about the extent to which it will exercise supervision over the decision by a government to declare a state of emergency justifying restrictions on Convention rights.[178]

---

[172] Arts. 2, 3, 4(1), and 7. See Art. 15(2) Convention.

[173] Shaw, above, note 106, at 445; EVANS, above, note 13, at 316.

[174] JACOBS AND WHITE, above, note 18, at 211; VAN DIJK AND VAN HOOF, above, note 56, at 557, argue that the application of Art. 15 to the *forum internum* is 'doubtful'.

[175] I.C.C.P.R., Art. 4(2). Limitations may still be placed on the right to manifest a religion or belief under Art. 18(3).

[176] CHOWDHURY, above, note 93, at 220–1.

[177] Art. 60 reads: 'Nothing in this Convention shall be construed as limiting or derogating from any of the human rights and fundamental freedoms which may be ensured under the laws of any High Contracting Party or under any other agreement to which it is a Party'; Shaw, above, note 106, at 446.

[178] On Art. 15 generally see JACOBS AND WHITE, above, note 18, chapter 21; MERRILLS, above, note 49, 152–5; JAMIE ORAÁ, HUMAN RIGHTS IN STATES OF EMERGENCY IN INTERNATIONAL LAW 16–22 (1992).

In *Lawless v. the United Kingdom*[179] the Court held that the words 'public emergency' referred to 'an exceptional crisis or emergency which affects the whole community of which the State is composed'[180] and it assessed the material presented by the State to determine whether a state of emergency was justified. In *Ireland v. United Kingdom*,[181] however, the Court was highly deferential to States in its approach to states of emergency. It held that by 'reason of their direct and continuing contact with the pressing needs of the moment, the national authorities are in principle in a better position than the international judge to decide both the presence of such an emergency and the scope of the derogations necessary to avert it. In this matter Article 15(1) leaves those authorities a wide margin of appreciation.'[182]

So far, Article 15 has had no role to play in justifying restrictions on Article 9. If Article 15 is ever invoked to override freedom of religion or belief, the State will still be required to show that any restrictions are strictly necessary in the circumstances. It is far more likely to be able to convince the Court of that in relation to restrictions on the right to manifest than would be possible in relation to the right to have or change a religion or belief. Nevertheless, Article 15 remains the only article in the Convention that arguably permits a restriction on the first half of Article 9(1) and it is possible that a State may at some point find it useful for this purpose. Given the inconsistency in approach to these types of cases, it is difficult to tell in advance what level of scrutiny the Court would be prepared to give to any such State action.[183] At any rate, the right to take action under Article 15 is limited[184] and less relevant to the everyday lives of people trying to live in compliance with their religion or belief than the way in which Article 9(2) is interpreted.

7.9 CONCLUSION

A religion or belief can be so all-embracing that it dictates the way in which some people live almost every aspect of their lives. This will tend to lead to conflicts with the plans of States and the way in which other individuals wish to live their lives and exercise their rights. Some compromise is

---

[179] *Lawless v. Ireland*, 3 Eur. Ct. H.R. (ser. A) (1961).

[180] *Id.* at 56.

[181] *Ireland v. the United Kingdom*, 25 Eur. Ct. H.R. (ser. A) (1979–80).

[182] *Id.* at 57. The Court did, however, reiterate that States do not have an 'unlimited power of appreciation'.

[183] ROBERTSON AND MERRILLS, above, note 2, at 183–90.

[184] A State is, for example, required to comply with Art. 15(3) which sets out the obligation of the derogating State to keep the Secretary-General of the Council of Europe informed of its measures, the reasons for them, and their duration.

inevitable and Article 9(2) reflects the need to balance complex factors against each other. Yet the limitation clause of Article 9 was drafted narrowly as compared to earlier suggested drafts and also to other comparable limitation articles in the Convention.[185] This suggests that the Court should not be too ready to blur the distinction between different heads of limitation or give the heads of limitation wide or vague definitions. This is particularly so in the Article 9 context where the *Arrowsmith* test often requires an applicant who makes an Article 9 claim to prove that it is necessary to his or her religion to behave in the way which the State has restricted. This very strict test at the Article 9(1) stage suggests that a more lenient test at the Article 9(2) stage would be appropriate, as the manifestation of religion or belief that is at stake is by definition one that is of great significance to the applicant. As a State must show that its actions are proportionate to the aims that are sought, the importance of the manifestation of religion or belief should figure in the weighing process that the Court undertakes to determine necessity.

At all stages of the process of determining whether a restriction on religion or belief is justified under Article 9(2) of the Convention, however, the Court and Commission have shown great deference to the claims of States. By regularly bypassing the Article 9(1) stage, they displace the applicant from the analysis at an early stage. The desire of the Court to focus on the specific facts of a case and come to a decision of limited scope has encouraged it to accept that broadly drafted rules are prescribed by law and have a legitimate aim, even when dissenting members of the Court have queried the purpose of a law or highlighted its discriminatory application. This has left the main focus on whether the actions of a State were necessary and proportionate to one of the aims set out in Article 9(2). Yet the controversial nature of religious and other beliefs has made it difficult for the Court to find much consensus on how to deal with conflicts between religion or belief and other legitimate concerns. This has led to a wide margin of appreciation and has made it difficult for applicants to prove their cases. This deference to State authority only tends to break down in cases where the State and its laws have deliberately targeted traditional religious behaviour, such as the establishment of places of worship or proselytism. While in these cases the Court has still taken a very narrow, factual approach to the issues raised, it has been more prepared to challenge the necessity of State actions and to look at the detail of the way in which laws have been applied. As the next chapter discusses, however, this still leaves unprotected a large group of applicants whose religion or belief is not restricted by specific legislation on religion but by general and neutral laws.

---

[185] See above at Chapter 3.2.3.

8

Neutral and Generally Applicable Laws

8.1 INTRODUCTION

One issue that has caused conceptual difficulties in other jurisdictions that deal with religious freedom but has not been discussed in any detail by the Commission or Court is the interaction between neutral and generally applicable laws and freedom of religion or belief. This is not because of a lack of cases dealing with the issue, but rather because neither the Court nor the Commission has given sophisticated consideration to such cases as a distinct group. The general and neutral law problem arises when a State passes legislation that does not on its face mention religious issues or appear to discriminate against a religious group. Sometimes this neutral appearance is deceptive and the law can either have been passed with the intention of curtailing the religious practices of a particular group[1] or is enforced or applied in a discriminatory manner.[2] These cases merely create the impression of laws that are general and neutral but the reality is otherwise and no particular problem arises in determining that they interfere with religion or belief.

This chapter deals with laws that are genuinely neutral regarding religion and general in their application, but that incidentally require people with a particular religion or belief to behave in a manner which is contrary to that religion or belief in order to comply with the law.[3] In increasingly pluralistic European societies this issue has the potential to be highly divisive. To allow a group to avoid a law that has been passed for the general social good seems to some people to be both unfair to those who have to

---

[1] For example, the regulations in issue in the US case of *Church of Lukumi v. City of Hialeah*, 113 S. Ct. 2217 (1993) were ostensibly about standards in animal slaughter, but had been deliberately drafted to apply only to the ritual animal sacrifices made by the Church of Lukumi. See Stephen L. Carter, *The Resurrection of Religious Freedom*, 107 HARV. L. REV. 118, 123–6 (1993).

[2] e.g. *Manoussakis and others v. Greece*, 17 Eur. Ct. H.R. (ser. A) 1347 (1996-IV), in which planning laws regarding places of worship were used in a way which discriminated against small, non-traditional religious groups. See also *Tsavachidis v. Greece*, App. No. 28802/95, Eur. Comm'n H.R., 4 Mar. 1997, unreported, in which the State used general national security surveillance laws to target such groups.

[3] While both the Court and the US Supreme Court have used terms such as 'general and neutral' a number of times, they have never been precise about the scope of the terms. Stephanos Stavros, *Freedom of Religion and Claims for Exemption from Generally Applicable, Neutral Laws*, 6 EUR. HUM. RTS REV. 607, 611 (1997), concludes that 'under the rubric "neutral and generally applicable" [are] those laws which in the process of advancing a legitimate secular public interest, have some incidental effects on some persons' religious beliefs'. This is the definition of general and neutral laws which is used in this chapter.

abide by the law and potentially dangerous to social cohesion and the common good.[4] To others, being forced to obey laws that conflict with their mostly deeply held beliefs is a serious interference with their religious or other beliefs, and they see themselves as being expected to pay too high a price for collective goals.[5]

Applicants in Article 9 cases generally, though not invariably, concede that States have the authority to make the general and neutral laws in question. Many of these cases have involved comprehensive legislative schemes in areas as diverse as cattle vaccination,[6] motor vehicle insurance,[7] pensions,[8] and taxation.[9] If States do not have the authority to make such laws for the general good then the power of the State would have been radically and inappropriately undermined by Article 9. Thus most applicants argue not that the laws themselves should not have been made, but that the applicant should be entitled to be exempted from them, or that their application in a particular case was inappropriate, or that the law should have been drafted in a more restrictive manner.

There are three basic responses that the Commission and Court have used in these cases. The first approach is to hold that, as long as a law is genuinely neutral and applied in a non-discriminatory manner, it cannot breach Article 9. The second approach is to hold that restricting a person's freedom of religion under a general and neutral law could breach Article 9(1), but that this breach could be justified in appropriate circumstances under Article 9(2). When the Commission and Court look at the Article 9(2) issue in this context, they tend to consider only whether the law as a whole is justified in a democratic society. Alternatively, they could look at whether the law, while pursuing a legitimate end, could have been drafted more narrowly to prevent the conflict with freedom of religion, or whether it would be appropriate to allow exemptions from the law for people who object to complying with it on the basis of their religion or belief. While the Court and Commission do not take such an approach, this would be more compatible with the protection of religious freedom than the current approach.[10]

---

[4] Ben Vermeulen, *Scope and Limits of Conscientious Objection*, in FREEDOM OF CONSCIENCE 87 (Council of Europe ed., 1993), regarding a Dutch law that allows tax-payers to contribute to a peace-fund the percentage of the taxes that would have otherwise been spent for military purposes, stated that, 'I believe it is incompatible with the equality principle and the democratic principle.'

[5] Steven D. Smith, *The Restoration of Tolerance*, 78 CAL. L. REV. 305 (1990).

[6] *X v. the Netherlands*, App. No. 1068/61, 5 Y.B. Eur. Conv. on H.R. 278 (1962).

[7] *X v. the Netherlands*, App. No. 2988/66, 23 Collection 137 (1967).

[8] *V v. the Netherlands*, App. No. 10678/83, 39 Eur. Comm'n H.R. Dec. & Rep. 267 (1984); *X v. the Netherlands*, App. No. 2065/63, 8 Y.B. Eur. Conv. on H.R. 266 (1965); *Reformed Church of X v. the Netherlands*, App. No. 1497/62, 5 Y.B. Eur. Conv. on H.R. 286 (1962).

[9] *Iglesia Bautista 'El Salvador' and Ortega Moratilla v. Spain*, App. No. 17522/90, 72 Eur. Comm'n H.R. Dec. & Rep. 256 (1992); *C v. the United Kingdom*, App. No. 10358/83, 37 Eur. Comm'n H.R. Dec. & Rep. 142 (1983).

[10] See below at Chapter 8.4.

The final way in which one type of general and neutral law has been dealt with is by specific reference to another article of the Convention. It is this type of reasoning that has traditionally been used in cases of conscientious objection to military service. Laws conscripting members of the public into the armed forces are general and neutral—it is clear that their aim is not to oppress religious minorities—but they place a far heavier burden on those who by religion or belief are pacifist. The policy debate in relation to conscientious objection to military service is very similar to any other form of conscientious objection to a general law. The law under the Convention is, however, quite different and thus it will be considered first.

8.2 CONSCIENTIOUS OBJECTION TO MILITARY SERVICE

Many Contracting Parties have some form of compulsory military service required of their young men by law. Historically, in some European States, military service was expected of all able-bodied young men and no exemptions on the basis of conscience were permitted.[11] Now, however, most European compulsory military service systems also permit conscientious objectors (variously defined) to perform substitute civilian service if they are opposed to armed service.[12] Generally a refusal to undertake either military or alternative service leads to a variety of punishments, which can include imprisonment. Until very recently conscientious objectors have had little assistance from the Convention.[13] Now, however, the Court has adopted a new approach that may provide a useful precedent for cases that deal with conscientious objection outside the military context.

8.2.1 The Traditional Approach to Conscientious Objection: Article 4 as an Exception to Article 9

In the first conscientious objection case in 1966 the Commission took the position that States are not compelled by Article 9 to recognize

---

[11] Greece, for example, only changed its laws to allow for the possibility of alternative service in 1997. Before that time it prosecuted and jailed thousands of conscientious objectors. See KEVIN BOYLE AND JULIET SHEEN, FREEDOM OF RELIGION AND BELIEF: A WORLD REPORT 338 (1997); AMNESTY INTERNATIONAL, 5000 YEARS IN PRISON: CONSCIENTIOUS OBJECTORS IN GREECE (1993).

[12] For a general overview of the constitutional provisions of many European States regarding compulsory military service, see Stefano Rodotà, *Conscientious Objection to Military Service*, in FREEDOM OF CONSCIENCE 98–102 (Council of Europe ed., 1993). The trend is towards the recognition of conscientious objection.

[13] While the term conscientious objection may apply to objectors to a range of laws, for the purposes of this section only conscientious objection to military service is intended by the use of the term.

conscientious objectors.[14] The reasoning of the Commission was based on Article 4 of the Convention, the article that prohibits slavery or forced or compulsory labour. In particular it was based on Article 4(3) which reads:

For the purposes of this Article the term 'forced or compulsory labour' shall not include: . . .

(b) any service of a military character or, in the case of conscientious objectors in countries where they are recognised, service exacted instead of compulsory military service.

As Article 4 refers to conscientious objectors in countries *where they are recognised* the Commission held that it followed that there was no obligation on States to recognize such objectors.[15] From this it has reasoned that arguments against military service based on reasons of conscience do not gain the protection of Article 9.[16] Furthermore, as substitute service is explicitly referred to as an exception to the forced labour rules, the Commission concluded that such service did not violate Article 9.[17] The Commission has also held that it falls within the margin of appreciation to make the length of civilian service greater than the length of military service as a form of disincentive to ensure that only those with a genuine conviction seek alternative service.[18] Such an extension of time is, however, subject to the principle of proportionality. States may extend the time to discourage all but genuine conscientious objectors from taking the easier option of substitute service, but they cannot use this extension in a manner that is unduly oppressive or punitive.[19] The Commission has not defined

[14] *Grandrath v. Federal Republic of Germany*, App. No. 2299/64, 10 Y.B. Eur. Conv. on H.R. 626 (1966); *DHI and X v. Germany*, App. No. 7705/76, 9 Eur. Comm'n H.R. Dec. & Rep. 196 (1977).

[15] *Grandrath v. Germany*, App. No. 2299/64, 10 Y.B. Eur. Conv. on H.R. 626 (1966); *X v. Austria*, App. No. 5591/72, 43 Collections 161 (1973); J. E. S. FAWCETT, THE APPLICATION OF THE EUROPEAN CONVENTION ON HUMAN RIGHTS 240–2 (1987); P. VAN DIJK AND G. J. H. VAN HOOF, THEORY AND PRACTICE OF THE EUROPEAN CONVENTION ON HUMAN RIGHTS 544–6 (3rd edn. 1997); FRANCIS JACOBS AND ROBIN WHITE, THE EUROPEAN CONVENTION ON HUMAN RIGHTS 217–20 (2nd edn. 1996).

[16] The United Nations Human Rights Committee has reached the same position following the same type of reasoning in *L.T.K. v. Finland*, Communication No. 185/1984, Inadmissibility decision of 9 July 1985, H.R.C. Rep., Pt 1, U.N. GAOR, 40th Sess. Supp. No. 40. For an overview of conscientious objection and the United Nations Human Rights Committee generally, see BAHIYYIH G. TAHZIB, FREEDOM OF RELIGION OR BELIEF: ENSURING EFFECTIVE INTERNATIONAL PROTECTION 280–6 (1996).

[17] See e.g. *Johansen v. Norway*, App. No. 10600/83, 44 Eur. Comm'n H.R. Dec. & Rep. 155, 165 (1985); *Autio v. Finland*, App. No. 17086/90, 72 Eur. Comm'n H.R. Dec. & Rep. 245, 249 (1990).

[18] *Conscientious Objectors v. Denmark*, App. No. 7565/76, 9 Eur. Comm'n H.R. Dec. & Rep. 117, 118 (1977); *Autio v. Finland*, App. No. 17086/90, 72 Eur. Comm'n H.R. Dec. & Rep. 245, 249 (1990).

[19] *Autio v. Finland*, App. No. 17086/90, 72 Eur. Comm'n H.R. Dec. & Rep. 245, 250 (1990). Vermeulen, above, note 4, at 88–9, argues that 'the only decisive test of the moral seriousness of the alleged conscientious objector is to impose on him a burdensome alternative'.

the point at which an extension would become disproportionate and it has never found a State in breach of the Convention for its system of substitute service. In most European States where conscientious objection is recognized, substitute service is longer in duration than military service and pay is often worse.[20]

As there is no right to be excused from substitute service in States where it is permitted, the Commission held that States are free to imprison those who refuse to undertake substitute service and, if necessary, to continue to do so to attempt to pressure recruits into complying with their obligations.[21] Of course, any such detention must be prescribed by law and must comply with the requirements of Article 5,[22] but the Commission held that there was no requirement that the determination that a person is required to undertake military or substitute service be made in accordance with the fair trial procedures set out in Article 6 if the purpose of the detention is coercive rather than punitive.[23]

There is certainly some justification for the Commission's decisions in the compulsory military service cases on the basis of a conflict between the general provision of Article 9 and the more specific provision in Article 4.[24] Article 4, however, does not deal primarily with freedom of religion or even with conscientious objection. Its primary concern is the prohibition on slavery and forced and compulsory labour. It certainly stands for the proposition that a State that has compulsory military or substitute service cannot be held to have breached the right not to be forced into labour. It does not stand so clearly for the proposition that compulsory military service can be forced upon a person regardless of their most deeply held religious beliefs.[25] It certainly *implies* this by the use of the phrase 'where they are recognised' in relation to conscientious objectors, but this merely sets up a conflict between the provisions of Article 4 and Article 9 that need not have been decided so conclusively in favour of Article 4.

---

[20] *Autio v. Finland*, App. No. 17086/90, 72 Eur. Comm'n H.R. Dec. & Rep. 245 (1990), held that recruits who opted for unarmed military service had to serve 120 days more, and those who opted for substitute service for 180 days more, than their military counterparts. However, States are increasingly reducing the length and stigma attached to alternative service. See Rodotà, above, note 12, at 99–100, 102.

[21] *Raninen v. Finland*, App. No. 20972/92, 84-A Eur. Comm'n H.R. Dec. & Rep. 17 (1996), in which the applicant was subject to a pattern of arrest, detention, release, and rearrest for continuing to refuse to undertake military or substitute service. His application was held to be manifestly ill-founded.

[22] *Johansen v. Norway*, App. No. 10600/83, 44 Eur. Comm'n H.R. Dec. & Rep. 155, 161–3 (1985).

[23] *Id.* at 164. That the detention had a coercive rather than punitive purpose could be seen by the fact that the applicant could have been released by indicating that he was prepared to fulfil his legal obligations.

[24] D. J. HARRIS, M. O'BOYLE, AND C. WARBRICK, THE LAW OF THE EUROPEAN CONVENTION ON HUMAN RIGHTS 369 (1995).

[25] Karel Rimanque, *Freedom of Conscience and Minority Groups, in* FREEDOM OF CONSCIENCE 155, 159–60 (Council of Europe ed., 1993).

The position reached by the Commission in conscientious objection cases was probably partly influenced by policy considerations, particularly the difficulties that States face in trying to develop fair systems for conscription.[26] Compulsory military service can be burdensome, unpleasant, and unwelcome to many conscripts who do not have a religious or philosophical objection to military service.[27] Even substitute service can take young men away from their ordinary lives, jobs, education, pay, and family.[28] Any reduction in the pool of young men available for military service may, therefore, increase the time in service or the workload of those who are conscripted and may create hostility in the wider community towards the group exempted.[29] In numerous cases, the Commission has made the point that 'any system of compulsory military service imposes a heavy burden on its citizens. The burden may be regarded as acceptable only if it is shared in an equitable manner and if exemptions are based on solid grounds. If some citizens were to be exempted without convincing reasons, a question of discrimination against the other citizens would arise.'[30]

8.2.2 The Traditional Approach to Discrimination Cases: Articles 9 and 14

The reluctance of the Commission to recognize a right to conscientious objection in the above cases was further underlined by cases where applicants claimed that they had been discriminated against by a State in its determination of who is entitled to claim exemptions from military service on the basis of conscience.[31] Generally in such cases the applicant has contested a State law that permits exemptions to military or substitute service for people of a particular religious belief, but does not give an exemption to people of other religions or beliefs. The conflict between Articles 4 and 9 is not of particular relevance in such cases, but again the Commission has traditionally been deferential to States' needs in applying Article 14 to conscientious objection cases.

In *N v. Sweden*,[32] for example, the Commission rejected a claim by a pacifist that a law that allowed conscientious objector status only to a person who could not perform military service 'in view of his affiliation

---

[26] *Autio v. Finland*, App. No. 17086/90, 72 Eur. Comm'n H.R. Dec. & Rep. 245, 250 (1990).

[27] EUROPEAN COUNCIL OF CONSCRIPTS, COMPULSORY MILITARY SERVICE IN CENTRAL AND EASTERN EUROPE: A GENERAL SURVEY (1996).

[28] *Id.*

[29] Krishnaswami study, at 44.

[30] *N v. Sweden*, App. No. 10410/83, 40 Eur. Comm'n H.R. Dec. & Rep. 203, 207 (1984); *Autio v. Finland*, App. No. 17086/90, 72 Eur. Comm'n H.R. Dec. & Rep. 245, 250 (1990); *Raninen v. Finland*, App. No. 20972/92, 84-A Eur. Comm'n H.R. Dec. & Rep. 17, 31 (1996).

[31] See discussion by JACOBS AND WHITE, above, note 15, at 217–20.

[32] *N v. Sweden*, App. No. 10410/83, 40 Eur. Comm'n H.R. Dec. & Rep. 203 (1984).

to a religious community' was discriminatory. In practice, such exemptions were granted only to Jehovah's Witnesses, although it was possible that similar religious communities might have been able to gain the protection of the provision.[33] There were no exemptions from service on the basis of philosophical beliefs. The applicant sought the right to be treated like the Jehovah's Witnesses in light of the fact that he shared their belief in pacifism.[34] The Commission rejected the application on the basis that the discrimination under the Swedish law was reasonably justified and objective[35] because 'members of Jehovah's Witnesses adhere to a comprehensive set of rules of behaviour which cover many aspects of everyday life' and that consequently

It follows that membership of the Jehovah's Witnesses constitutes strong evidence that objections to military service are based on genuine religious convictions. No comparable evidence exists in regard to individuals who object to compulsory service without being members of a community with similar characteristics.[36]

This narrow approach to the interpretation of Article 14 can be contrasted with the approach taken by the United Nations Human Rights Committee in dealing with an application based on very similar facts. It held:

[T]he exemption of only one group of conscientious objectors and the inapplicability of exemptions for all others cannot be considered reasonable. . . . [W]hen a right of conscientious objection is recognised by a State party, no differentiation shall be made among conscientious objectors on the basis of the nature of their particular belief.[37]

The Commission also took a narrow approach to discrimination when exemptions from military or other service were granted by a State to religious leaders in a manner that distinguished between ministers from different religions. The legislation in the *Grandrath* case,[38] for example, specified that ordained Evangelical ministers and Catholic priests would be automatically exempted from military service and that other equivalent ministers of religion would be exempted on application. In order to be considered 'equivalent' a religious leader had to show that being a religious leader was his or her main profession and full-time occupation. The applicant tried to claim the exemption on the basis that he was a Bible study leader in his religious community (the Jehovah's Witnesses). The State

---

[33] *Id.* at 207.   [34] *Id.* at 204.

[35] *Id.* at 207–8. This is the general test that the Court and Commission have developed to determine whether or not a discriminatory action is one which is prohibited under Art. 14.

[36] *Id.* at 208. See the defence of the case by Vermeulen, above, note 4, at 89–90. The same reasoning was used in *Raninen v. Finland*, App. No. 20972/92, 84-A Eur. Comm'n H.R. Dec. & Rep. 17, 33 (1996).

[37] *Brinkhof v. the Netherlands*, Communication No. 402/1990, Views of 2 July 1993, U.N. GAOR, 48th Sess., Supp. No. 40, Pt II, Annex X, Sect. S, para. 93, U.N. Doc. A/98/40 (1993).

[38] *Grandrath v. Federal Republic of Germany*, App. No. 2299/64, 10 Y.B. Eur. Conv. on H.R. 626 (1966).

rejected his application, saying that his main work was as a painter's assistant and his role as a Bible study leader was of no real importance either to his religious community or to his profession. The Commission upheld the decision of the State, saying that is was reasonable to distinguish between people who were full-time religious leaders and those who were not. It also held that it was permissible for the legislation to presume that Evangelical ministers and Catholic priests were to be exempted from service (even though, in a small number of cases, being a priest was not their main profession and the legislation also excused those in the seminary) and to require members of other faiths to prove their right to exemption. The Commission could have been expected to question more rigorously the issue of discrimination in regard to legislation that set out one test for Evangelical and Catholic ministers (that of their position) and another for other religious claims (that of function).[39]

8.2.3 Developments in International Law

While the Commission continued to refuse to recognize a right to conscientious objection arising from the Convention, various other international institutions showed increasing support for recognition of conscientious objectors. The Parliamentary Assembly of the Council of Europe, which had been tackling the issue of conscientious objection for some time, concluded that conscientious objection raised issues of freedom of religion or belief. It set out a series of principles for dealing with conscientious objection and called on member States to bring their national legislation into line, as far as possible, with the guidelines set out by the Assembly. The 'basic principles' that govern conscientious objection, according to the Assembly are

1. Persons liable to conscription for military service who, for reasons of conscience or profound conviction arising from religious, ethical, moral, humanitarian, philosophical or similar motives, refuse to perform armed service shall enjoy a personal right to be released from the obligation to perform such service.

2. This right shall be regarded as deriving logically from the fundamental rights of the individual in democratic Rule of Law States which are guaranteed in Article 9 of the European Convention on Human Rights.[40]

---

[39] JACOBS AND WHITE, above, note 15, at 219 argue that the reasoning of the Commission would 'have been acceptable if exemption from compulsory service had been based solely on the criterion of the minister's function; but it was not'. Compare with FREDE CASTBERG, THE EUROPEAN CONVENTION ON HUMAN RIGHTS 148, 164–5 (1974), who describes the reasoning as 'unassailable' even though it entails a finding that 'favouring one denomination or school of thought above another does not constitute a violation of Art. 9, either when examined in isolation or when interpreted in the light of Art. 14'. This is because conscientious objector status is a 'favour' that States may grant to anybody or nobody.

[40] Res. 337 (1976), Council of Europe, Cons. Ass., Eighteenth Ordinary Session (Third Part), Texts Adopted (1967); Parliamentary Assembly Res. 816 (1977), 7 Oct. 1977, reprinted

Thus the Assembly and later the Committee of Ministers[41] recognized the right to conscientious objection to military service (though not exemption from alternative service) as arising from Article 9. The United Nations Human Rights Committee has also recognized a right to conscientious objection that derives from the right to manifest a religion or belief under Article 18 of the I.C.C.P.R.[42] This approach has also been endorsed by the United Nations Commission on Human Rights.[43] Thus the Commission case law on conscientious objection and its relationship with freedom of religion or belief began to look increasingly out of step with international developments.

8.2.4 A New Approach to Conscientious Objection

Despite criticism the Commission maintained its narrow approach to conscientious objection for three decades. Two recent cases, however, indicate a change of attitude, particularly to the issue of discrimination in conscientious objection schemes. The first case, *Tsirlis and Kouloumpas v. Greece*,[44] involved the imprisonment of two Jehovah's Witness ministers by military courts for refusing to enlist for military service. The men claimed that they were entitled to be exempted from military service under Greek law as they were ministers of a 'known religion'. The Supreme Administrative Court eventually agreed that they were entitled to the exemption under Greek law and the men were released from prison but not given any compensation. The Commission held that their imprisonment breached Article 9 of the Convention in conjunction with Article 14, as the Jehovah's Witness ministers had endured lengthy periods of imprisonment before their right to an exemption was recognized, whereas Orthodox ministers had no difficulty in obtaining exemptions.[45] There were no objective and reason-

---

in Council of Europe, COLLECTED TEXTS 222–3 (1987). See also Council of Europe, Conscientious Objection to Military Service, Explanatory Report, CE Doc. 88.C55 (1988); Parliamentary Assembly of the Council of Europe, CE Doc. 7102, 10 June 1994; Report of Special Rapporteur Rodotà, Doc. 6752, 29 Jan. 1993 1404-28/1/93-1-E.

[41] Committee of Ministers, Recommendation No. R(87)8, Council of Europe, H/NF (87)1, 160 (9 Apr. 1987).

[42] United Nations Human Rights Committee, General Comment on Article 18, para. 11, which says that while the I.C.C.P.R. does not mention the right to conscientious objection as such, 'such a right can be derived from Article 18, inasmuch as the obligation to use lethal force may seriously conflict with the freedom of conscience and the right to manifest one's religion or belief'. Where conscientious objection is recognized it should not differentiate between objectors on the basis of their particular beliefs and there should be no discrimination against conscientious objectors for failing to do military service.

[43] Most recently in United Nations Human Rights Commission resolution E/CN.4/RES/1998/77 of 22 Apr. 1998 (adopted without a vote), which refers to previous resolutions and cites the work of the Human Rights Committee's General Comment on Article 18 to encourage States to permit conscientious objection and to treat conscientious objectors appropriately.

[44] *Tsirlis and Kouloumpas v. Greece*, 35 Eur. Ct. H.R. (ser. A) (1997-III).

[45] *Id.* at 942, annex to the judgment of the Court.

able grounds for such discrimination.[46] The Commission did, however, explicitly refer to the decision in *Grandrath* that ministers do not have a right to conscientious objection and it seemed to be taking only a slightly stricter approach to discriminatory applications of conscientious objection laws than it had in the past. The Court, in its judgment, focused on the trial and imprisonment of the men and held that there was no need to consider the issues raised by Articles 9 and 14 separately.[47]

One member of the Commission, however, in her partly dissenting opinion, directly challenged the orthodoxy that *Grandrath* rendered Article 9 irrelevant in conscientious objection cases. Commissioner Liddy held that the form of compulsion used to try to make the ministers enlist struck 'at the very substance' of the freedom to manifest a religion or belief.[48] In her analysis (drawing on the concurring judgment of Mr Eusthadiades in *Grandrath*) the provisions of Article 4 do 'not mean that Article 9 is inapplicable, but rather that the necessity for compulsory military or alternative service falls to be considered under paragraph 2 of Article 9, and that the margin of appreciation is extended as a result of Article 4(3)(b)'.[49]

While Mrs Liddy's opinion seemed to be a lone voice calling for a radically different interpretation of Article 9, only a short time later the case of *Thlimmenos v. Greece*[50] demonstrated wider concern within the Commission with the traditional approach to conscientious objection. This case involved a Jehovah's Witness who had been convicted and served two years' imprisonment for refusing to enlist in the army. Some years later he sat the test to become an accountant and passed with the second highest marks. He was refused entry into the profession, however, on the basis that he had been convicted of a serious criminal offence. The applicant claimed that this was a breach of his rights under Article 9 by itself and in conjunction with Article 14.

The majority of the Commission upheld the claim on the basis of a combination of Articles 9 and 14 and held that this made a decision under Article 9 by itself unnecessary. The majority commented, however, that, as there was no option of substitute service available at the time, 'Jehovah's Witnesses were faced with the choice of either serving in the armed forces or being convicted. In these circumstances, the Commission considers that the applicant's conviction amounted to an interference with his right to manifest his religion.'[51] They noted that the previous case law of the Commission had denied that a conviction for conscientious objection could amount to a breach of Article 9 but did not find it necessary to rule on that issue, in part because the case in question only challenged the

---

[46] *Id.* at 943.   [47] *Id.* at 926.
[48] *Id.* at 946, partly dissenting judgment of Mrs Liddy.   [49] *Id.* at 947.
[50] *Thlimmenos v. Greece*, App. No. 34369/97, Eur. Comm'n H.R., 4 Dec. 1998, unreported.
[51] *Id.* at para. 45.

decision to deny the applicant the right to become an accountant and not the original conviction.[52] The finding that the original conviction amounted to a breach of the right to manifest a religion or belief, however, seemed to challenge (without directly overruling) the orthodox position on conscientious objection set out in *Grandrath*.

A minority of the Commission, in a partly dissenting opinion, went further than the majority and decided the case directly on the basis of Article 9. The minority briefly discussed the past case law of the Convention but noted that, since the *Grandrath* case, the jurisprudence of the Convention had 'evolved in the interim to such an extent as to cast doubt' on the reasoning in the case.[53] They held that the original refusal of the applicant to serve in the armed forces attracted the protection of Article 9. His refusal to serve was a manifestation of his religion and thus could be distinguished from cases in which the individuals' actions did 'not actually express the belief concerned', such as *Arrowsmith*, and cases where the laws in question had no conscientious implications, such as general taxation laws. The minority therefore tried to limit the implications of their decision to conscientious objection to military service.

Thlimmenos went on to be heard by a Grand Chamber of the Court and the decision of the judges in that case focused on the issue of discrimination.[54] Unlike the Commission, the Court did 'not find it necessary to examine whether the applicant's initial conviction and the authorities' subsequent refusal to appoint him amounted to interference with his rights under Article 9(1). In particular, the Court [did] not have to address, in the present case, the question of whether sanctions on conscientious objectors to compulsory military service may in itself infringe the right to freedom of thought, conscience and religion guaranteed in Article 9(1).'[55] The Court restricted itself to an examination of Article 14 in conjunction with Article 9 and there is no *dictum* in the Court's decision that is comparable to the hints in the Commission decision that a re-examination of the position of conscientious objectors is likely. The Court did, however, hold that the refusal of the Greek government to allow the applicant to practise as an accountant was discriminatory as it 'failed to treat differently persons whose situations are significantly different'.[56] While the Court did not rule on whether it was appropriate to imprison people for conscientious objection it did hold that to further exclude them from the professions was disproportionate to the ends of punishing those who refuse to serve their country.[57]

---

[52] *Id.* at para. 46. As several years had passed since the conviction and imprisonment, any application directly challenging the original conviction would have been out of time.

[53] *Id.*, partly dissenting opinion of Commissioners Rozakis, Liddy, Marxer, Nowidie, Conforti, and Bratza, at para. 3. Note that Commissioners Rozakis, Conforti, and Bratza are now judges on the Court.

[54] *Thlimmenos v. Greece*, App. No. 34369/97, Eur. Ct. H.R., 6 Apr. 2000, unreported.

[55] *Id.* at para. 43.　　[56] *Id.* at para. 44.　　[57] *Id.* at para. 47.

The position of the Court in relation to the issue of conscientious objection to military service therefore remains unclear. While the *Grandrath* line of cases has come under attack in the Commission, the Court has refused to address the issue at this stage. The decision in *Thlimmenos*, however, that a regulation may be discriminatory because it does not make an exemption for people who cannot comply with the law for reasons based on religion or belief, has potentially far wider implications for the interpretation of Article 9. It is certainly a change from the position that the Commission and Court have taken in the past to cases in which people have refused to comply with a variety of general and neutral laws outside the military context on the basis of religion or belief. Were it to be extended to require States to grant exemptions on the basis of religion or belief outside the conscientious objection sphere, the decision could radically alter the position of the Court in relation to general and neutral laws.

8.3 THE CASE LAW ON GENERAL AND NEUTRAL LAWS

While conscientious objection to military service has a high profile and is attracting increased sympathy from States, there are general and neutral laws that do not relate to military service and thus cannot be dealt with by reference to Article 4. The question of whether those who object to such laws on the basis of religion or belief have a good claim under the Convention thus falls solely within the domain of Article 9. Even though the positions of the opposing parties in the military cases are more dramatic than the positions of the parties in more mundane conflicts of conscience, the policy arguments are similar.[58] On one hand, States are concerned to protect their right to make laws for the general good, to subject all members of society equally to all laws, and to ensure that any exemptions that are given are narrowly construed to avoid undermining the law or encouraging fraud. On the other hand, applicants claim that requiring them to obey such laws creates a conflict with their right to practise their religion or belief, and can lead to discrimination against minority groups.

Most of the cases dealing with general and neutral laws have been dealt with by the Commission rather than the Court and the reasoning of the Commission in these cases has been opaque and inconsistent. The Commission could deal with general and neutral laws in one of two broad ways. The first would be to hold that no general and neutral law can breach

[58] JOSEPH RAZ, THE AUTHORITY OF LAW 277 (1979), argues that, 'Conscientious objection is most often discussed nowadays in connection with military service. There may be practical reasons why it is difficult to extend the right to conscientious objection to other fields of the law, but whatever principles or moral reasons there are for recognising it with regard to conscription apply also to other areas of the law.'

Article 9. The second approach would be to hold that general and neutral laws can breach Article 9 in much the same way as laws specifically targeted at religious practice can. It would then be for the State to demonstrate that such interference with religious freedom was necessary under the provisions of Article 9(2). Unfortunately, the Commission has taken an awkward halfway position between these two clear alternatives. Sometimes it has held that laws that are general and neutral can restrict religious freedom, although in all these cases it has gone on to decide that such restrictions were justified under Article 9(2). Yet at other times it has referred to the general and neutral status of a law as though this was the determinative (or at least a highly relevant) factor in deciding that there was no breach of Article 9(1). Neither the Court nor the Commission has ever explicitly held that general and neutral laws cannot breach Article 9 but the pattern of case law suggests that this is the *de facto* position. It is necessary to look in some detail at the case law in order to extract the principles that apply in this area before considering what approach it would be appropriate for the Court to take in cases of this nature.

8.3.1 General and Neutral Laws and the *Arrowsmith* Test

Part of the explanation for this pattern of holding against applicants in cases regarding general and neutral laws comes from the use of the *Arrowsmith* test. The *Arrowsmith* test requires applicants to show that the actions restricted by the State were necessary manifestations of their religion or belief. In most cases involving conscientious objection to general legislative schemes the Commission has held that such actions are not necessary manifestations of a religion or belief. In cases where the law in question is general and neutral, the test seems to apply in an even more abbreviated form than it does in cases where the law is more specifically aimed at religious practices. The Commission pays almost no attention to the specific facts of the case or the claims of the applicant in regard to how the law interfered with their religion or belief, instead merely citing the *Arrowsmith* passage that Article 9 does not give individuals the right to behave in the public sphere in compliance with all the demands of their religion or belief. [59] The Commission has used this test to dismiss cases claiming a breach of Article 9 by general and neutral laws on issues such as cattle vaccination,[60]

---

[59] e.g. *Arrowsmith v. the United Kingdom*, App. No. 7050/75, 19 Eur. Comm'n H.R. Dec. & Rep. 5, 20 (1978); *Le Cour Grandmaison and Fritz v. France*, App. Nos. 11567/85 and 11568/85 (joined), 53 Eur. Comm'n H.R. Dec. & Rep. 150, 160 (1987); *McFeeley and others v. United Kingdom*, App. No. 8317/78, 20 Eur. Comm'n H.R. Dec. & Rep. 44, 77 (1980); *Stedman v. United Kingdom*, App. No. 29107/95, 89-A Eur. Comm'n H.R. Dec. & Rep. 104 (1997); *V v. the Netherlands*, App. No. 10678/83, 39 Eur. Comm'n H.R. Dec. & Rep. 267, 268 (1984).

[60] *X v. the Netherlands*, App. No. 1068/61, 5 Y.B. Eur. Conv. on H.R. 278 (1962).

taxation,[61] and mandatory voting.[62] The summary way in which the Commission deals with such cases suggests that the fact that a law is general and neutral is at least a powerful indication that it cannot interfere with freedom of religion or belief under the *Arrowsmith* test.

8.3.2 A More General Principle

Yet sometimes the Commission has indicated that the principle extends beyond a narrow application of the *Arrowsmith* test to the notion that the general and neutral nature of a law is determinative of the Article 9(1) question. The strongest evidence of a principle to the effect that general and neutral laws cannot breach Article 9 comes from comparing two cases that deal with taxation,[63] *Darby*[64] and *C v. United Kingdom*.[65] The applicant in *C v. the United Kingdom* was a member of the Society of Friends (commonly known as the Quakers) and, as such, a committed pacifist. He declined to pay the proportion of his income tax that would be spent on military purposes unless the government would give him assurances that it would spend that money on other, non-military purposes. Not surprisingly, the government refused to give such assurances and, eventually, sought to enforce a judgment debt against the applicant for refusal to pay taxes. The applicant petitioned the Commission in relation to the execution of the judgment debt.[66] The applicant argued that the Court had previously recognized pacifism as a 'belief' deserving of protection under Article 9.[67] He sought to bring his claim within the *Arrowsmith* test by arguing that his refusal to participate in military arrangements, even indirectly through taxation, was not merely incidental to or motivated by his religion but was *necessary* to it.[68]

The Commission set out the applicant's arguments and then held that

---

[61] e.g. *C v. the United Kingdom*, App. No. 10358/83, 37 Eur. Comm'n H.R. Dec. & Rep. 142, (1983). See discussion at Chapter 8.3.2.

[62] *X v. Austria*, App. No. 1718/62, 8 Y.B. Eur. Conv. on H.R. 168, 172 (1965); *X v. Austria*, App. No. 4982/71, 15 Y.B. Eur. Conv. on H.R. 468, 472–3 (1972).

[63] A number of cases have challenged taxation on Art. 9 grounds, *Iglesia Bautista 'El Salvador' and Ortega Moratilla v. Spain*, App. No. 17522/90, 72 Eur. Comm'n H.R. Dec. & Rep. 256 (1992); *C v. the United Kingdom*, App. No. 10358/83, 37 Eur. Comm'n H.R. Dec. & Rep. 142 (1983); *H and B v. the United Kingdom*, App. No. 11991/86, Eur. Comm'n H.R., 18 July 1986, unreported; *Ross v. the United Kingdom*, App. No. 10295/83, Eur. Comm'n H.R., 14 Oct. 1983, unreported.

[64] *Darby v. Sweden*, 187 Eur. Ct. H.R. (ser. A) (1990), annex to the decision of the Court.

[65] *C v. the United Kingdom*, App. No. 10358/83, 37 Eur. Comm'n H.R. Dec. & Rep. 142 (1983).

[66] *Id.* at 142–3.

[67] See *Arrowsmith v. the United Kingdom*, App. No. 7050/75, 19 Eur. Comm'n H.R. Dec. & Rep. 5 (1978).

[68] *C v. the United Kingdom*, App. No. 10358/83, 37 Eur. Comm'n H.R. Dec. & Rep. 142, 144 (1983).

Article 9 primarily protects the sphere of personal beliefs and religious creeds, i.e. the area which is sometimes called the *forum internum*. In addition, it protects acts which are intimately linked to these attitudes, such as acts of worship and devotion which are aspects of the practice of religion or belief in a generally recognised form.

However, in protecting this personal sphere, Article 9 of the Convention does not always guarantee the right to behave in the public sphere in a way which is dictated by such a belief:– for instance by refusing to pay certain taxes because part of the revenue so raised may be applied for military expenditure. The Commission has so held in Application No. 7050/75 (Arrowsmith v. the United Kingdom, Cmm Report, para 71, D.R. 19, p. 5) where it stated that 'the term "practice" as employed in Article 9(1) does not cover each act which is motivated or influenced by a religion or belief'.[69]

This passage suggests that the key issue had nothing to do with the general and neutral status of the law but was rather a simple application of the *Arrowsmith* test in the narrow form outlined above. Yet the Commission never addressed the particular facts of the case, or the fact that the applicant claimed that his actions were necessary manifestations of his religion, and later in the judgment the Commission held that

The obligation to pay taxes is a *general* one which has no specific conscientious implications in itself. Its *neutrality* in this sense is also illustrated by the fact that no tax payer can influence or determine the purpose for which his or her tax contributions are applied, once they are collected. Furthermore, the power of taxation is expressly recognised by the Convention system and ascribed to the State by Article 1, First Protocol.[70]

With this paucity of reasoning, the Commission dismissed the case as inadmissible. The first two sentences of the above quote beg the question. The applicant's contention was that taxes have serious implications for conscience and that, in certain areas, citizens should at least have a right to place limits on the purposes for which their taxes are spent. The Commission simply stating that this is not the case is hardly a convincing argument against the position and does not seem to be a serious application of the *Arrowsmith* test.[71] A later passage in the judgment further suggests that the justification for the decision in *C v. United Kingdom* is the nature of the law in question rather than necessity under *Arrowsmith*. The Commission held that 'It follows that Article 9 does not confer on the applicant the right to refuse, on the basis of his convictions, to abide by legislation, the operation of which is provided for by the Convention, and which *applies neutrally and generally in the public sphere*, without impinging on the freedoms guaranteed by Article 9.'[72] Again this reasoning

---

[69] *Id.* at 147.   [70] *Id.* (emphasis added).

[71] Malcolm Evans, Religious Liberty and International Law in Europe 310–11 (1997).

[72] *C v. the United Kingdom*, App. No. 10358/83, 37 Eur. Comm'n H.R. Dec. & Rep. 142, 147 (1983) (emphasis added).

suggests that general and neutral laws cannot breach Article 9, although the circularity in the last part of the sentence undermines the general principle.[73]

An alternative explanation[74] of *C v. United Kingdom*, and similar cases that have followed in the area of taxation, is that taxation laws cannot breach Article 9 because the State is given the power to tax under Article 1 of Protocol 1 of the Convention.[75] This argument is similar to the one used in relation to Article 4 and conscientious objection to military service. Yet the fact that States have the power to tax without thereby necessarily infringing the property rights of individuals (which is the concern of the first Protocol, Article 1) does not mean that all uses of the taxation system are above scrutiny by the European human rights system. A comparison of *C v. United Kingdom* and *Darby*[76] suggests that it was the general and neutral nature of the laws in the former case that was decisive, and not the fact that the laws dealt with taxation. In both cases the applicants argued that taxation laws should not be applied to them because to pay such taxes would be a violation of their religious freedom. In *Darby* the applicant was required to support a Church of which he was not a member. In *C v. United Kingdom* the applicant was required to support a military system that he felt was repugnant to his deepest beliefs. In the first case, the Commission held that there had been a violation of the *forum internum*, even though Sweden claimed that it had a right to tax under the First Protocol.[77] In the second case the Commission held that the applicant's case was manifestly ill-founded.[78] In distinguishing the cases, the Commission held that the difference between the cases was that in *Darby* 'the applicant's complaint is not that part of the tax money is used for a purpose which is contrary to his convictions but that he is obliged to pay a specific tax to the Church'.[79] It thus appears that the difference was in the directly religious nature of the taxation in *Darby* as compared to the more indirect and general taxation provisions in *C v. United Kingdom*.

Thus the fact that a law is general and neutral is a powerful factor in encouraging the Commission to hold that there has been no breach of

---

[73] Evans, above, note 71, at 311.

[74] *Id.* Evans considers the fact that States are specifically given the power to tax under the Convention to be the basis of the decision.

[75] Protocol 1, Art. 1 protects the right of 'every natural and legal person to the peaceful enjoyment of his possessions' but maintains the right of the State to control property to 'secure the payment of taxes'.

[76] *Darby v. Sweden*, 187 Eur. Ct. H.R. (ser. A) (1990), annex to the decision of the Court, at para. 51.

[77] *Id.* at para. 42. The submissions of the government included the claim that it 'must be free to use the taxes for purposes which the individual may object to'.

[78] *C v. the United Kingdom*, App. No. 10358/83, 37 Eur. Comm'n H.R. Dec. & Rep. 142, 147 (1983).

[79] *Darby v. Sweden*, 187 Eur. Ct. H.R. (ser. A) (1990), annex to the decision of the Court, at para. 48. See also paras. 56–7 distinguishing between 'general taxes' and direct contributions to a Church.

Article 9, even if it is not always determinative of the case.[80] Yet the Commission has never explicitly adopted this as a general principle and has not been prepared to apply it consistently in all cases. The position of the Court has been even more ambivalent. In the *Valsamis* and *Efstratiou*[81] cases, for example, the Court noted that the 'Commission considered that Article 9 did not confer a right to exemption from disciplinary rules which applied in a general and neutral manner'[82] but it did not explicitly adopt this reasoning or make any further comment on it. The Court also seemed to be hinting at the role of general and neutral laws in the *Kalaç* case, when it held that the applicant was not dismissed from his military post on the basis of his religion or belief but on the basis of his conduct and attitude, which breached *general* military disciplinary guidelines. It is perhaps more telling to note that almost all of the Article 9 cases that the Court has dealt with on the merits have involved laws that specifically targeted religious groups rather than general or neutral laws, which have tended to be dismissed by the Commission at the admissibility stage.

8.3.3 Inconsistency Towards General and Neutral Law Cases

While the Commission has generally denied that general and neutral laws can breach Article 9, this is not a strict rule. In a number of cases involving general and neutral laws the Commission has held that there was a breach of Article 9(1) and gone on to determine the case under Article 9(2). One of the areas in which the Article 9(2) approach tends to be used by the Court is in relation to freedom of worship. The case concerning the summer solstice worship of the Druids provides one example.[83] The law closing Stonehenge to the public on the solstice was general and neutral and for a clear public purpose that was unrelated to religion. The authorities did not apply it in such a way as to discriminate against the Druids, indeed they went to some lengths to try to accommodate them. Yet the Commission determined that, if Druidism were a religion, the regulations that prevented them from carrying out their summer rites were a limitation on their freedom of religion.[84] No reasoning was given for this decision and no mention of the general and neutral state of the law was made. Freedom of worship was also the right that was at stake in the two cases involving prisoners

---

[80] e.g. *Revert and Legallais v. France*, App. No. 14331/88 and 14332/88 (joined), 62 Eur. Comm'n H.R. Dec. & Rep. 309, 318 (1989). Application dismissed in part on the basis that the law making membership of the architects' association compulsory applied 'to every architect on a neutral basis, having no link whatsoever with his personal belief'.

[81] *Valsamis v. Greece*, 2 Eur. Ct. H.R. (ser. A) 2312 (1996-VI); *Efstratiou v. Greece*, 27 Eur. Ct. H.R. (ser. A) 2347 (1996-VI).

[82] *Id.* at para. 37 of each judgment.

[83] *Chappell v. the United Kingdom*, App. No. 12587/86, 53 Eur. Comm'n H.R. Dec. & Rep. 241 (1987).

[84] *Id.* at 246.

who complained of the application of general prison safety rules in a manner which meant that they were denied access to some religious services[85] and in the case of planning regulations that interfered with worship at a Hindu temple.[86] Extending the principle somewhat, the Court also held that requiring a Seventh Day Adventist schoolboy to attend school on a Saturday was an interference in his ability to manifest his religion of strict Sabbath observance, though one that was justified by the child's right to education.[87] In none of these cases was the fact that the restrictions on the right to worship were made under general and neutral laws determinative of the Article 9(1) issues or even mentioned by the Commission as relevant.

While it might be thought that freedom of worship is a special case, the Commission has also been inconsistent in its approach to the general and neutral issue in other areas. In *Håkansson v. Sweden*,[88] which involved a man who shouted out 'like a trumpet' about the sinfulness of alcohol and pornography, the application to him of the general law against disturbing the peace was seen by the Commission to be a breach of Article 9(1). In another, very similar case, the actions of a man who stood outside an abortion clinic and tried to dissuade women from having an abortion, in part by showing a picture of foetal remains in combination with images of Christ, were held to fall outside Article 9(1).[89] In both these cases the men involved were motivated by their religious beliefs to try to change what they perceived to be the sinful behaviour of others. In both cases they were restricted from doing so by the application of general civil laws that protected others from being unduly harassed by this sort of behaviour. Yet in one case the Commission easily concluded that there was a breach (albeit a justifiable one) of religious freedom, while in the other the Commission held that the applicant's activities were 'primarily aimed at persuading women not to have an abortion' and thus not a manifestation of his religion or belief.[90]

---

[85] *Chester v. the United Kingdom*, App. No. 9488/81, Eur. Comm'n. H.R., 6 Oct. 1982, unreported; *Pelle v. France*, App. No. 11691/85, Eur. Comm'n H.R., 10 Oct. 1986, unreported.

[86] *ISKCON v. the United Kingdom*, App. No. 20490/92, 76-A Eur. Comm'n H.R. Dec. & Rep. 90, 106 (1994). At 107 the Commission stated that it did not 'consider that Article 9 of the Convention can be used to circumvent existing planning legislation, provided that in the proceedings under the legislation, adequate weight is given to freedom of religion'. The first half of the sentence suggests that a general and neutral law cannot be the basis of an Art. 9 claim but the second half indicates that there are some limits to this proposition.

[87] *Casimiro and Ferreira v. Luxembourg*, App. No. 44888/98, Eur. Ct H.R., 27 Apr. 1999, unreported.

[88] *Håkansson v. Sweden*, App. 9820/82, 5 Eur. H.R. Rep. 297 (1983).

[89] *Van Den Dungen v. the Netherlands*, App. No. 22838/93, 80-A Eur. Comm'n H.R. Dec. & Rep. 147, 150 (1995).

[90] *Id.* at 150. Stavros, above, note 3, at 619 suggests that the distinction is that in religious speech cases the applicants must be people who 'pursue primarily religious aims and whose messages openly identify themselves as religious'. Yet the degree of religious identification in these cases is very similar and so this seems a tenuous ground of distinction.

Thus it is difficult to draw a general conclusion as to the relevance of general and neutral laws to the determination of Article 9 cases. In the vast majority of cases in which an applicant seeks to challenge a general and neutral law, the case is dismissed under Article 9(1) as manifestly unfounded. In addition, the Commission has referred to the generality and neutrality of laws as part of its reasoning in a significant number of cases. Yet the Commission has been inconsistent in its application of this principle and has sometimes found that there has been a breach of Article 9(1). In all these cases, however, the Commission has held that the restriction on religious freedom under a general and neutral law was justified under Article 9(2). Thus the *de facto* position of the Commission, based on the outcome in these cases, is that general and neutral laws do not breach Article 9. The conceptual confusion and inconsistency that permeate the reasoning in these cases, however, suggests that the Commission is not sure itself of the relevance of general and neutral laws to Article 9. Given the lack of clarity in the law surrounding this issue, it is worth considering some of the competing policy arguments that may help to explain the Commission's reluctance to adopt a clear legal position.

8.4   A POLICY ANALYSIS OF THE GENERAL AND NEUTRAL LAW PROBLEM

8.4.1 The Article 9(1) Approach

The Court is yet to clarify its position on general and neutral laws in the Article 9 context. A simple and consistent approach could be taken by the Court to general and neutral laws if it enunciated a principle that such laws could not raise Article 9(1) issues. As noted above, to many people such an approach appears to fulfil the requirements of fairness (as it subjects all people to the same rules) and of democracy (as it prevents minorities or 'fanatics' from undermining laws that are for the good of all). This approach is not, however, required by the wording of Article 9, which merely speaks of the right to manifest one's religion or belief. In order for Article 9 to be effective, it must sometimes prevail over the existing legal order.

Moreover, it should not be assumed that the fact that in theory a law applies to all people equally means that it is 'fair' in the sense of placing the same burdens on all. This general point has long been recognized in legal theory[91] and was reiterated by Krishnaswami in the context of

---

[91] John Edwards, *Preferential Treatment and the Right to Equal Consideration*, in MINORITY RIGHTS IN THE 'NEW' EUROPE 147–65 (Peter Cumper and Steven Wheatley eds., 1999); Sandra Fredman, *Equality Issues*, in THE IMPACT OF THE HUMAN RIGHTS BILL ON ENGLISH LAW (Basil S. Markesinis ed., 1998).

religion or belief. He observed that 'since each religion or belief makes different demands on its followers, a mechanical approach of the principle of equality which does not take into account the various demands will often lead to injustice and in some cases even to discrimination'.[92] He later concluded that 'certain limitations imposed upon particular manifestations of religion or belief, although apparently conceived in general terms, may in fact tend to affect only a particular group, or to affect it more than others'.[93] Thus it is recognized in many jurisdictions that a general law may be indirectly discriminatory because it places a heavier burden on a particular group of people to obey it than it places on the population as a whole and may interfere to a significant extent with their ability to manifest their religion or belief.[94] One example of this in the context of religious freedom is the Prohibition Laws in the United States. These applied to all people and were enacted for a general public good, but had they not included exemptions for celebrations of the Eucharist and Seder they would have directly interfered with some of the most sacred worship rituals of many Christian Churches and of American Jews.[95] Quite clearly a law that directly banned the Catholic Mass, for example, would have breached the right to religious freedom. A law that indirectly had the same effect by making it impossible to use the required facilities without breaching the criminal law would seem logically to equally breach the right to manifest one's religion or belief in worship.[96] Thus it is difficult to conclude that the Court should *prima facie* exclude general and neutral laws from the scope of Article 9 review.[97]

Yet a number of authors have suggested that courts concerned with religious freedom should take exactly that approach.[98] This debate has been

---

[92] Krishnaswami study, at 15.   [93] *Id.* at 20.

[94] Yoram Dinstein, *Freedom of Religion and Religious Minorities, in* THE PROTECTION OF MINORITIES AND HUMAN RIGHTS 165–7 (Yoram Dinstein ed., 1992) gives a number of examples; PATRICK THORNBERRY, INTERNATIONAL LAW AND THE RIGHTS OF MINORITIES 191 (1991); VAN DIJK AND VAN HOOF, above, note 15, at 550.

[95] An Act to Prohibit Intoxicating Beverages, 1919 (U.S.). Douglas Laycock, *Formal, Substantive, and Disaggregated Neutrality Toward Religion,* 39 DE PAUL L. REV. 993, 1000–1 (1990).

[96] This does not mean that one law may not be easier to justify than the other under Art. 9(2) but merely that the interference in religion or belief can be demonstrated in each case.

[97] *Employment Division, Department of Human Resources of Oregon v. Smith,* 494 U.S. 872, 893–4 (1990), concurring judgment of O'Connor J, with whom Brennan, Marshall, and Blackmun JJ joined. They held that, 'It is difficult to deny that a law that prohibits religiously motivated conduct, even if the law is generally applicable, does not at least implicate First Amendment concerns.'

[98] Stavros, above, note 3, at 627 concludes that when 'a law is shown after close scrutiny to be truly general and neutral, it should be immune from challenge under Article 9', and any objectionable effects of this immunity should be dealt with under other articles of the Convention. More cautiously VAN DIJK AND VAN HOOF, above, note 15, at 550 conclude that 'general regulations on a neutral basis may restrict the freedom of religion or belief in specific circumstances'. See also the approach of the High Court of Australia in *The Church*

fierce in the United States, where the Supreme Court has taken a variety of approaches to general and neutral laws. Originally, the Supreme Court took a narrow approach to the First Amendment as relating solely or primarily to the realm of belief and opinions rather than action.[99] Such an interpretation tends not to create a conflict between the court's conception of religious freedom and general and neutral laws.[100] After a time, however, the Supreme Court recognized that freedom of religion extended to some actions and that a general and neutral law could interfere with religious freedom. The high-water mark of this reasoning was *Wisconsin v. Yoder*,[101] in which the Supreme Court held that the First Amendment required States to give an exemption from the law making schooling compulsory up to the age of 16, as the Amish religion required the maintenance of a way of life that was incompatible with schooling beyond the age of 14. Now, however, the Supreme Court appears to have pulled back the scope of the religious freedom guarantee. In the case of *Oregon v. Smith*[102] the Supreme Court held that the First Amendment was not breached by a law that criminalized the taking of peyote, without any exemption for the Native Americans who used it in their traditional religious ceremonies. This decision was subject to great criticism[103] and Congress attempted to reverse it with the Religious Freedom Restoration Act in 1993.[104] The Act prohibited a government from 'substantially burdening' a person's religious freedom by a rule of general applicability unless the government could show that the burden was in 'furtherance of a compelling government interest' and that the regulation was the 'least restrictive means' of furthering that interest. The Supreme Court, however, found the legislation unconstitutional and reaffirmed its position in the *Oregon v. Smith* case.[105] Thus the debate in the United States, both by scholars and within the Court itself, can play a useful role in illuminating the issues at stake in cases dealing with general and neutral laws.

Some of the American critiques of 'accommodating' religious practices in relation to general laws stem from the concern to ensure the constitutional

---

of the New Faith v. The Commissioner of Pay-Roll Tax (Victoria), 154 C.L.R. 120, 136 (1983), which held that 'general laws to preserve and protect society are not defeated by a plea of a religious obligation to breach them'.

[99] *Reynolds v. U.S.* 98 U.S. 244, 250 (1878); *Cantwell v. Connecticut*, 310 U.S. 296 (1940).

[100] Thus in *Reynolds v. U.S.*, 98 U.S. 244, 250 (1878) laws against polygamy were held not to breach the First Amendment because they did not interfere with the beliefs of Mormons, only with their practices.

[101] *Wisconsin v. Yoder*, 406 U.S. 203 (1972).

[102] *Employment Division, Department of Human Resources of Oregon v. Smith*, 494 U.S. 872 (1990).

[103] e.g. Michael McConnell, *Free Exercise and the Smith Decision*, 57 U. CHI. L. REV. 1109 (1990).

[104] Religious Freedom Restoration Act 1993 (U.S.A).

[105] *City of Boerne v. Flores*, 117 S. Ct. 2157 (1997).

separation of the Church and State, which is not as significant an issue in the European context. There are, however, other policy issues that are relevant even when there is no legal separation of Church and State.[106] These reasons depend less on strictly legal argument than on policy concerns about the potential dangers of allowing individuals to resist general laws. Opponents of this viewpoint suggest two possible ways in which the general and neutral law issue could be dealt with in order to ensure that such laws do not become oppressive to religious freedom. The first is to allow for exemptions to the laws (for example, a right to conscientious objection in a system of compulsory military service) and the second is to require that the laws be drafted in a manner that is least restrictive[107] of religious freedom. Some of the policy arguments apply to both approaches but sometimes the distinction between the two can be important.

As the Court and Commission have generally rejected the claims of those who seek to avoid the application of a general and neutral law on the basis of Article 9 it is worth considering the reasons that support such a stance.

8.4.2 The Burden on the State

Those who argue against the notion that laws should have to be drafted in a manner that is least restrictive of freedom of religion or belief say that such a requirement would put too heavy a burden on the State.[108] This is particularly so as European societies become increasingly religiously pluralistic and numerous people have developed individualistic beliefs.[109] In this sort of context, it is argued, to expect States to be able to even know of, let alone accommodate, the beliefs of the numerous groups that may be affected by laws is not realistic. Governments must be able to govern for the general good, and to impose a 'least restrictive' requirement upon them would undermine their ability to do this.[110]

---

[106] Stavros, above, note 3, has written the most detailed analysis of this issue in the Art. 9 context. See also Joshua Puls, *The Wall of Separation: Section 116, the First Amendment and Constitutional Religious Guarantees*, 26 FED. L. REV. 139, 156–7 (1998).

[107] As some US Supreme Court cases have held: e.g. in *Scherbert v. Verner*, 374 U.S. 398, 400 (1963) the Court held that even if there were problems in granting exemptions to people on the basis of religion because of the problems of fraud, the State had to show that there were 'no alternative forms of regulation [that] would combat such abuses without infringing First Amendment rights'.

[108] e.g. *Lyng v. Northwest Indian Cemetery Protective Association*, 485 U.S. 439, 451–552 (1988), held that 'government simply could not operate if it were required to satisfy every citizen's religious needs and desires'.

[109] Stavros, above, note 3, at 626, argues that 'in times of extreme religious pluralism, courts cannot afford to balance the demands of each religion against the public interest pursued by each generally applicable, neutral law'.

[110] *City of Boerne v. Flores*, 117 S. Ct. 2157 (1997) held that the Restoration of Religious Freedom Act 1993 (U.S.) was a 'considerable intrusion into the States' traditional prerogatives and general authority to regulate for the health and welfare of their citizens'.

There is an element of truth in these arguments. Undoubtedly requiring States to adopt laws in a form which respects freedom of religion or belief would have some effect on their ability to quickly and efficiently pursue majoritarian goals. Yet that is the price that must be paid in societies that value rights. As Professor Dworkin admits, 'the majority cannot travel as fast or as far as it would like if it recognizes the rights of individuals to do what, in the majority's terms, is the wrong thing to do'.[111] Yet he argues that if we truly consider rights valuable this is an acceptable price to pay. The convenience of the majority is not a sufficient reason to disregard a fundamental right. The Court has recognized this by holding that 'although individual interests must on some occasions be subordinated to those of a group, democracy does not simply mean that the views of a majority must always prevail: a balance must be achieved which ensures the fair and proper treatment of minorities and avoids any abuse of a dominant position'.[112]

Others have argued against the proposition that it is unrealistic to expect States to be aware of the way in which laws could affect freedom of religion or belief. In the context of United States First Amendment protection of religious freedom, Stephen Carter draws an analogy with tort law to argue in favour of ensuring that laws do not unduly burden religion or belief.

Virtually any other plaintiff in a tort-style action has the freedom to rely on the sensible common law adage that people are presumed to intend the reasonably foreseeable consequences of their actions. By requiring a person who assesses the likelihood of a harm to compensate for it, this principle encourages private actors to take into account the harms that their actions might cause. Because the rational actor will then proceed only when the expected return outweighs the likely costs, net societal welfare is increased. But civil rights plaintiffs—and, now, free exercise plaintiffs as well—are mired in a bizarre jurisprudence under which government actors may proceed without considering the costs of their actions (measured in constitutional deprivations), as long as they act out of indifference rather than out of hostility. That was once the rule in torts as well, but the courts abandoned it long ago.[113]

He argues that allowing the government to take legislative action in any area as long as that law does not deliberately target religion encourages States to ignore religious freedom issues in the legislative process, whereas a rule that required them to justify the scope of legislation that interferes with religion or belief encourages them to be proactive in protecting the rights of believers.

---

[111] Ronald Dworkin, Taking Rights Seriously 204 (1977).

[112] *Young, James and Webster v. the United Kingdom*, 44 Eur. Ct. H.R. (ser. A) at 25 (1981).

[113] Carter, above, note 1, at 129.

While there are clear practical hurdles that a 'least restrictive' approach would require States to overcome, these are not as insurmountable as is sometimes suggested. In a number of States there are legislative committees or other organs of government that are charged with the responsibility of scrutinizing proposed legislation for compliance with human rights obligations.[114] If the Court were to take a clear line that laws should be drafted in a manner that was least restrictive to freedom of religion or belief, then general and neutral laws that may have an impact on religion or belief would fall within the competence of such committees. While no committee could be expected to have a sophisticated understanding of all religions and beliefs in a State, the members could utilize various mechanisms of consultation, such as public meetings, standing consultative groups made up of religious representatives, or ensuring widespread dissemination of information about proposed legislation to non-governmental organizations that represent various religions or beliefs. Also, religious or belief-based groups may often already be aware of the potential impact of the legislation on their community but lack an effective forum through which to ventilate their complaints or sufficient leverage to ensure that they are taken seriously by the government.[115] A least restrictive rule would give them such leverage and encourage States to seek to communicate with them. In short, there would seem to be a number of ways in which governments could ensure that they were well informed of the impact legislation was likely to have on religion or belief if they were serious about protecting the right.[116]

8.4.3 The Social Anarchy Argument

Another concern that arises when either exemptions from general and neutral laws or a least restrictive approach to religious freedom is proposed is that this will fragment the law and diminish social cohesion. The United States Supreme Court used the phrase 'courting anarchy' to dismiss the claim that all laws should be balanced against competing religious claims.[117]

---

[114] Michael Ryle, *Pre-legislative Scrutiny: A Prophylactic Approach to Protection of Human Rights*, 1994 PUB. L. 192.

[115] Steven Wheatley, *Minority Rights, Power Sharing and the Modern State, in* MINORITY RIGHTS IN THE 'NEW' EUROPE 210 (Peter Cumper and Steven Wheatley eds., 1999) argues that, 'Many problem issues relating to minorities are created as a result of the disenfranchisement of members of the minority group from the political processes—or at the very least a *feeling* of disenfranchisement.'

[116] Explanatory Report to the Framework Convention on National Minorities, Council of Europe, H(94)10 para. 80; Wheatley, above, note 115, at 208–10 each set out a number of proposals for ensuring better participation by minorities in the legislative process.

[117] *Employment Division of Oregon v. Smith*, 494 U.S. 872, 892 (1990); Gerard Quinn, *Conscientious Objection in Labour Relations, in* FREEDOM OF CONSCIENCE 109 (Council of Europe ed., 1993). Despite Quinn's strong support for conscientious objection he admits that 'at one level it is quite anarchic in its tendencies'.

This argument reflects a reasonable concern with ensuring that people do not become their own legislators, deciding for themselves what is compatible with their consciences and following only such laws as they decide are appropriate.[118] This is an even greater potential problem in Europe than it is in the United States, as the United States Constitution only protects freedom of religion rather than the more expansive religion or belief referred to in the Convention. The problems would be likely to be exacerbated by fraudulent claims made by those who use arguments of religious freedom to avoid onerous or unpleasant social obligations.[119] It may even be that the potential to avoid laws causes people to become mired in self-doubt or 'morbid introspection' about their own reasons for wishing to avoid a legal obligation and encourages people to claim a legal exemption when they would not otherwise have considered disobeying the law.[120]

These arguments apply more cogently in the context of exemptions than of least restrictive drafting of laws. A general principle that each person was entitled to an exemption to any law that restricted his or her ability to manifest a religion or belief would have potentially serious social consequences, although such a principle would still be limited by the right of the State to refuse an exemption on the grounds that refusing the exemption was necessary in a democratic society. There may be some areas, for example conscientious objection to military service, where the best way to balance the needs of the State against the compelling opposing claims of conscience is to institute some form of exemption. A general principle to this effect, however, may place too high a burden on the State to weed out undeserving cases while not unduly intruding into the *forum internum* of the applicants.

The same concerns do not apply with such force to the idea that a law should be drafted in a manner that is least restrictive of religious freedom (acknowledging that sometimes the best way to achieve this is to draft a general law with scope for exemptions). Professor Raz concludes that the best way of avoiding a conflict between State power and the conscience of

---

[118] *Reynolds v. U.S.*, 98 U.S. 244, 267 (1878), held that to permit a man to excuse practices contrary to law on the basis of his religious beliefs 'would be to make the professed doctrines of religious belief superior to the law of the land, and in effect to permit every citizen to become a law unto himself'.

[119] Though caution should be shown in holding that perfectly sincere applicants must forgo their rights in case other applicants take advantage of the system. See Jeremy Gunn, *Adjudicating Rights of Conscience under the European Convention on Human Rights, in* RELIGIOUS HUMAN RIGHTS IN GLOBAL PERSPECTIVE: LEGAL PERSPECTIVES 305, 311–12 (Johan D. van der Vyver and John Witte Jr. eds., 1996).

[120] RAZ, above, note 58, at 287 outlines three primary reasons that there should not be a unified, general rule allowing for conscientious objection to any law. The first is the danger of fraud, the second the likelihood of encouraging self-doubt of one's own motives and possibly self-deception to allow one to take advantage of exemptions, and the third that unless the right is based on the simple declaration of the believer, the State would become involved in assessing the private, moral claims of individuals. See also Laycock, above, note 95, at 1017.

the individual is to avoid laws in areas in which a conflict is likely. 'Freedom of conscience and the pluralistic character of a state are guaranteed by its self-restraint from dictating action in areas known to be subject to sensitive moral convictions and by the provision of facilities and services as required by people of different moral and religious convictions.'[121] Again, this does not require legislative restraint when dealing with the intolerable; religions or beliefs that are actively involved in harming others, endangering the State, or putting public health at risk may appropriately have their activities circumscribed for the reasons set out in Article 9(2). What such an approach requires is legislative constraint and creativity to ensure that freedom of religion or belief is not ignored in pursuit of other social goals. The reasons for restricting freedom of religion or belief may differ from society to society, and over time. It may be, for example, that the best way to avoid problems of fraud, discrimination, State intrusion into the *forum internum*, and the violation of conscience involved in compulsory military service, is to replace conscript soldiers with professional armed forces and greater reliance on military technology.[122] It may be, however, that some States with genuine concerns as to national security are unable to afford this type of change and will be able to show that it is necessary in their democratic society to maintain conscription, although it might be hard in these circumstances to also show a strong interest in not allowing for some exemptions.

Some laws must be drafted in a way that violates the conscience of some people without allowing for exemptions because important Article 9(2) considerations are involved. This will also help to prevent Article 9 becoming a source of complete fragmentation of the legal system. The farmers who refused to participate in a countrywide cattle vaccination scheme, for example, endangered the success of the whole scheme as infections from their cattle could have prevented the eradication of disease in the cattle of the Netherlands.[123] Compulsory insurance schemes would likewise become very difficult to operate with too extensive a scheme of exemptions, although the Netherlands (which has a minority Church that is deeply opposed to insurance) has tried a scheme that allows exemptions on religious grounds in exchange for a higher tax contribution.[124] The same may be said for

[121] RAZ, above, note 58, at 288.

[122] The majority of European States, however, continue to use some form of conscription despite economic and military arguments in favour of abandoning conscription for more professional armed forces. *Thinking Bigger*, THE ECONOMIST, 16 Oct. 1999, at 52–5.

[123] *X v. the Netherlands*, App. No. 1068/61, 5 Y.B. Eur. Conv. on H.R. 278 (1962).

[124] *X v. the Netherlands*, App. No. 2065/63, 8 Y.B. Eur. Conv. on H.R. 266 (1965); *X v. the Netherlands*, App. No. 2988/66, 23 Collection 137 (1967). In these cases the applicants protested that the obligation to pay the insurance contribution as taxation was a case of 'Etikettenschwindel' (false labelling) and still required them to participate in a compulsory insurance scheme. The Commission dismissed these cases as manifestly ill-founded on the basis that no breach of Art. 9(1) had been demonstrated.

compulsory pension schemes,[125] although there the burden of having to support oneself in old age falls on the individual who desires to opt out rather than the community as a whole.[126] In other cases, however, allowing exemptions or drafting laws in a more restrictive manner seems to raise less serious difficulties. The United Kingdom government decided that allowing an exemption to the motorcycle helmet laws for Sikhs was workable without endangering the whole legislation or seriously undermining its object.[127] Similarly a number of countries have tried to arrange their public holidays to coincide with religious festivals of a variety of religions, rather than simply the predominant or established religion.[128] This leads to fewer conflicts between the dictates of the religion or belief and the laws of a State.[129]

Thus the least restrictive law approach, and the creation of a limited number of exemptions from general and neutral laws, does not create the same danger of social chaos as is sometimes claimed in relation to a general principle requiring exemptions.[130] Rather than saying that the law must respect the right of each person to decide whether or not to comply with a law either in general or in the particular circumstances, it requires the legislature to think through the implications of its laws for freedom of religion or belief, and to consult with religious communities in advance about ways of shaping laws creatively to promote the general good without unnecessarily interfering with freedom of religion or belief.[131]

8.4.4 Weakening of Article 9(2)

Dr Stephanos Stavros, who is one of the few writers who have considered the general and neutral law issue in relation to the Convention, raises an

---

[125] *X v. the Netherlands*, App. No. 2065/63, 8 Y.B. Eur. Conv. on H.R. 266, 270 (1965).

[126] *Id.* The reason that the applicant wished to be exempt from the obligations to pay such contributions was in part because he would not accept support in his old age by the State. He thus wanted neither the benefit nor the burden of the legislation. This can be compared to compulsory third party car insurance where the rights of third parties are directly affected.

[127] *X v. the United Kingdom*, App. No. 7992/77, 14 Eur. Comm'n H.R. Dec. & Rep. 234 (1978). See the Road Traffic Act 1988 (U.K.) section 16(2) which reads, 'A requirement imposed by regulations under this section shall not apply to any follower of the Sikh religion while he is wearing a turban.'

[128] Thornberry, above, note 94, at 195; Krishnaswami study, at 35–6.

[129] Gunn, above, note 119, at 326–7, examines some of the cases in which the Commission did not even ask whether it was possible to frame the general rule in a way that accommodated the needs of people whose freedom of religion or belief was affected by them.

[130] Indeed, some authors claim that, in a pluralistic society, accommodation of religion decreases the likelihood of social disorder. Frederick M. Gedicks, *Public Life and Hostility to Religion*, 78 Va. L. Rev. 671, 690 (1992) argues that, 'Without exemptions, some religious groups will likely be crushed by the weight of majoritarian law and culture. Such groups pose no threat to public order. However, majoritarian dominance could radicalize some believers into destabilizing, antisocial activity, including violence.'

[131] Rodotà, above, note 12, at 96, notes the futility in a pluralistic society of trying in all circumstances to devise a legislative solution to such problems. He sees conscientious objection as an important way of overcoming conflict while respecting the position of all parties.

additional potential problem with allowing Article 9 claims to defeat a general and neutral law. He is concerned that if the Court is too willing to treat religion or belief as being infringed by general and neutral laws, it would be likely to compensate for this by watering down the requirements of Article 9(2) so that State action is not unduly restricted.[132] His evidence for this is the way in which the 'compelling interest' test that is normally required to justify abrogation of the United States First Amendment has been watered down in cases involving general and neutral laws.[133] He fears that a similar extension of Convention law could put at risk the protection that the Commission and Court have given against what he describes as 'old fashioned' religious persecution.[134] Dr Stavros is concerned to ensure that the important complaints about religious persecution are not endangered by jurisprudence that develops to deal with relatively minor restrictions imposed by general and neutral laws. For this reason he approves of the way in which the Commission and Court have usually treated general and neutral laws as not raising an Article 9 issue.[135]

Three points need to be made in response to this. The first is that, as discussed in Chapter 7, the Commission and Court are already deferential to State claims under Article 9(2). Refusing to entertain cases arising in relation to general and neutral laws is unlikely to change this. Second, in relation to other Convention rights, the Commission and Court change the margin of appreciation according to the factual circumstances. The margin of appreciation in relation to the freedom of expression in the political context is narrow,[136] and has not been endangered by a far wider margin of appreciation in areas such as pornography.[137] A law that is general and neutral is likely to comply more easily with the requirements of Article 9(2), and give States a wider margin of appreciation, than one that specifically sets out to limit religious activities. Indeed, it seems that the Commission is already applying such a test in the Article 9 context, by carefully scrutinizing State activity that intentionally targets minority religions[138] while deferring to the judgement of States in most matters relating to laws of general application. There is no reason to think that there would be negative implications for 'old fashioned' religious persecution cases if a wider range of cases were held to raise Article 9(1) issues.

The final problem with Dr Stavros's analysis is that he assumes that core cases of religious persecution can be clearly and easily isolated, and that

---

[132] Stavros, above, note 3, at 621–2.
[133] *Id.* at 625. [134] *Id.* at 626–7. [135] *Id.* at 626.
[136] *Sunday Times v. the United Kingdom*, 30 Eur. Ct. H.R. (ser. A) at 40 (1979); *Observer and Guardian v. the United Kingdom*, 126 Eur. Ct. H.R. (ser. A) (1991).
[137] See the discussion in *Wingrove v. the United Kingdom*, 23 Eur. Ct. H.R. (ser. A) 1937 (1996-V). *Otto-Preminger-Institut v. Austria*, 295 Eur. Ct. H.R. (ser. A) at 19 (1994), speaks of the obligation to avoid 'gratuitously offensive' expressions that do not 'further human progress'.
[138] This is conceded by Stavros, above, note 3, at 622.

serious persecution will not tend to take place under general and neutral laws. Yet understandings of what constitutes religious persecution depend on understandings of what it is to have a religion or belief. The Commission and Court have been more protective of traditional Christian practices, such as worship[139] and proselytism,[140] than they have of non-Christian practices, such as the wearing of head covering,[141] the possession of religious artefacts[142] and publicly trying to change the behaviour (compared with the religion) of others.[143] This is not to say that the Commission or Court is deliberately engaging in bias against non-Christian applicants, but rather that it is dangerous to assume that there is a common understanding of what is essential to the protection of religion or belief. For a Muslim woman required to appear in a photograph without a headscarf, for Jehovah's Witness children punished for refusing to participate in a parade, or for a pacifist denied the opportunity to argue against a particular military engagement, such laws are restrictions on their religion or belief— restrictions that they may feel as keenly as another would feel if denied the right to public worship. Rather than disguise the policy considerations inherent in this sort of question it is more appropriate to deal with them under Article 9(2) and to face the issue of general and neutral laws on a case by case basis. This may not be a neat solution to the problem, but it is preferable to denying that there is a problem, as many of the Convention cases do.

8.4.5 Minorities and Exemptions

One strength of admitting that a general and neutral law can breach Article 9 and that exemptions to the law or least restrictive drafting of a law may be required to protect religious freedom adequately is that it improves the position of adherents of minority religions and beliefs. While large religious groups will almost always be taken into account in the drafting of laws, smaller groups may find themselves overlooked, often as a result of ignorance or apathy rather than any desire to oppress them.[144] In the United States this can be seen by the fact that the exclusion of wine for sacramental purposes was an obvious exception to the Prohibition laws, as to

---

[139] *Manoussakis and others v. Greece*, 17 Eur. Ct. H.R. (ser. A) 1347 (1996-IV).

[140] *Kokkinakis v. Greece*, 260-A Eur. Ct. H.R. (ser. A) (1993); *Larissis and others v. Greece*, 65 Eur. Ct. H.R. (ser. A) 363 (1998-V).

[141] *Karaduman v. Turkey*, App. No. 16278/90, 74 Eur. Comm'n H.R. Dec. & Rep. 93 (1993); *X v. the United Kingdom*, App. No. 7992/77, 14 Eur. Comm'n H.R. Dec. & Rep. 234 (1978).

[142] *X v. Austria*, App. No. 1753/63, 16 Collections 20 (1965).

[143] *Håkansson v. Sweden*, App. 9820/82, 5 Eur. H.R. Rep. 297 (1983); *Van Den Dungen v. the Netherlands*, App. No. 22838/93, 80-A Eur. Comm'n H.R. Dec. & Rep. 147 (1995).

[144] Rimanque, above, note 25, at 145–65; Laycock, above, note 95, at 1014–18.

refuse such an exemption would have affected millions of people. In a more recent case, however, the conviction of members of a Native American tribe for using peyote in a traditional tribal ritual was held not to breach the First Amendment.[145] The general laws against the use of peyote did not give an exemption to the relatively small group for whom its use was an essential part of a religious rite. In the European context, traditional religions within a State may gain the benefit of funding for the maintenance of their Churches under laws regarding historical property, but newer religions are not permitted any such funding.[146] Large religious groups are difficult to ignore, even when drafting general and neutral laws. Minorities are easily overlooked.

Those who prefer the position that general and neutral laws cannot breach Article 9 often acknowledge that this does lessen the position of minorities. They suggest, however, that there are better ways of protecting such groups than a wide reading of Article 9. Professor Malcolm Evans, for example, notes that the exercise of religious freedom need not be without cost[147] and the Commission[148] and some authors[149] suggest that groups that are dissatisfied with the effect that a general law has on their religious practices should use the democratic processes to remedy this. The right to freedom of thought and expression should allow such minorities to communicate their concerns to the majority, and the democratic processes should then give relief to deserving minorities, either by way of exemptions or a redrafting of the law.

The problem with such a remedy is that the groups that tend to be most vulnerable to being overlooked in the legislative drafting process are small communities with little political influence, possibly living somewhat marginalized from the wider society.[150] These are precisely the groups that are least able to use the democratic processes to achieve their ends. This is especially so as some such groups can be viewed rather unsympathetically by the wider community and even the legal system,[151] as can be seen

---

[145] *Employment Division of Oregon v. Smith*, 494 U.S. 872 (1990); Carter, above, note 830, at 120–3.

[146] Antonio Perotti, *Freedom of Conscience and Immigrants, in* FREEDOM OF CONSCIENCE 183–5 (Council of Europe ed., 1993).

[147] EVANS, above, note 71, at 300.

[148] *C v. the United Kingdom*, App. No. 10358/83, 37 Eur. Comm'n H.R. Dec. & Rep. 142, 147 (1983). The Commission concluded that if the applicant 'considers the obligation to contribute through taxation to arms procurement an outrage to his conscience he may advertise his attitude and thereby try to obtain support for it through the democratic process'.

[149] Stavros, above, note 3, at 627.

[150] Perotti, above, note 146, at 185–6, notes the double discrimination against religious minorities that are also predominantly from immigrant communities, such as most European Muslims.

[151] *Employment Division, Department of Human Resources of Oregon v. Smith*, 494 U.S. 872, 902 (1990), concurring judgment of O'Connor J, with whom Brennan, Marshall, and Blackmun JJ joined. '[T]he First Amendment was enacted precisely to protect the rights of

for example in the judgments of the Greek courts to Jehovah's Witnesses, which refer to the Jehovah's Witnesses as a 'sect' numerous times, despite the fact that it is a recognized religion under Greek law.[152] For the Court to tell such groups that they must rely on being able to gain the support of the majority is to abrogate an important role that it should play in the protection of minorities.[153] If rights are to be meaningful, they must at times lead public opinion and grant protection to those who need it most—the very groups most ignored, despised, or marginalized by the broader society.

8.5   CONCLUSION

General and neutral laws that serve a public purpose have always been found by the Court and Commission either not to raise an issue of freedom of religion or belief or to comply with the requirements of Article 9(2). The Commission and Court seem to adopt a universally hostile attitude to adherents of religions or beliefs who claim the right to opt out of comprehensive legal schemes, and sometimes do not seem to give sufficient consideration to the details of the particular case. While such legal schemes serve a useful social purpose and a scheme of exemptions or less restrictive drafting imposes some burden on States, it is important not to lose sight of the fact that general legislation may impose serious restrictions on religion or belief, particularly the religion or belief of relatively small and powerless groups. Such groups cannot necessarily rely on the democratic processes to see to their needs.

It is clear from the number of cases that have been brought in relation to general and neutral laws that many applicants consider their religion or belief to be threatened by laws that *prima facie* have little or nothing to do with religion. Most of the people bringing such cases belong to minority groups or have beliefs that do not associate them with an institutional structure. They have been unable to use the democratic process to change

those whose religious practices are not shared by the majority and may be viewed with hostility. The history of our free exercise doctrine amply demonstrates the harsh impact majoritarian rule has had on unpopular or emerging religious groups such as the Jehovah's Witnesses and the Amish.'

[152] *Kokkinakis v. Greece*, 260-A Eur. Ct. H.R. (ser. A) at 4–6 (1993), which quotes the Greek domestic courts using the term 'sect'. See also the same terminology in the dissenting opinion of Judge Valticos.

[153] Steven Wheatley, *Minority Rights, Power Sharing and the Modern Democratic State*, in MINORITY RIGHTS IN THE 'NEW' EUROPE 204 (Peter Cumper and Steven Wheatley eds., 1999) argues that, 'It is insufficient merely to allow the national minority the freedom to compete for resources in the face of a majority able to outvote it and outbid it.' See also John Packer, *On the Content of Minority Rights*, in DO WE NEED MINORITY RIGHTS? 121 (J. Räikkä ed., 1996).

the law or to gain themselves exemptions from it in a way that more numerous groups might be able to do. To tell such groups that the law that they believe has a profound effect on their religion or belief is not actually a restriction on their ability to manifest their religion or belief (or not a serious enough restriction to trigger Article 9 protection) is to deny them fair protection under the Convention. This does not mean that such groups should always be entitled to exemptions or to have the law interpreted or applied in a way that does not interfere with their religion or belief. The limitation clauses in the Convention demonstrate an understanding that individual rights cannot always defeat broader social purposes. At least dealing with such issues under Article 9(2) rather than dismissing them under Article 9(1) requires States to justify their restrictions on individual rights, thereby providing a greater measure of protection for freedom of religion or belief.

The decision in *Thlimmenos v. Greece*[154] could signal a marked shift in the thinking in this area. The ruling that a general and neutral law may be discriminatory if it does not allow for exemptions for people on the basis of religion is unprecedented in the Article 9 case law. If it were applied outside the military context, it could revolutionize the approach of the Court to general and neutral laws. Applicants would still need, however, to convince the Court that their actions were a manifestation of their religion and belief, and States would probably still be given a wide margin of appreciation in such cases. If the discrimination principle becomes used as a matter of routine in Article 9 cases it is possible that many types of claims that have been rejected routinely by the Court or Commission in the past will now be far more likely to succeed.

[154] *Thlimmenos v. Greece*, App. No. 34369/97, Eur. Ct. H.R., 6 Apr. 2000, unreported.

9

Conclusion

Freedom of religion or belief is a fundamental human right that protects a vital aspect of human integrity and autonomy. In recognition of this fact the Convention, along with numerous other international human rights treaties, sets out a protection for both the right to have and the right to manifest a religion or belief. The drafters of the Convention were clear both about the importance of freedom of religion or belief and about the need to restrict the circumstances in which the right to manifest a religion or belief could be limited. Thus freedom of religion or belief appears to have been given significant protection under the Convention. Yet the case law interpreting Article 9 has not demonstrated an appropriate understanding of the importance of freedom of religion or belief in the lives of individuals and has shown an undue deference to the concerns of States.

9.1 PROBLEMS WITH THE CONVENTION CASE LAW

The decisions in Article 9 cases reveal a narrow and often confused concept of religious freedom. While the term 'religion or belief' has been interpreted widely (thus avoiding some complex but important issues), this seemingly liberal approach to Article 9 has been undermined by the narrow scope that has been given to the right to have and to manifest a religion or belief. This approach makes it difficult for applicants acting outside the traditional, European model of religious practice to make successful Article 9 claims. Even when applicants do manage to bring their claims within the ambit of Article 9(1), Article 9(2) has been interpreted so as to give States great leeway in their treatment of religion or belief. The difficulties faced by applicants reveal a number of problems in the approach that the Court and Commission have taken toward freedom of religion or belief.

9.1.1 Failure to Recognize the Importance of the Right

There are numerous, often conflicting conceptions of freedom of religion and belief. Yet, with the exception of one rather bland paragraph in *Kokkinakis v. Greece*[1] that notes the importance of religious freedom to individuals and to pluralistic democracy, the Court seems not to have given any consideration to the importance of freedom of religion or belief. The

---

[1] *Kokkinakis v. Greece*, 260-A Eur. Ct. H.R. (ser. A) at 13 (1993).

words from *Kokkinakis* have been repeated talismanically in all the later cases, but the implication of the words have been largely ignored. Freedom of religion or belief is acknowledged to be a 'precious asset' but the Court has not been prepared to accord it significant scope or protection. The failure of the Article 9 cases to take freedom of religion or belief seriously can be seen in the cases dealing with the *forum internum* and with the right to manifest a religion or belief.

The right to have a religion or belief was said in *Kokkinakis* to be at the heart of Article 9. The text of the Convention reiterates this by not subjecting the *forum internum* to limitations under Article 9(2). Yet despite its acknowledged importance, neither the Court nor the Commission has ever developed any sophisticated notion of what the first limb of Article 9 protects or how it can be breached by States. Even in the area of children's education, where there is a clear danger of inappropriate interference with the *forum internum*, a simplistic approach to the issue of indoctrination has allowed schools considerable scope to pressure children to take religious education classes. In other areas, the Court and, to a slightly lesser extent, the Commission have rejected the notion that even serious burdens on belief, such as dismissal from employment or denial of the right to sit in Parliament, are sufficient to constitute an interference with internal belief as well as with manifestation. Cases that have involved religious discrimination (e.g. for public service jobs), a requirement to reveal one's religion, or an obligation to act in contradiction to deeply held beliefs have been held to raise issues of manifestation only. Yet the distinction between belief and action is not as clear and simple as the cases suggest. While there is a danger in allowing too great a scope to the *forum internum* (in particular because it is not subject to restrictions under Article 9(2)), there must come a point at which State coercion of actions interferes in both the internal and external right to religious freedom. At present the case law denies the relevance of the *forum internum* even in cases in which States place significant burdens on belief. The relationship between action and belief is complex, and the case law does not adequately reflect this complexity. By so narrowing the scope of the first limb of Article 9(1), the Court and Commission have trivialized a right that the Court has said is of great importance both to individuals and to the creation of pluralistic democracies.

The fundamental importance of religion or belief in allowing individuals to create their self-identity and to live autonomously is also undermined by the readiness of the Court and Commission to dismiss claims about the importance of particular practices in the lives of believers. Freedom of religion or belief is said to be important in part because of its role in the development of tolerant and pluralistic societies. Yet the Court and Commission seem often to dismiss cases, such as the school marching case or most of the cases involving general and neutral laws, in part because of the unusual or eccentric nature of the claims. Applicants whose concept of religion or belief does not fit the very limited model adopted by the Court and Commission are simply assumed not to fall within the protection of Article 9. A theory of religious freedom that truly took account of the role of religion or belief as one of the most important components of a freely chosen life would be more flexible and readier to acknowledge that religion or belief may be manifested in a variety of ways. What may be essential to one religion (public worship or dietary practices for example) may be irrelevant or marginal to another. By imposing on non-traditional religions or beliefs too narrow a conception of a 'proper' manifestation, the Court and Commission have failed to respect the diverse ways in which religion or belief are expressed. The importance of freedom of religion or belief to both individuals and society is thus not adequately acknowledged in the case law.

9.1.2 Inconsistency and Lack of Clarity

Even the limited conception of religion or belief that has been developed in the cases has not been applied consistently. The conceptual confusion over the role of the *Arrowsmith* test in limiting the scope of protected manifestations illustrates this point, as does the inconsistent approach to general and neutral laws.

The *Arrowsmith* test was developed to determine when an action should be protected under the second limb of Article 9(1) by reference to the objective test of whether a particular action is necessary to the practice of a religion or belief. Yet it has not proved a useful guide to resolving complex questions. First of all, it is unclear whether it applies only to limit the term 'practice' or whether it also applies to worship, teaching, and observance. Second, it is unclear whether the test states that the actions in question be required by the religion or belief, or whether the actions must merely be strongly connected to religion or belief. Whichever version of the test is used, it raises particular difficulties for those who belong to non-hierarchical religions or have individualistic beliefs. Finally, the Commission has sometimes simply failed to apply the test, even when faced with an applicant claiming that an action was a practice that was necessary to his or her religion or belief. This most often happens in cases where the law in question was of a general and neutral kind. The relationship between the *Arrowsmith* test and such laws is far from clear, despite the fact that cases that claim that a religious practice requires the applicant to breach a general and neutral law are the most common type of case to be raised under Article 9.

Thus at the heart of the interpretation of Article 9(1) lies a test that is unclear in its scope, uncertain in its application, and inconsistent in its usage. The vagueness of the test opens up the potential for judges to determine cases based only on their own perceptions of the importance of actions for which protection is claimed.

9.1.3 Evidence and Objectivity

The potential for such subjective judgments is increased by a lack of clarity as to what evidence can be used by an applicant to make out his or her case. Vague tests create evidential as well as conceptual difficulties. For example, the lack of a clear definition of religion or belief makes it difficult to know how an applicant who claims to be a member of an obscure religion or to hold an individualistic belief can establish this to the Court's satisfaction. The practical importance of this can be seen by the fact that the Commission has rejected a small number of claims on the grounds that the applicants have not proved the existence of their religion or belief.

This problem is compounded in relation to manifestation. The *Arrowsmith* test was intended to introduce an element of objectivity into the determination of whether an action is a 'practice' for the purposes of Article 9(1) but objective forms of evidence have rarely been used to make determinations about whether an action was necessary or not. The use of evidence from religious organizations or leaders has been sparing and haphazard, and the evidence of applicants themselves seems to be treated as largely irrelevant to the determination of necessity. No recourse is had to United Nations documents, such as the Declaration on Religious Intolerance and Discrimination, or the Krishnaswami study. Thus, while the *Arrowsmith* test itself appears to be objective, the Court and Commission have tended to rely on their own subjective judgements as to necessity rather than utilizing more truly objective sources of evidence.

A different type of evidential problem arises in relation to the Article 9(2) cases. The wording of the Article suggests that the State must discharge a high burden of proof to show that its actions were '*necessary* in a democratic society' for one of the limited number of reasons that constitute a legitimate aim. Yet the Court and Commission when dealing with Article 9(2) claims have generally simply accepted the word of the State as sufficient evidence of whether the law had a legitimate aim. Evidence from applicants of abuses of a law or discriminatory implementation or enforcement of seemingly general laws has been ignored. Similarly, the margin of appreciation, which is wide in most Article 9 cases, gives States a clear evidential advantage as little evidence is required to substantiate claims that a law is necessary and proportionate for the ends that the State wishes to achieve. Unless an applicant can show that the State is using a law in a deliberate and hostile manner to undermine a religion or belief, the claim is likely to be held to fall into the margin and the Court will then defer to the judgement of the State as to whether the restrictions on religious freedom were necessary.

9.1.4 Deference to States

The evidential advantage given to States is only one way in which the Article 9 case law demonstrates that the Court and Commission have had greater sympathy with the concerns of States than with the position of applicants. The very limited scope given to Article 9(1), combined with an expansive approach to Article 9(2), has denied relief to almost all applicants who have claimed a breach of their freedom of religion or belief. The narrow approach to Article 9(1) creates particular difficulties for applicants because it absolves the State from having to show any justification for its actions or from having to prove that its actions were proportionate.

There are good reasons for States to be concerned to limit the right to freedom of religion or belief, particularly the desire to ensure that they can deal effectively and coherently with social problems without being frustrated by small, sometimes unreasonable groups of believers. Yet there are also bad reasons for States to favour a limited concept of religion or belief. People who choose to exercise their autonomy in religious matters may use this as a basis for resisting social control. Religions may also be independent voices that speak with some authority to challenge government corruption, to champion the marginalized, or to criticize the predominant political morality. This makes them uncomfortable for the authorities, but it is one of the reasons why religious freedom is worth protecting. Yet the narrow scope given to Article 9(1) means that these activities are generally outside the protection of the Convention. Religion or belief are largely limited to the church, synagogue, temple, or mosque and to closely associated activities. This reflects the view of most States as to what a religion should be, but it does not reflect the reality of religious experience for many people. The Court and Commission have simply accepted a view of religion or belief that reflects the concerns of States without considering the implications of their position for applicants. Such consideration should lead to a reconceptualization of both Article 9(1) and 9(2).

9.2 RECONCEPTUALIZING FREEDOM OF RELIGION OR BELIEF

9.2.1 Article 9(1)

In order to give fuller protection to freedom of religion or belief, the Court needs to take the claims of applicants more seriously than they are currently taken. This is most important in determining whether there has been a breach of Article 9(1). Clearly the Court cannot simply accept any claim by applicants about competing interests under Article 9(2) or about what is necessary in a democratic society, but it could take a more applicant-focused approach to Article 9(1).

One important aspect of such an approach would be to better define the scope and function of the *forum internum*. At present it plays almost no practical role in Article 9 cases, and it is difficult to see how a State could interfere with the *forum internum* short of brainwashing. The Court needs to develop a more sophisticated definition of what the *forum internum* is and to explain in greater detail how it can be interfered with. In particular, there should be a recognition that there is a point where State coercion to force someone to act in a certain way is so severe that it interferes with belief as well as with manifestations. The Court should also pay greater attention to the areas where there is often potential for subtle interference with the *forum internum*, in particular in education and the treatment of State Churches.

The Court could also deal far more respectfully with the subjective claims of applicants about whether a law or regulation interferes with the practice of their religion or belief. A number of members of the Court and Commission have set out tests of manifestations under Article 9(1) that pay more attention to the views of applicants and are less prone to privilege traditional, mainstream practices of religion. A model of religious freedom that treated belief with respect would adopt an approach that treated the claims of applicants about the ways in which they manifested their religion or belief more seriously. If an applicant claimed that acting in a particular way was a manifestation of his or her religion or belief and could provide some evidence to support the claim, this should be sufficient to constitute a manifestation for the purposes of Article 9(1), without the applicant also having to show that the action in question was necessary to his or her religion or belief. This would be a more subjective test than the one currently used but, to limit concerns about abuse or fraud, reference could usefully be made to United Nations documents and other reputable, scholarly studies that discuss religious practices world-wide to illustrate the types of actions that are accepted as important religious practices. This could help to shift the Court's approach away from the traditional Christian perspective of religion that is evident in some of its judgments and could help to ensure that minority practices are less marginalized in cases on manifestations.

Another problem with the case law on manifestations at present is that the *Arrowsmith* test is used in such a way that it is virtually impossible to show a breach of Article 9(1) arising from a general and neutral law. A more sophisticated model of freedom of religion or belief would recognize that a law may be indirectly and unintentionally discriminatory or restrictive of freedom of religion or belief. There are legal and policy reasons for clarifying that general and neutral laws can breach Article 9(1) and requiring States, when such a breach is shown, to illustrate that such laws were necessary in the terms of Article 9(2). While it would be inappropriate for the Court to formulate a rule that required States to grant exemptions to religious groups from any law that interfered with their religion or belief, by recognizing that general and neutral laws can interfere with religious freedom the Court would encourage States to adopt a variety of strategies to ensure that their laws do not improperly restrict that freedom. Such strategies might include exemptions from some laws but may also include greater consultation with religious communities about proposed laws, more restrictive drafting of certain regulations, or a decision not to legislate in some areas. Such an approach would be particularly helpful to minority groups that are often overlooked in the legislative process.

9.2.2 Article 9(2)

While freedom of religion or belief is an important right, the free practice of religion or belief should sometimes be limited. Even if a believer claims an absolute and divinely mandated obligation to behave in a particular manner, it does not follow that the State or human rights bodies should support those claims. Religions or groups of believers may be involved in stirring up hatred against people who do not share their beliefs and they may actively oppose the notion of religious freedom. Religions have also historically tended to discriminate against women and some religions have been involved in promoting notions of racial inequality or inciting persecution against homosexuals. While Article 9(2) requires States to show good reasons to justify interference with religion or belief, such reasons often do exist. States, however, are often reluctant to challenge religions (especially well-established, majority religions) on these types of grounds, and the Court and Commission likewise appear to prefer not to become involved in the competing claims of, for example, women's equality and religious freedom. Instead the reasons given for limiting manifestations of religion or belief have tended to focus more on administrative convenience and broad concepts of public order. In *Karaduman v. Turkey*,[2] for example, the Commission brushed over the complicated issues of whether women being allowed to wear headscarves in public universities would put pressure on other women to do the same (thus limiting their freedom of religion) and promote gender inequality. Instead the dubious device of voluntarism was employed to avoid the issues and to resolve the case in a way that failed to acknowledge the importance of religious apparel to many Muslims. The Court needs to be prepared to deal directly with these conflicts and develop principles to adjudicate between the competing claims.

---

[2] *Karaduman v. Turkey*, App. No. 16278/90, 74 Eur. Comm'n H.R. Dec. & Rep. 93 (1993).

Such principles are not easy to develop and every claim will still need to be assessed on its own merits. The case law on Article 9(2), however, suggests that the Court and Commission have been too willing to accept even reasonably trivial reasons for interfering with religious freedom and that they have given considerable weight to State claims involving public order and administrative convenience. While religious freedom cannot be given absolute priority over all other considerations, it should be given sufficient respect to outweigh these relatively trivial concerns.

9.3 TRENDS IN THE COURT

While there have been significant problems with the way in which the Court and Commission have dealt with freedom of religion or belief in the past, there is room for some optimism in the way in which the Court established under Protocol 11 will deal with Article 9. While the Court did not deal in a very sophisticated manner with the scope of Article 9(1) (particularly with the *forum internum*) in *Buscarini v. San Marino*,[3] it unanimously found a breach of Article 9 and dismissed the claims of San Marino about the importance of religious tradition to public order. Also in *Tsavachidis v. Greece*[4] a number of members of the newly constituted Court were prepared to hold that government surveillance of a minority religious group, when there were no grounds for believing that it was involved in criminal or anti-social behaviour, was a breach of the *forum internum*. While the majority was not prepared to subscribe to such a view, it suggests that at least some members of the Court take a broader view of the first limb of Article 9(1) than the current case law supports. Were the Court to extend its decision in *Thlimmenos v. Greece*[5] and require States to grant exemptions to some general and neutral laws on the basis of religion or belief, it would greatly extend the protection of the Convention, particularly in the way in which it protects minorities. Finally, the decision in *Serif v. Greece*,[6] in which the Court reiterated the importance of religious pluralism and the role of the government in the promotion of tolerance, could signal a shift away from the unthinking deference of the Court to State claims of the tension that is likely to be caused if religious freedom is not restricted. The number of cases decided since Protocol 11 entered into force is too limited to draw any firm conclusions, but there does seem to be room for cautious optimism.

[3] *Buscarini and others v. San Marino*, App. No. 24645/94, Eur. Ct. H.R., 18 Feb. 1999, unreported.
[4] *Tsavachidis v. Greece*, App. No. 28802/95, Eur. Comm'n H.R., 4 Mar. 1997, unreported.
[5] *Thlimmenos v. Greece*, App. No. 34369/97, Eur. Ct. H.R., 6 Apr. 2000, unreported.
[6] *Serif v. Greece*, App. No. 38178/97, Eur. Ct. H.R., 14 Dec. 1999, unreported.

9.4 CONCLUSION

Freedom of religion or belief will always be a controversial right, in part because its importance to many people makes it a potent source of social conflict. No judicial model of religious freedom should ever give absolute primacy to the right to have and to practise a religion or belief. There are other important social goals that such an approach would undermine and other important aspects of autonomy that could be restricted were religious freedom given priority over all other rights. The current case law, however, gives inadequate scope to religious freedom and does not deal respectfully with the most deeply held beliefs of many applicants. Rather than disguising complex policy questions about what type of religion or belief is protected under Article 9 in discussions of the right to manifest a religion or belief, the Court should define religion or belief in a more sophisticated and narrow manner. It should then take a far more applicant-oriented approach to the determination of what constitutes a manifestation of religion or belief, paying more attention to the subjective claims of applicants and to the United Nations studies of religious practice. Such an approach would treat religions and beliefs with more respect and it would acknowledge that the State has interfered in an important aspect of religious practice on more occasions than the current case law. This would leave the role of balancing the importance of those practices against other social goods to Article 9(2)—the appropriate place to make such trade-offs. There are many good reasons for limiting religious freedom, but an approach that focused more on Article 9(2) as a way of limiting religious freedom and less on narrowing the scope of Article 9(1) would at least require States to demonstrate that such reasons exist and would allow individuals the chance to argue for the importance of their religious practices.

Too often claims concerning freedom of religion or belief have been dismissed out of hand by the Court and Commission. While freedom of religion or belief in Europe may not be in the same perilous state that it is in some other parts of the world, even seemingly minor intrusions on freedom of religion or belief can cause great hardship and suffering to those whose freedom is restricted. Religion and belief have been important sources of inspiration for moral and political development, for artistic and literary endeavours, and, most importantly, for individuals seeking to live their lives meaningfully and with integrity. Undoubtedly religious freedom has certain social costs and gives rise to the potential to create conflict, but it is nevertheless worthy of far greater protection than it is currently given under the Convention. If religious vitality and tolerance is undermined, European democracy and pluralism will be the weaker for it. In the words of Aristotle,

[W]e ought not to listen to those who warn us that 'man should think the thoughts of man' or 'mortal thoughts fit mortal minds'; but we ought, so far as in us lies, to put on immortality, and do all that we can to live in conformity with the highest that is in us; for even if it is small in bulk, in power and preciousness it far excels all the rest.[7]

[7] ARISTOTLE, THE NICOMACHEAN ETHICS 31 (J. A. K. Thomson trans., 1953).

Select Bibliography

BOOKS

Aristotle, The Nicomachean Ethics (London: Penguin Classics, J. A. K. Thomson trans., 1953).

Beddard, R., Human Rights and Europe (Cambridge: Grotius Publications, 3rd edn., 1993).

Boyle, Kevin and Sheen, Juliet (eds.), Freedom of Religion and Belief: A World Report (London: Routledge, 1997).

Burns, Gene, The Frontiers of Catholicism: The Politics of Ideology in a Liberal World (Berkeley: University of California Press, 1992).

Cantwell Smith, Wilfred, The Meaning and End of Religion (New York: New American Library, 1962).

Castberg, Frede, The European Convention on Human Rights (Leiden: Oceana, 1974).

Chowdhury, Subrata Roy, Rule of Law in a State of Emergency: The Paris Minimum Standards of Human Rights Norms in a State of Emergency (London: Pinter, 1989).

Council of Europe (ed.), Freedom of Conscience (Strasbourg: Council of Europe, 1993).

Cumper, Peter and Wheatley, Steven (eds.), Minority Rights in the 'New' Europe (The Hague: M. Nijhoff, 1999).

Denzinger, Henry (ed.), The Sources of Catholic Dogma (St Louis: Herder, 1957).

Dickson, Brice (ed.), Human Rights and the European Convention (London: Sweet & Maxwell, 1997).

Dinstein, Yoram (ed.), The Protection of Minorities and Human Rights (Dordrecht: M. Nijhoff, 1992).

Drzemczewski, Andrew, European Human Rights in Domestic Law: A Comparative Study (Oxford: Clarendon Press, 1983).

Dworkin, Ronald, Taking Rights Seriously (London: Duckworth, 1978).

European Council of Conscripts (ed.), Compulsory Military Service in Central and Eastern Europe: A General Survey (European Council of Conscripts, 1996).

Evans, Malcolm D., Religious Liberty and International Law in Europe (Cambridge: Cambridge University Press, 1997).

Fawcett, J. E. S., The Application of the European Convention on Human Rights (Oxford: Clarendon Press, 1987).

Flanz, Gisbert (ed.), Constitutions of the Countries of the World (New York: Oceana Publications, 1971–).

Ganji, Manouchehr, International Protection of Human Rights (Geneva: Librairie E. Droz, 1962).

Gomien, D. and Zwack, L., Law and Practice of the ECHR and the European Social Charter (Strasbourg: Council of Europe, 1996).

Goonesekere, Savitri, Children, the Law and Justice (New Delhi: Sage, 1998).

Harris D. J., O'Boyle M. and Warbrick C., The Law of the European Convention on Human Rights (London: Butterworths, 1995).

Jacobs, Francis G. and White, Robin C. A., The European Convention on Human Rights (Oxford: Clarendon Press, 2nd edn., 1996).

Janis, Mark and Evans, Carolyn (eds.), Religion and International Law (Dordrecht: M. Nijhoff, 1999).

Janis, Mark, Kay, Richard and Bradley, Anthony, European Human Rights Law: Text and Materials (Hartford, Conn.: University of Connecticut Law School Foundation Press, 1995).

Khadduri, M., The Islamic Concept of Justice (Baltimore: Johns Hopkins University Press, 1984).

Kurland, Philip, Religion and the Law: Of Church and State and the Supreme Court (Chicago: Aldine Pub. Co., 1961).

Lerner, Natan, Group Rights and Discrimination in International Law (Dordrecht: M. Nijhoff, 1991).

Loucaides, Loukis G., Essays on the Developing Law of Human Rights (Dordrecht: M. Nijhoff, 1995).

Merrills, J. G., The Development of International Law by the European Court of Human Rights (Manchester: Manchester University Press, 1993).

Mill, John Stuart, On Liberty (Hertfordshire: Wordsworth Classic edition, 1996).

Oraá, Jamie, Human Rights in States of Emergency in International Law (Oxford: Clarendon Press, 1992).

Rawls, John, A Theory of Justice (Oxford: Oxford University Press, 1972).

Raz, Joseph, The Authority of Law (Oxford: Clarendon Press, 1979).

Raz, Joseph, The Morality of Freedom (Oxford: Clarendon Press, 1986).

Robertson, A. H. (ed.), *Travaux Préparatoires* of the European Convention on Human Rights, vols. i–viii (Strasbourg: Council of Europe, 1973).

Robertson, A. H. and Merrills, J. G., Human Rights in Europe (Manchester: Manchester University Press, 3rd edn., 1993).

Schuster, Joseph, The First Amendment in the Balance (San Francisco: Austin & Winfield, 1993).

Steiner, Henry J. and Alston, Philip, International Human Rights in Context (Oxford: Oxford University Press, 1996).

Tahzib, Bahiyyih G., Freedom of Religion and Belief: Ensuring Effective International Protection (The Hague: Kluwer Law International, 1996).

Thornberry, Patrick, International Law and the Rights of Minorities (Oxford: Clarendon Press, 1991).

Traer, Robert, Faith and Human Rights (Washington, DC: Georgetown University Press, 1994).

Van Bueren, Geraldine, The International Law on the Rights of the Child (Dordrecht: M. Nijhoff, 1998).

van Dijk, P. and van Hoof, G. J. H., Theory and Practice of the European Convention on Human Rights (Deventer: Kluwer Law & Taxation 3rd edn., 1997).

Williams, John Fisher, Some Aspects of the Covenant of the League of Nations (London: Oxford University Press, 1934).

Yourow, Howard Charles, The Margin of Appreciation Doctrine in the Dynamic of European Human Rights Jurisprudence (The Hague: Kluwer Law International, 1995).

CHAPTERS

Bassiouni, M. Cherif, *Sources of Islamic Law and the Protection of Human Rights in the Islamic Criminal Justice System, in* The Islamic Criminal Justice System 3 (M. Cherif Bassiouni ed., London: Oceana, 1982).

Boyle, Kevin, *Freedom of Conscience in International Law, in* Freedom of Conscience 37 (Council of Europe ed., Strasbourg: Council of Europe, 1993).

Boyle, Kevin, *Religious Intolerance and the Incitement of Hatred, in* Striking a Balance: Hate Speech, Freedom of Expression and Non-discrimination 61 (Sandra Coliver ed., London: Article 19, 1997).

Capotorti, Francesco, *Are Minority Groups Entitled to Collective International Rights?, in* The Protection of Minorities and Human Rights (Yoram Dinstein ed., Dordrecht: M. Nijhoff, 1992).

Cohen, Cynthia Price, *The Relevance of Theories of Natural Law and Legal Positivism, in* Ideologies of Children's Rights (Michael Freeman and Philip Veerman eds., Dordrecht: M. Nijhoff, 1992).

Cumper, Peter, *The Rights of Religious Minorities: The Legal Regulation of New Religious Movements, in* Minority Rights in the 'New' Europe (Peter Cumper and Steven Wheatley eds., The Hague: M. Nijhoff, 1999).

Dickson, Brice, *The Common Law and the European Convention, in* Human Rights and the European Convention (Brice Dickson ed., London: Sweet & Maxwell, 1997).

Dinstein, Yoram, *Freedom of Religion and Religious Minorities, in* The Protection of Minorities and Human Rights 152 (Yoram Dinstein ed., The Hague: M. Nijhoff, 1992).

Edwards, John, *Preferential Treatment and the Right to Equal Consideration, in* Minority Rights in the 'New' Europe (Peter Cumper and Steven Wheatley eds., The Hague: M. Nijhoff, 1999).

Evans, Carolyn, *Religious Freedom in European Human Rights Law: The Search for a Guiding Conception, in* Religion and International Law (Mark Janis and Carolyn Evans eds., Dordrecht: M. Nijhoff, 1999).

Fredman, Sandra, *Equality Issues, in* The Impact of the Human Rights Bill on English Law 111 (Basil Markesinis ed., Oxford: Clarendon Press, 1998).

Gunn, T. Jeremy, *Adjudicating Rights of Conscience under the European Convention on Human Rights, in* Religious Human Rights in Global Perspective: Legal Perspectives (Johan D. van der Vyver and John Witte Jr. eds., The Hague: M. Nijhoff, 1996).

Liskofsky, S., *The UN Declaration on the Elimination of Religious Intolerance and Discrimination: Historical and Legal Perspectives, in* Religion and State: Essays in Honour of Leo Pfeffer 441 (J. Woods ed., 1985).

Locke, John, *Letters on Toleration, in* Works of John Locke vol. vi (London: Bell, 1823).

Packer, John, *On the Content of Minority Rights, in* Do We Need Minority Rights? 121 (J. Räikkä ed., Boston: M. Nijhoff, 1996).

Partsch, K. J., *Freedom of Conscience and Expression and Political Freedoms, in* The International Bill of Human Rights: The Covenant on Civil and Political Rights 209 (L. Henkin ed., New York: Columbia University Press, 1981).

Perotti, Antonio, *Freedom of Conscience and Religion and Immigrants, in* Freedom of Conscience 179 (Council of Europe ed., Strasbourg: Council of Europe, 1993).

Quinn, Gerard, *Conscientious Objection in Labour Relations, in* Freedom of Conscience 107 (Council of Europe ed., Strasbourg: Council of Europe, 1993).

Rimanque, Karel, *Freedom of Conscience and Minority Groups, in* Freedom of Conscience 144 (Council of Europe ed., Strasbourg: Council of Europe, 1993).

Robert, Jacques, *Freedom of Conscience, Pluralism and Tolerance, in* Freedom of Conscience 22 (Council of Europe ed., Strasbourg: Council of Europe, 1993).

Rodotà, Stefano, *Conscientious Objection to Military Service, in* Freedom of Conscience 94 (Council of Europe ed., Strasbourg: Council of Europe, 1993).

Shaw, Malcolm, *Freedom of Thought, Conscience and Religion, in* The European System for the Protection of Human Rights 445 (R. StJ. McDonald *et al.* eds., Dordrecht: M. Nijhoff, 1993).

Teitgen, P. H., *Introduction to the European Convention on Human Rights, in* The European System for the Protection of Human Rights (R. StJ. McDonald *et al.* eds., Dordrecht: M. Nijhoff, 1993).

Vermeulen, Ben, *Scope and Limits of Conscientious Objection, in* Freedom of Conscience 74 (Council of Europe, ed., Strasbourg: Council of Europe, 1993).

Wheatley, Steven, *Minority Rights, Power Sharing and the Modern State, in* Minority Rights in the 'New' Europe (Peter Cumper and Steven Wheatley eds., The Hague: M. Nijhoff, 1999).

ARTICLES AND REPORTS

Amnesty International, *5000 Years in Prison: Conscientious Objectors in Greece* (1993).

An-Na'im Abdullahi, A., *Religious Minorities Under Islamic Law and the Limits of Cultural Relativism*, 9 HUM. RTS. Q. 1 (1987).

Artz, Donna, *The Application of International Human Rights Law in Islamic States*, 12 HUM. RTS. Q. 202 (1990).

Bassiouni, M. Cherif, *Paper to Panel on Religious Discrimination and Blasphemy*, 83 AM. SOC. INT'L L. 432 (1989).

Boulware-Miller, Kay, *Female Circumcision: Challenges to the Practice as a Human Rights Violation*, 8 HARV. WOMEN'S L.J. 155 (1985).

Carter, Stephen L., *Evolutionism, Creationism and Treating Religion as a Hobby*, 6 DUKE L.J. 977 (1987).

Carter, Stephen L., *The Resurrection of Religious Freedom*, 107 HARV. L. REV. 118 (1993).

Choper, Jesse, *Defining 'Religion' in the First Amendment*, U. ILL. L. REV. 579 (1982).

Churchill, R. R. and Young, J. R., *Compliance with the Judgments of the European Court of Human Rights and Decisions of the Committee of Ministers: The Experience of the United Kingdom 1975–1983*, 62 BRIT. Y.B OF INT'L L. 283 (1992).

Clark, Roger S., *The United Nations and Religious Freedom*, 11 N.Y.U.J. INT'L L. & POL. 197 (1978).

Clarke, Desmond, *Freedom of Thought in the UN Declaration and Covenants*, 28 IRISH JURIST 121 (1993–1995).

Cook, Rebecca, *Reservations to the Convention on the Elimination of All Forms of Discrimination Against Women*, 30 VA. L. INT'L L. 643 (1990).

Dickson, Brice, *The United Nations and Freedom of Religion*, 44 INT'L & COMP. L.Q. 327 (1995).

DiPietro, Melanie, *Fact Finding Faith*, 3 J. OF CONTEMP. HEALTH L. & POL. 185 (1987).

Drzemczewski, Andrew and Meyer-Ladewig, Jan, *Principal Characteristics of the New European Convention on Human Rights Mechanism, as Established by Protocol 11, signed on 11 May 1994*, 15 HUM. RTS. L.J. 81 (1994).

Edge, Peter W., *Current Problems in Article 9 of the European Convention on Human Rights*, 1996 JURID. REV. 42.

Edge, Peter W., *Holy War on the Doorstep*, 1996 NEW L.J. 146.

Edge, Peter W., *The European Court of Human Rights and Religious Rights*, 47 INT'L & COMP. L.Q. 680 (1998).

Evans, Malcolm D., Religion, Law and Human Rights: Locating the Debate, unpublished paper delivered at a meeting of the British Institute for International and Comparative Law at Charles Clore House on 2 March 1998.

Fawcett, J. E. S., *Reform of the European Convention on Human Rights*, 1983 PUB. L. 468.

Feoanov, Dmitry N., *Defining Religion: An Immodest Proposal*, 23 HOFSTRA L. REV. 309 (1994).

Fish, Stanley, *Liberalism Doesn't Exist*, 6 DUKE L.J. 997 (1987).

Freeman, H. A., *A Remonstrance for Conscience*, 106 PA. L. REV. 806 (1958).

Gedicks, Frederick M., *Public Life and Hostility to Religion*, 78 VA. L. REV. 671 (1992).

Greenawalt, Kent, *Religion as a Concept in Constitutional Law*, 72 CAL. L. REV. 753 (1984).

Hannum, Hurst, *Collected Travaux Préparatoires of the European Convention on Human Rights*, 82 AM. J. INT'L L. (1988) (BOOK REVIEW).

Hayden, Paul, *Religiously Motivated 'Outrageous' Conduct: Intentional Infliction of Emotional Distress as a Weapon Against 'Other People's Faiths'*, 34 WM & MARY L. REV. 579 (1993).

Johnson, Phillip E., *Concepts and Compromise in the First Amendment Religious Doctrine*, 72 CAL. L. REV. 817 (1984).

Jones, Timothy H., *The Devaluation of Human Rights Under the European Convention*, 1995 PUB. L. 430.

Laycock, Douglas, *Formal, Substantive and Disaggregated Neutrality Toward Religion*, 39 DEPAUL L. REV. 993 (1990).

Lerner, Natan, *Toward a Draft Declaration Against Religious Intolerance and Discrimination*, 11 ISR. Y.B. OF H.R. 84 (1991).

Lerner, Natan, *The Final Text of the U.N. Declaration Against Intolerance and Discrimination Based on Religion and Belief*, 12 ISR. Y.B. OF H.R. 187 (1992).

McConnell, Michael, *Free Exercise and the Smith Decision*, 57 U. CHI. L. REV. 1109 (1990).

McDougal, Myres S., Lasswell, Harold and Chen, Lung-chu, *The Right to Religious Freedom and World Public Order: The Emerging Norm of Non-Discrimination*, 74 MICH. L. REV. 865 (1976).

Malecha, Wayne F., *Faith Healing Exemptions to Child Protection Legislation: Keeping the Faith vs. Medical Care for Children*, 12 J. OF LEGIS. 243 (1985).

Mansfield, John, *The Religion Clauses of the First Amendment—the Philosophy of the Constitution*, 72 CAL. L. REV. 857 (1984).

Marston, G., *The United Kingdom's Part in Preparation of the European Convention on Human Rights*, 42 INT'L & COMP. L.Q. (1993).

Moens, Gabriel, *The Action–Belief Dichotomy and Freedom of Religion*, 12 SYDNEY L. REV. 195 (1989).

Note, *Defining 'Religion' in the First Amendment: A Functional Approach*, 84 CORNELL L. REV. 532 (1986).

Note, *Jehovah's Witnesses and the Refusal of Blood Transfusions: A Balance of Interests*, 33 CATH. LAW. 361 (1991).

O'Donnell, Thomas, *The Margin of Appreciation Doctrine: Standards in Jurisprudence of the European Court of Human Rights*, 4 HUM. RTS. Q. 474 (1982).

O'Frame, Richard, *Belief in a Non-Material Reality—A Proposed First Amendment Definition of Religion*, U. ILL. L. REV. 819 (1992).

Panel, *Resolving Conflicting Human Rights Standards in International Law*, 85th Meeting ASIL Proc. 336 (1991).

Poulter, Sebastian, *Rights of Ethnic, Religious and Linguistic Minorities*, 3 EUR. HUM. RTS. L. REV. 254 (1997).

Poulter, Sebastian, *Muslim Headscarves in Schools: Contrasting Legal Approaches in England and France*, 17 OXFORD J. LEGAL STUD. 43 (1997).

Puls, Joshua, *The Wall of Separation: Section 116, the First Amendment and Constitutional Religious Guarantees*, 26 FED. L. REV. 139 (1998).

Ricks, Val D., *To God God's, To Caesar Caesar's, and to Both the Defining of Religion*, 26 HOFSTRA L. REV. 309 (1994).

Ruparell, Shantilal, *ISKCON: More than a Planning Dispute*, 6(43) LAWYER 10 (1992).

Ryle, Michael, *Pre-legislative Scrutiny: A Prophylactic Approach to Protection of Human Rights*, 1994 PUB. L. 192.

Sadurski, Wojciech, *On Legal Definitions of 'Religion'*, 63 AUSTL. L.J. 834 (1989).

Scheiderer, Judith Inglis, *When Children Die as a Result of Religious Practices*, 51 OHIO ST. L.J. 1429 (1990).

Slack, Alison T., *Female Circumcision: A Critical Appraisal*, 10 HUM. RTS. Q. 437 (1988).

Smith, Steven D., *The Restoration of Tolerance*, 78 CAL. L. REV. 305 (1990).

Stavros, Stephanos, *Freedom of Religion Claims for Exemption from Generally Applicable and Neutral Laws: Lessons from Across the Pond?*, 6 EUR. HUM. RTS REV. 607 (1997).

Sturn, Douglas, *Repentance, Constitutionalism and Sacrality*, 42 DEPAUL L. REV. 61 (1992).

Sullivan, Donna, *Advancing the Freedom of Religion or Belief Through the UN Declaration on the Elimination of Religious Intolerance and Discrimination*, 82 AM. J. INT'L L. 487 (1988).

Sullivan, Donna, *Gender Equality and Religious Freedom: Towards a Framework for Conflict Resolution,* 24 N.Y.U.J. LAW & POL. 795 (1992).

Trahan, Jennifer, *Constitutional Law: Parental Denial of a Child's Medical Treatment for Religious Reasons,* ANN. SURV. AM L. 307 (1989).

Treen, Eric, *Prayer-treatment Exemptions to Child Abuse and Neglect Statutes, Manslaughter Prosecutions, and Due Process of Law,* 30 HARV. J. ON LEGIS. 135 (1993).

Van Boven, Theo, *Advances and Obstacles in Building Understanding and Respect between People of Diverse Religions and Beliefs,* 13 HUM. RTS. Q. 437 (1991).

COUNCIL OF EUROPE DOCUMENTS

Council of Europe, COLLECTED TEXTS (1987).

Council of Europe, CONSCIENTIOUS OBJECTION TO MILITARY SERVICE, EXPLANATORY REPORT C.E. Doc. 88.C55 (1988).

Council of Europe, HUMAN RIGHTS IN EUROPE (1986).

Council of Europe, *Reform of the Central System of the European Convention on Human Rights,* Doc. H(92)14, reprinted in 14 HUM. RTS. L.J. 81 (1994).

Council of Europe, SURVEY OF ACTIVITIES AND STATISTICS (1996) AND (1998).

Council of Europe, *Monitoring of Compliance with the Commitments Entered into by Council of Europe Members: An Overview,* MONITOR/INF(97).

Council of Europe and Hanna Suchocka (eds.), *General Report on the European Regional Colloquy: The Effectiveness of Human Rights Protection 50 Years after the Universal Declaration,* 5 ODUDH(98).

Committee of Ministers, Standard Minimum Rules for the Treatment of Prisoners, Resol. (73)5.

Committee of Ministers, Recommendation no. R(87)8,Council of Europe, H/NF (87)1, 160 (9 April 1987).

Parliamentary Assembly, Res. 337(1976), Council of Europe, Cons. Ass., Eighteenth Ordinary Session (Third Part), Texts Adopted (1967), Parl. Ass. Res. 816 (1977).

Rodotà, Stefano, Report of Special Rapporteur Rodotà, Doc. 6752 (1993), 1404-28/1/93-1-E.

Index